Can You
Outsmart
an
Economist?

BOOKS BY STEVEN E. LANDSBURG

The Armchair Economist:
Economics and Everyday Life

Fair Play:
What Your Child Can Teach You About
Economics, Values, and the Meaning of Life

More Sex Is Safer Sex:
The Unconventional Wisdom of Economics

The Big Questions:
Tackling the Problems of Philosophy with Ideas
from Mathematics, Economics, and Physics

Can You Outsmart an Economist?
100+ Puzzles to Train Your Brain

Can You Outsmart an Economist?

100+ PUZZLES TO TRAIN YOUR BRAIN

Steven E. Landsburg

MARINER BOOKS
Houghton Mifflin Harcourt
Boston • New York
2018

For information about permission to reproduce selections
from this book, write to trade.permissions@hmhco.com or to
Permissions, Houghton Mifflin Harcourt Publishing Company,
3 Park Avenue, 19th Floor, New York, New York 10016.

hmhco.com

Library of Congress Cataloging-in-Publication Data
Names: Landsburg, Steven E., 1954- author.
Title: Can you outsmart an economist? : 100+ puzzles to train
your brain /Steven Landsburg.
Description: Boston : Mariner Books/Houghton Mifflin Harcourt, [2018] |
Identifiers: LCCN 2018006350 (print) | LCCN 2018028468 (ebook) |
ISBN 9781328489821 (ebook) | ISBN 9781328489869 (trade paper)
Subjects: LCSH: Economics—Problems, exercises, etc. |
Puzzles. | Logic puzzles.
Classification: LCC HB171.5 (ebook) |
LCC HB171.5 .L35143 2018 (print) | DDC 330—dc23
LC record available at https://lccn.loc.gov/2018006350

Book design by Chrissy Kurpeski
Typeset in Chronicle Text

Printed in the United States of America
DOC 10 9 8 7 6 5 4 3 2 1

Illustration Credits

Figures and illustrations by Jesse Raymond: pages 2, 4, 7, 13, 39 (bottom), 123,
127, 129, 132–35, 144, 151, 153, 191, 249, 280–81. Figures by Chrissy Kurpeski:
pages 6, 39 (top), 212, 261, 275. Charts and tables by Mapping Specialists,
Ltd.: pages 162, 244, 252, 253 (bottom). Cartoon from the *Wall Street Journal,*
permission Cartoon Features Syndicate: page 255.

Contents

Acknowledgments   vii

Introduction   ix

1. Warm-Ups   1

2. Inferences   19

3. Predictions   45

4. Explanations   69

5. Strategy   93

6. How Irrational Are You?   119

7. Law School Admissions Test   143

8. Are You Smarter Than Google?   157

9. Backward Reasoning   173

10. Knowledge   185

11. *Now* Are You Smarter Than Google?   199

12. How to Make Decisions   207

13. Matters of Life and Death   225

14. The Coin Flipper's Dilemma   237

15. Albert and the Dinosaurs   249

16. Money, Trade, and Finance   259

Appendix   275

Acknowledgments

First: I am grateful to Alex Littlefield at Houghton Mifflin Harcourt for his enthusiasm, insight, and good-natured persistence in the face of my occasional failures to recognize his wisdom. I am equally grateful to Lisa Glover, whose deft management has allowed me to labor under the illusion that the production process is pretty much effortless. And I am grateful to Pilar Garcia-Brown for coordinating everything behind the scenes, and allowing me to believe that everything else is effortless too. Every one of these people has been absolutely terrific to work with.

And Margaret Wimberger is the best copyeditor ever.

Next: I am enormously indebted to Lisa Talpey, Ken Braithwaite, Bennett Haselton, Romans Pancs, and Ron Tansky for detailed and helpful comments, many of which improved the exposition and a few of which saved me from embarrassing myself in print.

I am indebted also to the many brilliant commenters who have shown up over the years to join the discussion on my blog at TheBigQuestions.com and to remind me that they like thinking about this stuff. I hope you do too.

Introduction

*T*his is a different sort of puzzle book. If you solve the puzzles in this book — or even if you just cheat and read the solutions — you'll learn a lot about economics, a lot about how to interpret statistics, and maybe a bit about law, math, science, and philosophy. As you might expect if you're familiar with some of those subjects, not every puzzle has a clear, unambiguous answer. But that doesn't mean that all answers are equally good, and the "solutions" will at least aim to sort out the best from the worst.

There is, though, one way this book is just like every other puzzle book: it's meant to be fun. To that end, I've scattered in a few puzzles that I think are especially fun, even when they have no deep lessons to teach.

Here and there I've also indulged in some (occasionally rambling) commentary that I hope will make the lessons of the puzzles either clearer or more entertaining — or, ideally, both.

If this book has a moral, it is this: *think beyond the obvious*. What seems obvious is often wrong. That's both why puzzles are fun and why economics is important. Economics is, first and foremost, a collection of intellectual tools for seeing beyond the obvious.

When 46 percent of male applicants but only 30 percent of equally qualified female applicants are accepted to grad school, what can we infer? When a strong pig and a weak pig compete for food, what should we expect? If you impose a price ceiling on wheat, what will happen to the price of bread? Why do appliance manufacturers prohibit retailers from discounting their merchandise? Can a series of perfectly rational choices lead to inevitable bankruptcy? In each case, the obvious answer is wrong, and economists know why. When you've finished reading this book, so will you.

Economists are not the only explorers in the land beyond the obvious. Philosophers, psychologists, legal scholars, scientists, and statisticians map the same territory, each equipped with a different intellectual toolkit. It would be foolish to ignore their hard-won discoveries. Nineteenth-century Arctic explorers routinely died of such foolishness when, disregarding the freely offered wisdom of the natives, they refused to wear animal skins and therefore froze to death in woolen clothes issued by the Royal Navy. The navy, you see, trusted only ideas that came from people like themselves. I'd prefer not to make the same mistake, even in a less deadly context. So while most of the puzzles in this book are designed to showcase the power of economics, I am delighted to share some of the limelight with the worthy insights of non-economists.

Anyway, even if I wanted to, it would be quite impossible to fence economics off from all other disciplines, because disciplines overlap. A handful of numbers can either reveal a deep and important truth or mislead us into accepting a dangerous falsehood. How do you tell the difference? Both economists and statisticians worry about that question. Is the answer part of economics or statistics? It's part of both. And when lawyers have to settle cases based on a handful of possibly deceptive facts, they face essentially the same set of issues. Are they practicing law, or are they practicing statistics or economics? They're practicing all three.

That's not the only way economics overlaps with the law. Much of economics is about facing up to trade-offs. Is it better to have a bigger fire department or a cut in taxes? Is it better to have more cars or less pollution? Is it better to have a safer investment portfolio or one with more upside potential? Legal scholars face exactly the same sort of trade-offs when they ask questions like: Is it better to risk more false convictions (say, by loosening the rules of evidence) or to risk more false acquittals (by tightening those rules)? When they debate that trade-off, are they being lawyers or are they being economists? They're being both.

Much of economics is about what it means to be rational, and the extent to which human behavior *is* rational, and why anyone should care. In other words: How do people make decisions, how could they make better decisions, and would better decisions improve their lives? These are also central questions in philosophy. Indeed, there's a whole subject called *decision theory,* which draws on ideas from both economics and philosophy — and statistics and mathematics, for that matter. Are decision theorists economists, or are they philosophers? Sometimes they're one, sometimes they're the other, and often they're both.

And so on. The analysis of strategic behavior lies at the core of both economics and political science. Finding the right way to think about uncertainty is key to both economics and the branch of mathematics called *probability theory* (though philosophers and statisticians weigh in heavily here also). It's quite simply impossible to just "do economics" without simultaneously doing a whole lot of other things.

Now and then, when you're reading this book, you might be

tempted to ask, "But what has this got to do with economics?" Please resist that temptation! If what you're reading has anything to do with interpreting data, or with strategic behavior, or with decision making, or with calculating probabilities, or with facing trade-offs, then it not only has something to *do* with economics, it *is* economics. If what you're reading has anything to do with thinking beyond the obvious, then economics has something to contribute.

This is not a textbook. A textbook on economics would have chapters on consumer behavior, profit maximization, supply and demand, market structures, and cost-benefit analysis. There are plenty of good textbooks out there, but this book is different. It's organized according to the sorts of questions that people (including economists) ask naturally, and the habits of thinking that economists (and others) have found useful.

The book starts off (after some largely just-for-fun warm-up puzzles) with chapters on inferences, predictions, and explanations — corresponding roughly to questions that ask "What's happening?" "What's likely to happen?" and "Why?" These are the sorts of questions we all ask every day, and there are no hard-and-fast dividing lines among them. Does smoking cause cancer? I might be able to draw an *inference* from data showing that smokers have higher cancer rates — at least if I can rule out other possibilities, such as a single gene that causes both cancer and a propensity to smoke. Based on that inference, I can make a *prediction* that people who smoke more today are more likely to get cancer tomorrow. And I can look for an *explanation* for the observed correlation, which might involve cell damage. The lines between the inference, the prediction, and the explanation are a little blurry. So please don't take the chapter headings too seriously; many of these puzzles, with a slight twist or two, could have fit just as well in one chapter as another.

Within each of these chapters, I've felt free to draw on many different branches of economics and schools of thought — calling on whatever helps to illuminate the issue at hand.

Economists aspire to understand, predict, and explain all human behavior. We believe that much of that behavior is *strategic,* which just means that people try to anticipate how others will respond to their behavior and plan accordingly. Sometimes thinking one obvious step ahead is all it takes to succeed. More often, thinking one step ahead is an excellent recipe for losing out to those who think two or three less obvious steps ahead — until they, in turn, have lost out to those who think all the way to the even less obvious endpoint. You can see how that plays out in the chapter on strategy.

We also believe that much human behavior is *rational,* which just means that it serves some purpose. Other people's apparently irrational choices — in politics, in business, and in their private lives — are sometimes genuinely irrational. More often those choices serve a perfectly rational but non-obvious purpose. Discovering that purpose can make you a more compassionate person, a more effective competitor, and a wiser voter. In the other direction, when you make your own meticulously rational choices, you always risk exploitation at the hands of those who can spot the non-obvious inconsistencies in your plan. You can test your own vulnerability by taking the quiz in the chapter titled "How Irrational Are You?"

The remaining chapters offer a potpourri of techniques and topics that economists (and others!) find useful — calculating probabilities, reasoning in reverse, the best ways to make decisions, distinguishing right from wrong (particularly when lives are at stake), and more. Near the end I've included two chapters — "The Coin Flipper's Dilemma" and "Albert and the Dinosaurs" — that invite the reader to contemplate some simple problems that look very much like economics but where the usual tools of economics break down. The final chapter returns to some of the areas where economists are most sure of themselves: money, trade, and finance.

Feel free to read these in any order. A few hark back to ideas from earlier chapters, but most stand alone. Dip into whatever looks inviting. Engage with the ideas. Join the conversation on my blog at TheBigQuestions.com. And above all, have fun.

Can You
Outsmart
an
Economist?

CHAPTER 1

Warm-Ups

*L*et's get started with a few warm-up exercises. These are largely just for fun, though there are lessons lurking in the background. Like most good puzzles, many of them are designed to mislead — sometimes with words and sometimes with numbers. Refusing to be misled by a puzzle can be good practice for refusing to be misled by a journalist, a politician, a Facebook friend — or even an economist.

1

State Boundaries

The border between Delaware and its neighbors includes a section with a circular arc (on the circle ten miles from a church in Dover, Delaware). Can you name another state border that is partially defined by a circular arc?

SOLUTION: The borders of Colorado consist of four circular arcs. They might look straight on a map, but they can't be. They lie, after all, on the surface of the earth. Wyoming's another good example.

In fact, forty-nine of the fifty states have borders that are partially defined by circular arcs. Can you name the one exception?

2

Games of Chance

The bad news is that you need $20 right away to pay off the loan shark who will otherwise break your knees. The good news is that you've already got $10, and you're at a carnival with games of chance.

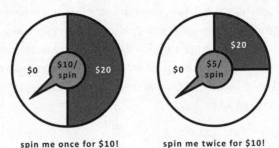

spin me once for $10!   spin me twice for $10!

Here are your choices:

a) Spin the first wheel once, and win $20 if the pointer lands in the dark area, giving you a 50 percent chance to win.
b) Spin the second wheel twice, and win $20 if the pointer lands in the dark area either time, giving you two 25 percent chances to win.

Which do you choose?

SOLUTION: Did you fall into the trap of thinking that it's a mistake to put all your eggs in one basket, so it's safer to go for two spins of the second wheel?

Imagine for a moment that 100 people have found themselves in your situation, all of whom choose the first wheel. Then we expect 50 payoffs, saving 50 sets of knees.

Now imagine instead that the same 100 people all choose the second wheel, spinning twice each. Once again, we expect 50 payoffs. But occasionally the same person wins twice. So those 50 payoffs go to fewer than 50 people, which saves fewer than 50 sets of knees.

That tells us that the first wheel is better at saving knees than the second wheel—and therefore that's the wheel you should bet on.

Of course you *could* have solved that one with a quick calculation: The first wheel gives you a $\frac{1}{2}$ chance of losing your kneecaps. The second wheel gives you a $\frac{3}{4}$ chance of hitting white on either spin; hence a $\frac{3}{4} \times \frac{3}{4} = \frac{9}{16}$ chance of hitting white twice in a row and losing your kneecaps. Because $\frac{9}{16}$ is bigger than $\frac{1}{2}$, the second wheel is the poorer choice. But I think it's a lot more satisfying to solve these things without resorting to arithmetic.

3

Get Off the Earth

Tie a string at ground level all the way around the 24,000-mile circumference of the earth.

Now tie a second string all the way around but supported by posts to keep it 1 foot off the ground.

How much longer is the second string than the first?

SOLUTION: You've added 1 foot to the radius of the string circle. Because the circumference of a circle is 2π times the radius, you've added 2π feet — that is, about 6.28 feet — to the circumference. Most people guess somewhere in the thousands of miles.

4

The Kool-Aid Test

Bob and Alice are both mixing giant vats of Kool-Aid to serve at a party. They started with equal amounts of powder and then added water. Bob's mix is 99 percent water; Alice's is 98 percent water. How much bigger is Bob's batch than Alice's?

SOLUTION: Many people jump to the guess that Bob's batch is only slightly bigger than Alice's. After all, 99 percent is more or less the same as 98 percent, right?

But let's reword what we know: Bob's batch is 1 percent powder, while Alice's is 2 percent powder. Her batch is twice as concentrated as his, even though they started with equal amounts of powder. That can happen only if her batch is exactly half the size of his.

5

Flu Count

The countries of Bobovia and Alovia have equal numbers of deaths from flu each year. In Bobovia, 99 percent of flu victims recover; in Alovia, 98 percent recover. Which country has more flu victims, and by how much?

SOLUTION: The same number of deaths accounts for 1 percent of Bobovia's batch of flu victims and for 2 percent of Alovia's. This can happen only if Alovia's batch is exactly half the size of Bobovia's. Or to say that another way, Bobovia has twice as many flu victims as Alovia.

6

Doctors and Lawyers

My friends Albert and Betty have a son named Xerxes, a daughter-in-law named Yolanda, and a grandson named Tom. The family tree looks like this:

```
ALBERT ——————— BETTY
           |
       XERXES ——————— YOLANDA
           |
          TOM
```

Albert, Betty, and Yolanda are lawyers. Tom is a doctor. *True or False:* In this family, the child of two lawyers is always a lawyer.

SOLUTION: False, though I can't tell you exactly why. Xerxes either is or is not a lawyer. So:

- If Xerxes is a lawyer, then Xerxes and Yolanda are both lawyers but their child is not.
- If Xerxes is not a lawyer then Albert and Betty are lawyers but their child is not.

I don't know which bullet point applies, but I do know that *one* of them applies, and either way the statement is false.

I like this last problem because I think it's cool that you can know for sure that a statement is false without having to know exactly why it's false. Mathematicians love this kind of trick. See the appendix for a math proof that uses the same sort of sneaky logic.

7

The Hungry Bookworm

On my shelf I have a three-volume set of encyclopedias, shelved in the usual order. Each volume is 2 inches thick, with the front and the back covers accounting for ⅛ inch each and the pages accounting for 1¾ inches. One day a hungry bookworm, starting on the first page of volume 1, burrowed its way through pages and covers until it reached the last page of volume 3. How far did the bookworm travel?

SOLUTION: The bookworm traveled 2¼ inches — through the ⅛-inch front cover of volume 1 (which is adjacent to the back cover of volume 2), then through all 2 inches of volume 2, and finally through the ⅛-inch back cover of volume 3, which is also adjacent to volume 2.

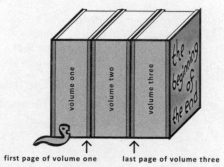

first page of volume one   last page of volume three

If you think I've labeled this diagram incorrectly, I encourage you to look at an actual real book on an actual real shelf and think about it before you email to complain.

The Hungry Bookworm problem is an old chestnut; I remember it from a puzzle book that I had in my childhood. The great

Russian mathematician V. I. Arnold loved challenging children with this problem and was delighted by those who solved it correctly. He once tried to refer to it in a professional article about the varieties of logical thinking but was dismayed when his editors missed the point and "fixed" the wording to say that the bookworm starts on the *last* page of volume 1 and ends on the *first* page of volume 3. He later included the same problem in a book called *Problems for Children from 5 to 15,* with a footnote warning that this problem is "absolutely impossible for academicians, though some preschoolers handle it with ease."

The next problem is another old chestnut, followed by a new version with a remarkable twist.

8

Boys, Boys, Boys

A two-child family is chosen at random.

a) If at least one of the children is a boy, what is the probability they're both boys?
b) If at least one of the children is the blind poet Homer, author of *The Iliad* and *The Odyssey,* what is the probability they're both boys?

SOLUTION:
a) There are three equally likely ways a family can have two children, one of whom is a boy: in birth order, they can be boy/boy, boy/girl, or girl/boy. In exactly one of these three cases, both are boys. So the probability is ⅓.
b) There are four equally likely ways a family can have two children, one of whom is Homer: in birth order, they can be

Homer/boy, Homer/girl, boy/Homer, girl/Homer. In exactly two of these four cases, both are boys. So the probability is ²⁄₄, or ½.

You might find it a little surprising that the answers to parts (a) and (b) are different, when the only difference is that in (b) you've got the apparently irrelevant information that one of the boys is the author of *The Iliad*. The moral — and you'll need this elsewhere in this book — is that "apparently irrelevant" is not always the same thing as "irrelevant."

9

More Boys

A two-child family is chosen at random. If at least one of the children is a boy born on a Thursday, what is the probability they're both boys?

I know, I know, "born on a Thursday" appears to be quite irrelevant. But haven't we already learned our lesson about jumping the gun on what's irrelevant? So let's run with this.

SOLUTION: There are 14 equally likely kinds of children: boys born on a Monday, girls born on a Monday, boys born on a Tuesday, and so forth. There are several ways a family can have two children, one of whom is a Thursday boy: in birth order, they can be

Thursday boy/any of 14 possibilities

or

any of 14 possibilities/Thursday boy

That looks like a total of 28 cases, but the case of two Thursday boys has been counted twice, so it's really only 27.

In how many of those 27 cases does the family have two boys? They'd have to be either

Thursday boy/any of seven possibilities

or

any of seven possibilities/Thursday boy

That looks like a total of 14 cases, but once again we've double-counted the case of two Thursday boys, so it's really only 13.

Bottom line: Out of 27 possible cases, 13 involve two boys. The probability that this family has two boys is $^{13}/_{27}$, or about 48 percent.

When my daughter was in second grade, she was assigned to write a paragraph on the question "Which is heavier, a pound of lead or a pound of feathers, and why?" She wrote: "A pound of lead and a pound of feathers weigh exactly the same, because lead is extremely heavy and so are feathers." Let's see if you can outsmart a second grader.

10

A Weighty Problem

a) What's heavier, a pound of feathers or a pound of gold?

b) What's heavier, an ounce of feathers or an ounce of gold?

Hint: the two parts of this problem have opposite answers!

SOLUTION:

a) According to Standard English usage, the unmodified word "pound" refers to an avoirdupois pound (453.6 grams) —

unless the item being weighed is a precious metal, in which case it refers to a troy pound (373.2 grams). Therefore a pound of gold weighs about 17.7 percent less than a pound of feathers.

b) While a troy pound is less than an avoirdupois pound, a troy ounce is *more* than an avoirdupois ounce (31.1 grams versus 28.35 grams). Therefore an ounce of gold weighs about 9.7 percent more than an ounce of feathers.

A pound (or an ounce) of silver, however, weighs exactly as much as a pound (or an ounce) of gold, and a pound (or an ounce) of lead weighs exactly as much as a pound (or an ounce) of feathers. So my second grader was right, though not, perhaps, for exactly the right reason!

11

Another Weighty Problem

In an attempt to control my weight, I've started rolling a die every morning and eating dessert only on days when I roll a 6. It's Monday morning and I'm about to roll. On which day this week am I most likely to have my next dessert?

SOLUTION: In order to have my next dessert today, I must roll a 6 today. In order to have my next dessert tomorrow, I must roll a 6 tomorrow *and* fail to roll a 6 today. So I'm more likely to have my next dessert today than tomorrow, and by the same sort of logic I'm more likely to have my next dessert today than on any other day of the week.

12

Trainspotting

The Reading Railroad numbers its train cars consecutively, beginning with 1. The only one of these cars you've ever seen is 1547. What's your best guess for the highest number on any train car owned by the railroad?

SOLUTION: The problem is a little ambiguous, because it asks for your "best guess" without specifying what it means for one guess to be better than another.

But statisticians would typically interpret "best guess" to mean *maximum likelihood estimate,* which is a fancy term for the guess that makes your observation most likely.

We know that there are at least 1547 train cars. If there are exactly 1547, then the probability that you'd have seen this particular train car is $\frac{1}{1547}$. If there are exactly 1548, then the probability that you'd have seen this one is the slightly smaller $\frac{1}{1548}$, and so on. The guess that makes your observation most likely is that there are exactly 1547 train cars.

13

Donuts

Three friends are down to their last donut. They want a fair and random method to decide who gets it, and unfortunately they have never heard of rock-paper-scissors. All they have is a fair coin. How can they decide who gets the donut?

SOLUTION: One option: Flip the coin twice. If it comes up HH, the first friend gets the donut. If it comes up HT, the second friend gets the donut. If it comes up TH, the third friend gets the donut. If it comes up TT, start over.

An inferior option: Everyone flips the coin, and whoever doesn't match the others wins. If all match, flip again. This is inferior because it tends to require more flips. With the first method, you're usually finished after two flips. With the inferior method, you always need at least three.

14

The Tortoise and the Hare

Alice and Bob ran a marathon (exactly 26.2 miles long), with Alice running at a perfectly uniform 8-minute-per-mile pace and Bob running in fits and starts, but taking exactly 8 minutes and 1 second to complete each mile interval (so, for example, it takes him exactly 8 minutes and 1 second to get from the 3.78-mile mark to the 4.78-mile mark, exactly 8 minutes and 1 second to get from the 3.92-mile mark to the 4.92-mile mark, and so on). Is it possible that Bob finished ahead of Alice?

SOLUTION: Yes, it is possible!

First, here's a simple (though not terribly realistic) solution:

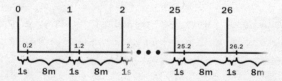

The vertical lines are the mileposts at 0, 1, 2, and so forth, and the hash marks are the mileposts at 0.2, 1.2, 2.2, and so forth.

Bob runs the first fifth of each mile in 1 second and the remaining ⅘ in 8 minutes (at one steady pace for the first fifth and a much slower steady pace for the rest). It takes him 208 minutes and 26 seconds to reach the 26 milepost. Alice reaches that milepost in just 208 minutes, so at this point she's ahead of him.

But Bob saves the day by running the last .2 miles in 1 second, finishing in 208 minutes and 27 seconds, while Alice continues to plod along at her 8-minute-mile pace, requiring well over 209 minutes to finish.

Okay, so now we know the answer is yes, at least for a theoretical Bob who can run a fifth of a mile in a second. What about a more realistic Bob?

The same idea still works: We can let Bob run the first fifth of each mile in anything less than 70 seconds and finish the mile at whatever pace is necessary to keep him at 8 minutes and 1 second per mile. Alice will reach the 26-mile marker 26 seconds ahead of him, but she'll need 96 seconds to cover the remaining .2 miles, while he needs less than 70 — which gives him time to catch up.

15

Fuel Efficiency

Which would save more gas — replacing my wife's 12-mile-per-gallon SUV with a 15-mile-per-gallon SUV, or replacing my 30-mile-per-gallon car with a 40-mile-per-gallon car?

Well, of course it's quite impossible to answer this without some information about our driving habits. If, for example, my car never leaves the garage, then its fuel efficiency doesn't matter. So let's start over.

16

Fuel Efficiency, Take Two

My wife and I each drive exactly the same number of miles each day. *Now* which would save more gas—replacing her 12-mile-per-gallon SUV with a 15-mile-per-gallon SUV, or replacing my 30-mile-per-gallon car with a 40-mile-per-gallon car?

It's *still* quite impossible to answer, without some information on how our driving habits might change. A more efficient car might inspire me to take a longer and more scenic route to work. Or maybe I'll save so much money on gas that I can afford to cut my workweek back from five days to four, so I end up driving less. So let's start over once more:

17

Fuel Efficiency, Take Three

My wife and I each drive exactly the same number of miles every day *and would continue to do so even if we upgraded our vehicles. Now* which would save more gas—replacing my wife's 12-mile-per-gallon SUV with a 15-mile-per-gallon SUV, or replacing my 30-mile-per-gallon car with a 40-mile-per-gallon car?

SOLUTION: Finally, a question we can answer! And you might find the answer mildly surprising. You might have reasoned that we're contrasting a 25 percent increase in fuel efficiency with a 33 percent increase in fuel efficiency for the car—and you might have been tempted to conclude that the latter saves more gas.

But here's what this overlooks: the SUV uses so much gas to begin with that a little added efficiency goes a long way.

If, for example, we each drive 120 miles a day, then replacing my 30-mpg car with a 40-mpg car cuts my gas consumption from 4 gallons a day to 3—a saving of just 1 gallon. But replacing my wife's 12-mpg SUV with a 15-mpg SUV cuts her gas consumption from 10 gallons a day to 8—a saving of 2 gallons.

One moral of that story is: Don't rely blindly on numbers. Of *course* a 33 percent improvement is better than a 25 percent improvement—except when it's not.

The bigger moral lies in it having taken three tries to construct a sensible version of this problem. How does a new car affect your fuel consumption? Until we know how the new car affects your driving habits, it's impossible to say.

This is a moral that runs at large. If Americans spend $80 billion a year on cigarettes, how much revenue will be raised by a new 10 percent tax on cigarettes? Until we know how the tax affects smoking habits, it's quite impossible to say.

Or try this one: Infants traveling on airplanes are currently permitted to ride in their parents' laps. Every five years, approximately two of those infants die from injuries sustained during turbulence. If a new rule required each infant to be strapped into a separate seat, how many infant lives could be saved? The obvious answer is two every five years. The correct answer requires more information. Under the new rule, how many families would choose to drive rather than pay for an extra airline seat? How many of those families would be involved in car accidents? How many of those car accidents would result in infant fatalities?

One reason why regulators still allow infant flyers to ride on their parents' laps is that economists have investigated these questions, and have estimated that for every two infant lives saved in the air, there would be about seven infant lives lost on the roads. So if infant air travelers were required to have their own seats, then every five years the total number of infant deaths would go *up* by a total of five, not down by two.

Notice the pattern: How does a new car affect fuel consumption? It depends on how driving habits change. How does a smoking tax affect government revenue? It depends on how smoking habits change. How does a new rule about infant seating on airlines affect infant mortality? It depends on how traveling habits change.

In our artificial problem about fuel consumption, we dispensed with this issue via the arbitrary (and probably quite unrealistic) assumption that driving habits don't change at all. If you want to understand the real world, arbitrary and unrealistic assumptions won't do — though sometimes it pays to *start* with an arbitrary and unrealistic assumption just to get a feel for the problem, and then come back to rework it later.

These issues will pop up repeatedly to challenge us in this book (as they pop up repeatedly to challenge economists). Now that we're warmed up and ready to face them, let's get started.

CHAPTER 2

Inferences

*T*he single dumbest thing I've ever seen in an academic journal — and believe me, the competition is stiff — is an article by two "researchers" about the relative generosity of college students taking different classes.

It turns out that students taking economics classes are, on average, less willing to contribute to certain left-of-center political organizations. From this, the authors conclude that students taking economics classes are, on average, less generous.

It apparently never entered their heads that economics students might, on average, be less sympathetic to those particular organizations, and therefore inclined to direct their generosity elsewhere. Or even that economics classes might teach precisely the sort of critical-thinking skills that could lead students to be skeptical of certain agendas.

This becomes pretty plausible when you read a little more about the organizations involved. One of them is dedicated to the cause of lower tuition at state universities. Now, I am guessing that the average economics student is somewhat more aware than, say, the average anthropology or chemistry student, that lower tuition for college students is likely to entail higher taxes and/or reduced services for families who are less well off than the families of college students. I might therefore expect that the very most generous economics students — those, that is, who care the most about families worse off than their own — would be the least likely to support this organization.

One might just as well conclude that among all students, physics majors are the least compassionate because they are the least likely to offer encouragement to the inventors of perpetual-motion machines. Or that history majors are the least open-minded, because they are the least willing to consider the possibility that Millard Fillmore might have served as Abraham Lincoln's vice president. Or that chemistry majors are the least ambitious, because they are the least likely to invest in lead-to-gold conversion kits, even when they are easily available on the Internet. Or that geology students are the least socially conscious, because they are the least willing to join in coordinated meditation to prevent earthquakes, even when hundreds of thousands of lives might be at stake.

At first the whole thing seemed so absurd that I had to believe I'd misunderstood it. But this theory was laid definitively to rest in the comments section of my blog, where one of the authors showed up to repeat and defend his conclusions. You can make your own judgment about his logical skills by reading the conversation that followed at www.TheBigQuestions.com/yoram.html.

Interpreting evidence is always perilous, even when you've brought quite a few more IQ points to the table than these authors appear to have done. When a university admits 46 percent of its male applicants and only 30 percent of its (equally qualified) female applicants, can we infer gender discrimination? Several high-powered attorneys thought so, which is why they brought suit against the University of California at Berkeley in 1973. They managed to run up a lot of bills before someone observed that not a single one of Berkeley's individual departments appeared to be discriminating.* Instead, women were being disproportionately rejected because women were disproportionately applying to the most selective departments.

Here are the actual admissions statistics. (The numbers are part of the public record, but the names of the departments are not, so they are referred to here simply as Departments A, B, C, D, E, and F.)

	Dept. A	Dept. B	Dept. C	Dept. D	Dept. E	Dept. F	Total
MEN	$512/825$ (62%)	$353/560$ (63%)	$120/325$ (37%)	$138/417$ (33%)	$53/191$ (28%)	$16/272$ (6%)	$1192/2590$ (46%)
WOMEN	$89/108$ (82%)	$17/25$ (68%)	$202/593$ (34%)	$131/375$ (35%)	$94/393$ (24%)	$24/341$ (7%)	$557/1835$ (30%)

As you can see, four out of six departments admitted women at a higher rate than men, and the other two (Departments C and E) admitted men at only a slightly higher rate than women. When this was pointed out in court, the lawsuit against Berkeley collapsed — but not before a lot of lawyers had spoken a lot of nonsense.

The mistake those lawyers made was to focus on the *aggregate* statistics — that is, the numbers in the "total" column — without breaking things down. That's what created the illusion of discrimination where none existed. But exactly the same mistake can just as easily create the *opposite* illusion, by creating the illusion of *non*discrimination where discrimination *does* exist.

For example:

---

* The lawsuit involved Berkeley's graduate program, where each department makes its own admissions decisions.

1

Jury Selection

A political activist complains that blacks are systematically un-
derrepresented on American juries. An investigation reveals that
exactly 25 percent of white Americans have served on juries and
exactly 25 percent of black Americans have served on juries.
Can we dismiss the activist's complaint?

SOLUTION: Not at all. Those aggregate statistics tell us practi-
cally nothing. Suppose, for example, that blacks live primarily in
cities, where it's very common to be called for jury duty, while
whites live disproportionately in rural areas, where jury service is
rare. In that case, you'd expect to see a much bigger fraction of
blacks than whites serving on juries. If you don't see that bigger
fraction, you're right to suspect discrimination — no matter what
the aggregate statistics seem to show.

Here's a concrete (though hypothetical) example:

	Urban	Rural	Total
Whites	$^{50}\!/_{100}$ (50%)	$^{50}\!/_{300}$ (17%)	$^{100}\!/_{400}$ (25%)
Blacks	$^{10}\!/_{30}$ (33%)	$^{0}\!/_{10}$ (0%)	$^{10}\!/_{40}$ (25%)

The chart tells us, for example, that there are 100 urban
whites, 50 of whom have served on juries. If you prefer a more
realistic (though equally hypothetical) example, just tack a few
zeroes onto all the numbers in the chart, which won't affect the
percentages.

What you can see here is that even though 25 percent of

blacks and 25 percent of whites have served on juries, blacks are apparently being discriminated against in *both* the urban and rural areas.

In the case of the Berkeley lawsuit, a focus on aggregate statistics created the illusion of discrimination where in fact there was none. In the jury example, a focus on aggregate statistics creates the illusion that discrimination is absent when it is in fact pervasive. The moral, then, is not that discrimination is always either more or less a problem than it appears. The moral is to beware of aggregate statistics.

Here's another example, where aggregate statistics mislead in a slightly different way:

2

Income Trends

In a recent 25-year period, the median income of all American workers increased by a paltry 3 percent. Over the same period, the median income of *white male* American workers increased by a much heftier 15 percent. Can you conclude that for at least one other demographic group (white females, nonwhite males, or nonwhite females), the increase must have been even *less* than 3 percent?

SOLUTION: You can conclude nothing of the kind.

The period in question is 1980–2005.* Here's what happened

---

* I chose this period because it predates the great crash of 2008, so that the apparently paltry 3 percent growth rate is not an artifact of the recession that followed.

to median incomes (after correcting for inflation) for each demographic group over that period:

	1980 Median	2005 Median	% Increase
All Workers	25,000	25,700	3%
White Men	30,700	35,200	15%
Nonwhite Men	19,300	22,300	16%
White Women	11,200	19,600	75%
Nonwhite Women	10,200	16,500	62%

That's right. White males had 15 percent growth, and every
other group had even larger growth — as high as 75 percent for
white women — even though the aggregate growth was only 3
percent.

That's possible partly because the sizes of the groups
changed. In 1980 the median worker was a white man. By 2005,
enough women had entered the workforce that the median
worker was a woman. Women do indeed earn less than men,
which is why the income of the median worker came down. But
that tells us exactly nothing about income growth for men, or for
women, or for whites, or for nonwhites, or for anyone else.

Similarly, the average math scores of seventeen-year-olds have
dropped slightly over the past twenty years or so — even though
the scores of the average white student, the average black student, and the average Hispanic student have all increased (by
1.3 percent, 12.6 percent, and 8.7 percent). How can this be? It's
simple: blacks and Hispanics, who on average score lower than
whites, now make up a larger percentage of the population. If you
focus on the grim-looking aggregate statistic, you'll miss the fact
that every group has improved.

In case that's not crystal clear, here's a much simpler example
of exactly the same phenomenon:

3

Animal Farm

A farmer keeps both goats and cows. Ten years ago, his median animal weighed 1,000 pounds. Then he adopted a new feeding technique, and today his median animal weighs 300 pounds. Should we conclude that his new feeding technique was a failure?

SOLUTION: Here's what I left out: Ten years ago, the farmer had ten 100-pound goats and twenty 1,000-pound cows. Today he has fifty 300-pound goats and forty 3,000-pound cows. His median goat and his median cow have both tripled in size — but his median animal, which used to be a 1,000-pound cow, is now a 300-pound goat.

An unscrupulous rival might point to that reduction as proof that the farmer's techniques have failed — when in fact they proved to be a great success for both the goats and the cows. Likewise, an unscrupulous politician might point to the paltry 3 percent growth rate in median income as proof that the American economy wasn't working very well — when in fact it worked quite well for every demographic group.

One more example of the pitfalls inherent in aggregate statistics:

4

The Smoking Gun

A tobacco company claims to have evidence that cigarettes prevent cancer. You've managed to get ahold of all the data from its study, which clearly shows that in a representative sample of the population, only 5 percent of nonsmokers get cancer, while 20 percent of smokers do. Can you conclude that the tobacco company was lying (or at least mistaken)?

SOLUTION: No, you cannot. It is in fact perfectly possible for a single legitimate study to show both that smoking prevents cancer and that cancer strikes smokers disproportionately.

For example, there might be a single gene (call it the STRS gene) that makes people highly sensitive to stress. All of that stress, in turn, causes both a higher susceptibility to cancer and a desire to smoke. That by itself could account for a strong correlation between smoking and cancer *even if smoking actually helps to prevent cancer.*

More concretely (though still, of course, hypothetically): suppose that out of every 110 people, 13 are STRS positive and 8 of those smoke, while 97 are STRS negative and 2 of those smoke. Like so:

	STRS-Positive	STRS-Negative
Smokers	8	2
Nonsmokers	5	95

Now suppose that among the STRS positive, smoking reduces cancer risk from 80 percent to 75 percent, while among the STRS negative, smoking reduces cancer risk from about 1 percent to 0 percent. Then, in each group, here are the numbers we should expect to see getting cancer:

	STRS-Positive	STRS-Negative	Total
Smokers	2/8 = 25%	0/2 = 0%	2/10 = 20%
Nonsmokers	4/5 = 80%	1/95 ≈ 1%	5/100 = 5%

As you can see, 20 percent of smokers get cancer and only 5 percent of nonsmokers get cancer, just as the problem asks us to assume. But as you can also see, smoking reduces your cancer risk whether or not you have the STRS gene.

Does smoking in fact prevent cancer? I very much doubt it. In fact, I'd bet with considerable confidence that smoking *causes* cancer. But my *reason* for believing that is not simply that smokers are more cancer prone. As we've just seen, that kind of aggregate statistic proves nothing.

Instead, the best evidence comes from two sources: First, there are natural experiments where, for example, one state or another suddenly raises the tax on cigarettes, leading people to cut back on smoking *for reasons that we can be pretty sure have nothing to do with genetics or other factors that might affect cancer risk*. When cancer rates start to fall after the tax increase, we *are* entitled to draw the kind of causal inference that raw correlations would not justify.

The second good reason to believe that smoking causes cancer is that doctors are pretty sure they understand the *mechanism* by which smoking causes cancer, starting with cell damage. That's pretty convincing, especially since each step in the mechanism can be tested in a lab. But without *some* additional argument, aggregate statistics tell you nothing.

Another example: Aggregate statistics show that urban areas with large police presences tend to have a lot of crime. Should we conclude that policing causes crime? More plausibly, it's the other way around: More police are assigned to areas where crime is most rampant. Do those additional police do any good? The raw numbers won't tell you.

Economists Jonathan Klick and Alex Tabarrok attacked this problem by observing that the city of Washington, DC, substantially increases its police presence whenever the national terror alert status is raised from yellow to orange. This has the flavor of a controlled experiment, because changes in the terror alert status are not caused by changes in urban crime levels and so can be thought of as random events. The result of this controlled experiment is that when the alert level is orange and there are more police on the streets, crime rates fall substantially. In other words, policing appears to work.

For yet another example, we know that college graduates typically earn higher wages than high school graduates. Is that because a college education tends to boost your wages? Or is it because those who already expect to be high earners figure they can afford to waste four years in college? Or maybe because a single genetic makeup leads to both a strong work ethic and a taste for higher education?

The gold standard would be another controlled experiment: if you could *randomly* assign 1,000 fresh high school graduates to go to college and another 1,000 to go straight into the workforce, and then observe their wages ten years down the line, you could be pretty sure that any wage differences were *caused* by differences in education. Unfortunately, that's not the kind of experiment that subjects are likely to volunteer for.

So we do the best we can with the data we've got. Ideally, you'd compare college grads with high school grads who, except for their educational choices, are as similar as possible. Of course, it's not always an easy business to figure out who is "as similar as possible" to whom, as the next problem demonstrates.

5

Twin Studies

Which of the following provides the strongest evidence that college *causes* higher wages?

a) Mark and Clark are total strangers. Mark went to college; Clark did not. Mark earns more than Clark.
b) Fred and Ed are brothers, three years apart in age. Fred went to college; Ed did not. Fred earns more than Ed.
c) Spike and Ike are identical twins. Spike went to college; Ike did not. Spike earns more than Ike.

SOLUTION: We can probably dispense with Mark and Clark. There are a thousand possible reasons why Mark might earn more than Clark does. Maybe he's smarter, or more ambitious, or has a more supportive family.

Fred and Ed, the brothers, provide somewhat better evidence, because brothers (as opposed to total strangers) tend to be closer in brainpower, closer in ambition, and closer in family background. (Of course not all brothers fit this pattern, but we're playing the odds here.)

You might think that Spike and Ike, the twins, provide even better evidence, because identical twins (as opposed to brothers generally) tend to be even more alike in brainpower, ambition, and family background.

But I suspect that Spike and Ike are exceptions to that rule. After all, there must be *some* reason why Spike went to college and Ike didn't. Presumably there was already some important difference there.

You could, of course, say the same about Fred and Ed. But for them, there's a three-year age gap. A lot can happen in three years. The family might have gone bankrupt; a parent might have died; a new factory might have opened up and offered tempting alternatives to college. Any of these could explain why Fred went to college and Ed didn't, *even if they're very similar in brains and temperament.*

For Spike and Ike (the twins), there are many fewer possible explanations. Yes, maybe Ike skipped college because he broke his leg—but you could say exactly the same about Ed. If you're playing the odds, you might well judge that there are more likely to be important differences—such as a big intelligence gap—between Spike and Ike than between Fred and Ed.

Even identical twins are never truly identical, and the *very fact that Spike and Ike made different choices* probably means they're less identical than most. Moreover, their having made very different choices *in the same year, facing exactly the same family circumstances,* makes this even more likely.

If you were to tell me that Spike spent a year in the hospital at age twenty-three while Ike worked as a lumberjack, and that Spike dropped dead at twenty-five, I'd be reluctant to conclude that hospital stays cause early deaths. Instead, I'd start with the presumption that there was a *reason* that Spike, but not Ike, went to the hospital. And if you tell me that Spike went to college while Ike stayed home, I'm going to start with the presumption that, compared with Ike, Spike was more academically inclined.

I'm not sure, then, whether the answer is (b) or (c).

Do you see a pattern emerging? Instead of looking at the overall admission rates to graduate school, you get a clearer picture by looking separately at each department. Instead of looking at the overall racial makeup of juries, you get a clearer picture by looking separately at each geographic area. Instead of looking at the overall rise in median income over some period, you get a clearer picture by looking separately at each demographic group. Instead of looking at the overall correlation between smoking and cancer, you get a clearer picture by looking separately at smokers with different genes. Instead of looking at the overall correlation between policing and crime, you get a clearer picture by looking separately at crime rates on yellow and orange alert days.

The obvious moral, once again, is: Don't jump to conclusions based solely on aggregate statistics. Instead, break things down (say, by department or by geography or by demographics or by genetics). But a far better moral, once again, is don't jump to conclusions, period. Because sometimes it's the breakdown statistics that mislead and the aggregate statistics that paint the accurate picture. For example:

6

Inside Baseball

In 1923, Lou Gehrig's batting average was .423, while Babe Ruth's was only .393.

In 1924, Lou Gehrig's batting average was .500, while Babe Ruth's was only .378.

In 1925, Lou Gehrig's batting average was .295, while Babe Ruth's was only .290.

Who had the higher batting average for the three years combined?

SOLUTION: There's not enough information here to tell, but the answer happens to be Babe Ruth. Here is the missing information:

	1923	1924	1925	1923–1925
GEHRIG	$11/26 = .423$	$6/12 = .500$	$129/437 = .295$	$146/475 = .307$
RUTH	$205/522 = .393$	$200/529 = .378$	$104/359 = .290$	$509/1410 = .361$

If Gehrig was the more valuable player in each individual year, how can Ruth be the more valuable player for the three years combined? Answer: Gehrig's best years—1923 and 1924—were years when he had very few at-bats, so they contribute very little to his three-year average.

The moral of this problem is exactly opposite to the morals of the preceding few. There the aggregate statistics told a misleading story. Here, it's the *non*-aggregate statistics (that is, the statistics that are broken down year by year) that tell the misleading story, making Gehrig look more valuable (relative to Ruth) than he really was. The übermoral, then, is not that aggregate statistics always mislead *or* that non-aggregate statistics always mislead. It's that *all* statistics can mislead if you interpret them carelessly.*

An even broader moral is: Don't jump to conclusions. Here are some more problems to test how jumpy you are.

7

The Teacher's Dilemma

You're an elementary school teacher, and over the years you've been keeping tabs on the effectiveness of your methods. You've discovered that when you praise students for their success, they don't usually improve very much. In fact, they often *dis*-improve. But when you speak harshly to a weak student, that student usu-

---

* The fact that aggregate and broken-down statistics can tell very different (and even contradictory) stories — and that, depending on circumstances, *either* story can mislead — is known as *Simpson's paradox* and was first explicitly noted by the British statistician Edward H. Simpson in 1951.

ally improves. Can you conclude that harsh words are more effective than praise?

SOLUTION: Here's the thing: it's pretty likely that 70 percent of the time, no matter *what* you do, the weak students will improve — for the simple reason that weak students have a lot of room for improvement. So it's not clear that your harsh words had any effect at all.

Likewise, no matter what you do, strong students will tend to dis-improve, because they have a lot more room to slide downward than to climb upward.

We can add a little flesh to that story: When a student performs poorly on an exam, it's probably because of some combination of innate (dis)ability, failure to study, and just plain having a bad day. The next time around, the ability and the study habits might be entirely unchanged, but it's unlikely that the same student will have two bad exam days in a row, for the same reason that if you throw a die twice, and if the first one comes up six, you're still unlikely to throw double sixes. So those students will tend to improve.

You might have heard of the *Sports Illustrated* jinx — sports teams and players who appear on the cover of *Sports Illustrated* tend to suffer performance declines. Of course they do! To make the cover of *Sports Illustrated,* you usually have to have had a particularly good year, which means you probably had some particularly good luck that can't be expected to continue. Making the cover of *Sports Illustrated* is like being praised by your teacher — it only happens when you're already poised for a fall.

The Teacher's Dilemma and the *Sports Illustrated* jinx are examples of the statistical phenomenon called *regression to the mean.* As a quite general rule, in any activity where chance plays a role (such as success in school, sports, or business), those who perform best on a given day are likely to have been unusually lucky that day. Because luck does not persist the way skill does, those people are likely to perform less well in the future. Likewise, those who perform worst on a given day are likely to have been unusually unlucky, which means that their luck — and their performance — is likely to improve.

8

College Education

Moosylvania State University has determined that its weakest third-year students are generally being held back by poor writing skills. Therefore, to improve the student success rate, MSU plans to require all freshmen to pass a writing proficiency test and take remedial writing courses as needed. Is this policy justified by the evidence?

SOLUTION: On the contrary. Despite their poor writing skills, these students are still in school in their third year. That's evidence that poor writing skills are *not* the key barrier to success.

The least successful students are those who flunked out in their first and second years, possibly for reasons that are quite invisible when you look at those who are just managing to scrape by.

If, for example, solid math skills are absolutely necessary to survive the first two years, then the weakest third-year students, having made it that far, will all have solid math skills. This masks the fact that weak math skills are the main barrier to success.

There's a famous and apparently true story about the British Royal Air Force adding armor to its World War II warplanes. To minimize the weight of the plane, they wanted to add armor only in spots where it would do the most good. So they inspected planes returning from battle, determined that the majority of the bullet holes were in a few particular locations on the fuselage, and figured that's where they'd add the armor.

It was the great statistician Abraham Wald who more than earned his entire lifetime's income by pointing out that if planes could return safely with bullet holes in these locations, then these weren't the locations that needed armor. It's the locations with *no* visible bullet holes that need the armor — because the planes that were shot in *those* locations were the ones that never made it back.

Probationary students are like warplanes that got shot up pretty badly but (so far at least) have survived. If the visible holes are in their writing skills, it might not be the writing skills that need to be patched.

Incidentally, Moosylvania State is particularly proud of its small class sizes, and advertises that its average class has just 20 students. What they don't tell you is that despite those impressive numbers, most students most of the time are enrolled in nothing but huge lecture classes.

You see, Moosylvania, true to its word, does offer a lot of small classes. But there's almost nobody *in* those classes — that's what keeps them small.

In fact, Moosylvania offers 149 classes each term. Of those, 140 are seminars with just two students each; the remaining nine are big lecture classes with 300 students. That does average out to just 20 per class, just as advertised. Better yet, nearly 94 percent of the classes have fewer than three students!

But in any given semester there are only 280 enrollments in those 140 tiny two-person seminars, while there are 2,700 enrollments in those nine giant 300-person lectures. Lecture enrollments outstrip seminar enrollments by a factor of almost ten-to-one, which means that over the course of a college career the average student must take about ten times as many lecture courses as seminars.

Prospective students should beware of aggregate statistics!

(Come to think of it, if I were running a college, and if I were more unscrupulous than I like to believe I am, I would create a huge number of "classes" with their sizes capped at exactly zero students. It would cost me nothing to staff those courses, but boy, would it bring my average class size down!)

And while we're talking about higher education:

9

Good-Looking Teachers

At most American colleges, students periodically evaluate the performance of their professors. A recent study shows that professors who are perceived as physically beautiful generally receive much higher ratings. Is this evidence of superficiality on the students' part?

SOLUTION: More likely it's evidence that the evaluations are accurate—because you should have expected all along that the prettiest teachers would be among the best.

That's not just because the teachers who bother to comb their hair and the teachers who bother to prepare their lectures are likely to be the same teachers. It's true for a much deeper reason.

There are a great many jobs in which physical beauty is a considerable advantage—not just jobs like "fashion model" or "movie star" but pretty much anything in sales or retailing. By and large, you'd expect physically attractive people to gravitate toward those jobs. Those who choose to teach instead presumably have either a particular talent for teaching or a particular love for it. So of course you should expect them to be better than the average teacher.

I'd expect this to be even more the case in occupations where physical beauty is even more irrelevant than it is in the classroom. You show me a lighthouse keeper with movie-star good looks, and I'll show you (at least probably) a really really good lighthouse keeper — one who has such a passion for lighthouse keeping that he resisted every temptation to cash in on those looks. And if your cable guy looks like Brad Pitt, he's probably a hell of a cable guy.

In fact, three researchers at the University of Nevada recently found evidence that attractive teachers really are more effective, in the sense that their students retain more knowledge. But the Nevada researchers failed to look beyond the obvious. Instead, they offer two possible explanations:

> First, it is possible that the attractiveness of the instructor produces a self-fulfilling prophecy effect, where student expectations influence teacher behavior. Second, it is possible that instructor attractiveness has a more direct impact on learning by changing the students' responses to the instructor. It is conceivable that attractive instructors command more attention from students than less attractive instructors.

Either of these alternatives assumes that, one way or another, attractive teachers do a better job because students notice their attractiveness. But that misses the larger point. You should expect more attractive teachers to do a better job even if students are completely blind to their physical beauty.

Of course, there's nothing special about education when it comes to statistical fallacies. Medical statistics can be just as misleading, as the following example shows.

10

Hospital Patients

There's only one hospital in the Land of Nod, where, on the average day last year, there were 80 patients being treated for cancer and 80 being treated for heart attacks. From this, does it appear that the average Noddian is about equally likely to be struck by a heart attack as by cancer?

SOLUTION: Certainly not. For all we know, there are 80 cancer patients who have been in the hospital for a year, while 80 new heart attack victims were admitted each day and released the next — for a total of 80 cancer patients and 365 × 80 = 29,200 heart attack victims.

The mistake here is to overlook the fact that some hospital stays are longer than others. If you count the patients on, say, August 1, most of the year's short-term patients don't get counted — because they came and went in February or April, or won't arrive until October.

How are you doing so far? If you've gotten most of these puzzles wrong, you're not alone. After all, I *chose* these puzzles because *most* people get them wrong. I could just as easily (though far less interestingly) have compiled a collection of equally complicated and subtle puzzles that most people get right.

In fact, psychologists tell us that human beings are hardwired to draw inferences faster and more accurately in some circumstances than others. They've devised experiments to determine just what those circumstances are. One of those experiments — a highly replicated one — forms the basis for the following three puzzles.

11

Checking Cards

I have four cards, each with a letter on one side and a number on the other. Here they are, some with their letters face up and some with their numbers face up:

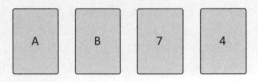

You want to know whether every card with an A on one side has a 7 on the other. Which cards must you flip?

12

Barefoot Cheaters

Here are four patrons who have just shown up at your seaside diner, where you've posted a sign reading ALL CHILDREN MUST WEAR SHOES:

To catch all the potential rule breakers, which black boxes must you peek behind?

13

Which Is Harder?

Which is harder — problem 11 or problem 12?

SOLUTIONS: For problem 11, you have to turn over the first and fourth cards. There's no need to check the second card because it doesn't have an A and therefore doesn't need a 7. There's no need to check the third card because it's got a 7 whether it needs one or not.

For problem 12, you need to remove the first and the fourth black boxes. You don't need to check the second patron, because he's not a child. You don't need to check the third patron, because she's wearing shoes whether she needs them or not.

Problem 13 is where things get interesting. Problems 11 and 12 are, in essence, exactly the same problem, and their solutions follow exactly the same logic. But psychologists have found that only about 10 percent of people solve problem 11 correctly (so don't feel too bad if you got it wrong!) whereas a great many more solve problem 12 correctly. (The exact number depends on experimental conditions.) The most widespread interpretation is that our critical faculties kick into high gear in social situations, and particularly when we're on the lookout for cheaters.

Indeed, it's been argued that a well-developed instinct to root out cheating, deception, and other "unfair" behaviors is part of what makes us uniquely human, and perhaps a driving force behind the evolution of our enormously sophisticated brains. But that well-developed instinct sometimes has a tendency to go into overdrive, which is what allows nonsensical conspiracy theories to thrive. The antidote, of course, is logic. See how you do with this one:

14

Gas Prices

Following a recent interruption in the supply of crude oil, the price of gasoline rose so high that oil company profits actually increased. *True or False:* This is evidence that the oil companies collude to keep prices high.

SOLUTION: Not only is this false; it is precisely the opposite of the truth. The big hike in gas prices is evidence—in fact, it's pretty much *proof*—that the oil companies *don't* collude.

Here's why: If it were this easy for the oil companies to raise their profits, then they wouldn't have waited for a supply interruption. They'd have raised their prices long ago.

Gasoline customers kept right on buying a lot of gas after the price hike, so they must be quite price insensitive. But no monopolist, and no successful cartel, ever faces price-insensitive customers. If your customers *were* price insensitive, you'd raise your prices, and you'd keep on raising them until your customers were no longer price insensitive. (This has to happen eventually, if only because you reach a point where they just can't afford to pay anymore.)

The only force that prevents this from happening is competition. You might be willing to pay $1,000 a gallon for gasoline, but no competitive oil company will try to charge you that much, for fear of losing your business to a rival. So whenever we see price insensitivity, we know there's competition afoot.

When you start to get drunk on conspiracy theories, logic is the friend who hangs on to your car keys. Be sure to thank it the next day. But sometimes you need a little help that logic alone can't give you. Sometimes you also need a few facts.

15

The Gender Gap

Alice has just heard that on average, women are paid 77 cents for every dollar earned by equally skilled men.

Bob, who has just completed his first course in economics, explains to Alice that this is impossible. If it *were* true, he says, profit-maximizing firms would clamor to hire cheap women instead of expensive men, and men would be unemployable until the wage rates equalized.

Alice, who has a little more experience in the real world, observes that the people who run corporations are not always single-minded rational profit maximizers. Therefore, it's perfectly possible for discriminatory wages to survive.

Carlita, who has studied more economics than Bob and worked in industry longer than Alice, points out that they're both right and both wrong. Corporate managers routinely overlook small profit opportunities but rarely pass up large ones. So the right question to ask is, If Alice is right, how big is the profit opportunity that Bob is pointing to?

Pure logic can't settle this one. But a little back-of-the-envelope calculation can point to the most probable resolution. Supply the needed back-of-the-envelope calculation.

SOLUTION: We'll need some numbers. First, the workforce is currently (to a rough but reasonable approximation) about 50 percent female.

The next number is one you're less likely to have at your fingertips — unless you have the fingertips of an economist: To the same sort of rough but reasonable approximation, corporations pay out about ⅔ of their revenue in employee compensation. The remaining ⅓ goes to stockholders and bondholders.

The next number is one I wasn't sure of myself until I Googled it: To a very rough approximation, the total value of the bond market and the total value of the stock market are equal. So for our back-of-the-envelope purposes, we can assume that of every $300 that comes in, about $200 goes to the employees and the remaining $100 is split equally, with $50 going to the bondholders and $50 to the stockholders.

Now suppose Alice is right about that 77 percent bit. Then employers face the opportunity to fire half their workforce (i.e., the males) and replace them with workers who are 23 percent cheaper. That's a saving, on average, of 11.5 percent per worker. Instead of paying your workers $200, you're now paying them 89.5 percent of that, or $179—a saving of $21. All of that goes to the stockholders. (After all, where else could it go?)*

Bottom line: Instead of earning $50 for each $300 of corporate revenue, the stockholders now earn $71. That's a 42 percent increase. The company's stock is now 42 percent more valuable.

That's huge. A corporate manager who raises the company's stock price by 42 percent in a single stroke is on the road to a brilliant career and perhaps the status of a legend. If Alice is right, corporate managers everywhere are seeing that opportunity and choosing not to grab it.

Might there be a manager here and there who chooses to ignore such opportunities? Absolutely, and Bob is wrong to deny it. But might such laziness be as widespread as it would have to

---

* Once the workers and the bondholders are paid, everything else either gets paid out directly to the stockholders in dividends or indirectly to the stockholders via capital improvements, supply purchases, and other expenditures that increase the value of the company's stock.

be to sustain what Alice claims is a 23 percent wage differential? That's too implausible to take seriously.

Notice that the numbers really matter here. If our calculation had come out with a number like 2 percent instead of 42 percent, then Alice's theory would have been at least plausible. At 42 percent it's not. Calculation, like logic, is your friend.

This leaves unanswered the question of what *does* account for gender gaps in wages. The answer surely is a conglomeration of a great many factors, possibly including differences in ability, differences in training, differences in interests, differences in wage-negotiation tactics, differences in career choices, differences in priorities, and, yes, discrimination. We've determined that discrimination can't account for a 23 percent wage gap or anything close to that. Might it still be a significant contributing factor? The evidence, pro and con, could fill a book — a different book, because this book is largely about other things. The further evidence that will be collected and analyzed in the next couple of years will probably be enough to fill a second volume. People are working on this. They're making progress. They're not finished yet.

Often progress takes the form of *ruling out* some inference that seems plausible on the surface or — once again — recognizing that what seems obvious is not always true. That will be a good lesson to keep in mind as we turn to the next chapter, where we'll still be drawing inferences — inferences about the future. We call them predictions.

CHAPTER 3

Predictions

*N*ever make predictions, especially about the future." At the moment I'm typing this, there are 47,600 Google hits attributing that quote to Baseball Hall of Famer Casey Stengel and 56,300 attributing it to Baseball Hall of Famer Yogi Berra. I have no idea who actually said it, which suggests that one should be cautious even in making predictions about the past.

The future is even harder. Around the year AD 100, the Roman senator Sextus Julius Frontinus pronounced that "inventions have long since reached their limit, and I see no hope for future development." In 1943, Thomas J. Watson, a pioneer in electronic computing and the president of IBM, predicted that "there is a world market for maybe five computers." In 1955 the entrepreneur and inventor Alex Lewyt predicted that we were no more than ten years away from having a nuclear-powered vacuum cleaner.

As there are failed predictions, so there are failed anti-predictions. My treasured copy of the 1985 humor classic *Science Made*

Stupid (a spot-on parody of the popular-science genre) contains a "Wonderful Future Invention Checklist," offered tongue-in-cheek, because of course the joke was that there was little chance we'd see any of this in our lifetimes. Just twenty-five years later I was able to check off about a third of the entries: household robot (does my Roomba count?); magnetic train (check!); flat-screen TV (check!); flat-screen 3-D TV (check!); two-way wrist radio (we are so far past this!); two-way wrist TV (ditto); instant access to all human knowledge (check!!! — and as a bonus we also have instant access to all human stupidity); human clones (getting there); first black president (check!); spelling reform (OMG! I cn chk this 1 off 2!).

Of course I'm cherry-picking; history affords many examples of spectacularly accurate predictions as well. (Think of Dmitry Mendeleyev, in 1863, using his Periodic Table to correctly predict the properties of more than forty chemical elements that hadn't yet been discovered.) In any event, predict we must or we simply can't go on. I am writing these words, for example, based on the (cautious) prediction that somebody might want to read them.

The puzzles in this chapter call for predictions. Not all of them call for *perfect* predictions; in some cases the best you can do is argue that one outcome is more likely than another, or that the answer depends on some additional fact beyond what's given. In some cases, the answer might even be that prediction is impossible. But each problem does call for some genuine insight beyond what you might think is obvious.

Start here.

1

Pigs in a Box

An experimenter places two pigs in a box—one very large pig and one very small pig. At one end of the box is a lever. At the far end of the box—several pig's lengths away—is a bowl that fills with food whenever the lever is pressed. Which pig do you predict will eat better?

SOLUTION: When real-life pigs are placed in a real-life box under these circumstances, the big pig does most of the work and the small pig does most of the eating.

That's because the little pig has absolutely no incentive to press the lever, having quickly learned that if he does, the big pig will steal all the food.

So the big pig, in order to get fed at all, has to do all the lever pushing. While he's getting ready to push the lever, the small pig is waiting by the food bowl. The big pig pushes the lever and runs to the bowl. By the time he gets there, the small pig has scarfed down most of the food. But the big pig shoves the small pig aside and gets whatever's left, which is enough to teach him that it's worth pushing the lever.

The immediate moral is that sometimes it pays to be small. The bigger moral is that even in very simple situations, outcomes are not always what you'd first guess—and if you're making predictions, a little bit of logic goes a long way.

2

Boys or Girls?

You've just opened an adoption agency in a time and place where it's well established that most parents prefer sons to daughters. Do you expect to get more requests for boys or for girls?

SOLUTION: I can't be sure, but my guess is that you'll get more requests for girls.

That's because prospective parents, even when they have a strong preference for boys, tend to have a lot of other strong preferences — including a strong preference for healthy, well-behaved children.

Who gets put up for adoption? Disproportionately, kids who are less wanted. And who are those kids? They're kids with health problems, kids with behavior problems, kids whose parents can't raise them, and (given what the problem tells us about parental preferences in this time and place) girls.

So if I were looking to adopt a healthy, well-behaved child, I might very well choose a girl *even if, like most parents, I had a strong preference for a boy.*

As long as parents prefer boys, they'll tend to cut their sons more slack than they cut their daughters. Therefore (on average, of course), boys have to be *really* bad to get thrown into the adoption pool, whereas girls are sometimes thrown in just for being girls. If you're fishing in that pool, it can make good sense to steer clear of the boys, no matter how much you prefer boys in general.

So as long as prospective parents think this through — and when you're adopting a child, you tend to spend a lot of time thinking things through—your agency might quite likely get a lot more requests for girls than for boys.

You might think this all comes down to which is stronger—the preference for boys or the preference for healthy, well-behaved kids. But that cuts both directions. If you're an adoptive parent with a very strong preference for boys, you might choose a boy despite the risk. But if you're an adoptive parent in a time and place where others have a very strong preference for boys, then the risk of choosing a boy is elevated even further, giving you all the more reason to opt for a girl.

Way back in 2003 I wrote a couple of columns for *Slate* magazine on the subject of whether parents in general prefer boys or girls. I pointed to several bits of relevant evidence: All over the world, parents of boys are less likely to divorce than parents of girls. Again all over the world, parents of girls are more likely to try for another child than parents of boys. Unmarried couples, upon learning the sex of their unborn child, are more likely to marry if the child is a boy. None of these things proves conclusively that parents prefer boys, but I argued that, taken altogether, the evidence seems to point that way. (I'm less convinced of that now than I was in 2003, but that's not relevant here.)

A great many readers chimed in to say I must be wrong, because adoption agencies get more requests for girls—and this (according to those readers) proves that people on average prefer girls! The preceding problem is dedicated to those readers.

Incidentally, Amazon offers for sale a device that's advertised to predict the sex of a child in the womb only six weeks after conception. Here's the distribution of customer reviews for that product:

Customer Reviews

⭐⭐⭐☆☆ 1,034
2.9 out of 5 stars ▾

5 star	▰▰▰▱▱▱▱▱▱▱	33%
4 star	▰▱▱▱▱▱▱▱▱▱	7%
3 star	▰▱▱▱▱▱▱▱▱▱	10%
2 star	▰▱▱▱▱▱▱▱▱▱	9%
1 star	▰▰▰▰▱▱▱▱▱▱	41%

Apparently this product predicts very accurately just about half the time!

3

Kids at School

Studies show quite conclusively that, on average, children from four-child families do significantly worse in school than children from three-child families. You already have three children and have just discovered that you're pregnant with a fourth. Do you predict that your first three children's school performance is likely to suffer?

SOLUTION: You shouldn't. It's true that family size is strongly correlated with educational achievement: once you get past two children, the larger the family, the worse the kids perform. But there's ample evidence that this correlation is not causal. Parents who choose to have four children are generally less educated than parents who choose to have three, and this (along with other demographic differences), not the family size itself, is why their children do less well in school.

   (The effect persists as family sizes get larger; children from five-child families do worse than children from four-child families, and so on.)

But of course your own decision to have a fourth child doesn't change you into a different sort of person. Even if most four-child parents have less education than you do, having a fourth child won't cause your alma mater to revoke your MBA. So your first three children will probably do just as well (or just as poorly) with a fourth sibling as without.

How do we know that it's the demographic characteristics of large families, and not the family size itself, that drives differences in school performance? The simplest test would be a statistical study that controls for demographic characteristics. But that's an imperfect strategy if you're not sure which characteristics are important to control for. So researchers have aimed to be a little more clever. For example, they've looked at families with four children where the last two are twins. Many of these are families who chose to have three children but ended up with four. It turns out that their children tend to perform a lot like children from three-child families, which suggests that it pays not to come from a three-child family but to come from the sort of family where the parents aim for three children.

Another clever strategy is to look at four-child families with, say, three boys followed by a girl (or the same pattern with the sexes reversed). A lot of these families probably planned to stop at three but then took one final stab at gender diversity. Once again, their kids perform a lot like children from three-child families.

Incidentally, even after we make all the corrections for demographics, children from four-child families still do slightly worse on average than children from three-child families (and children from larger families do even worse), but this can be explained away as a birth order effect: fourth children do worse in school than third children, and therefore bring down the family average without bringing down their older brothers and sisters. Fifth, sixth, and seventh children do even worse. Of course it should go without saying that there's plenty of variation around these averages. Wolfgang Mozart was the youngest of seven children, and Benjamin Franklin was the youngest of fifteen.

4

Birth Control

If a new method of birth control is safer, cheaper, more effective, and easier to use than any existing method, what do you predict will happen to the number of unwanted pregnancies?

SOLUTION: It is a safe bet that if a new method of birth control is safer, cheaper, more effective, and easier to use than any existing method, some people will switch from other methods to the new one. It is also a safe bet that some people will switch from abstinence to the new method, or switch from having sex once in a while to twice in a while. So unless the method is *perfectly* effective, the number of unwanted pregnancies can go either up or down.

5

Cutting Back on Smoking

Nosmo King is an antismoking crusader who finds that people who don't recognize him sometimes offer him a cigarette. He always takes the cigarette and throws it away, figuring that if he does this 20 times a year, there will be 20 fewer cigarettes smoked. Is his prediction correct?

SOLUTION: Nosmo is correct that as long as he accepts and discards 20 free cigarettes a year, there will be less smoking. He is wrong to think there will be 20 fewer cigarettes smoked.

After all, once you give a cigarette to Nosmo, you run out a little sooner, and buy a new pack a little sooner. The convenience store where you do your shopping runs low on inventory just a little sooner and reorders just a little sooner, leading its supplier to run out a little sooner. This (ever-so-slight) increase in the demand for cigarettes percolates up the supply chain all the way to the tobacco companies, which notice that buyers want ever so slightly more cigarettes than they'd planned to manufacture — and that they can afford to ask for a slightly higher price.

At the new, higher price, the tobacco companies are willing to produce a few extra cigarettes. If they produce, say, an additional 7, and if Nosmo discards 20, then the number smoked falls not by 20 but by 13.

The same process works in reverse whenever an activist group asks people to go meatless for a day or a week in order to make more food available for others. I've seen the slogan "Eat a pound less so someone else can eat a pound more." But when you and others eat a pound less, the fall in demand leads to a fall in price, which leads producers to provide less meat — so your sacrifice might mean others can eat more, but it does not mean they can eat a pound more.

6

Cutting Hairs

Over the next few decades it's expected that technological improvements will vastly increase worker productivity in many industries but not in all. Barbers, for example, will probably be no more productive in the year 2050 than they are today. Do you predict that the wages of the average barber, relative to those of the average worker, will be higher or lower in 2050 than they are today?

SOLUTION: The safe prediction is that wages will rise for more productive workers—and that barbers, even though they'll be no more productive, will see their wages rise in tandem with everyone else's.

That's because higher wages on (say) the auto assembly line tend to lure barbers away from haircutting. The supply of haircuts falls, so the price of a haircut—along with the wage of the average barber—must rise.

And if the wages of barbers rise only a little bit, then the exodus from haircutting to auto assembling will continue, raising barbers' wages further, until they're high enough to keep the barbers in the barbershops.

The fact that rising productivity in some industries leads to higher wages in other industries is known to economists as the *Baumol effect*. The Baumol effect not only predicts the future, it also explains the past. It takes your barber about ten minutes to provide a basic haircut. It took your grandfather's barber about the same. In other words, your barber is no more productive than your grandfather's. But your barber is a lot *richer* than your grandfather's barber, and the reason is that productivity has risen in *other* industries.

As a teacher, I'm very glad to report that the same reasoning applies to teachers. While today's farmer feeds twelve times as many people as a farmer of fifty years ago, I still grade essays at about exactly the same rate as my predecessors in the seventeenth century. Nevertheless, I earn a lot more than they did, because a lot of potential teachers have instead become, if not farmers, then computer programmers or financial analysts, whose productivity has also skyrocketed.

7

The Organ Eater

Leopold is a great consumer of mutton kidneys.

a) If Leopold comes into a nice inheritance, what happens to his kidney consumption? Does it increase or decrease?

b) If the price of mutton kidneys rises, what happens to Leopold's kidney consumption?

c) If I tell you that the answer to (a) is that Leopold's kidney consumption increases, does that change your answer to (b)?

d) Extra credit: What is Leopold's last name?

SOLUTION:

a) When I left graduate school and started to earn a decent living, I started eating a lot more steak and a lot less bologna. If Leopold thinks of kidneys the way I thought of steak, he'll eat more of them. If he thinks of kidneys the way

I thought of bologna, he'll eat fewer of them. That's about all we can say.

b) There are two factors in play here. First, when the price of kidneys rises, Leopold has an excellent reason to consume fewer: his fourth or fifth kidney might just not be worth it to him at the new price.

But there's also a second factor: A rise in the price of kidneys means Leopold can no longer continue to live quite as well as he's accustomed to. In other words, he's effectively poorer. We saw in (a) that when Leopold becomes richer (or poorer), his kidney consumption could either rise or fall.

Bottom line: The first factor gives Leopold a good reason to cut back on his kidney consumption. The second factor—the effect of feeling poorer—might give him either a second reason to cut back or a reason to do the opposite. We have no idea which reason is more compelling, so we have no idea whether his overall consumption goes up or down.

c) We still have the same two factors in play. The first factor remains a good reason for Leopold to eat fewer kidneys. As for the second factor, the price increase makes Leopold effectively poorer, and we're now given the additional information that when he's poorer, he eats fewer kidneys. (Actually we're told that when he's *richer,* he eats *more* kidneys, but that comes down to the same thing.) Now both factors point in the same direction, so there are two good reasons for his consumption to fall and zero good reasons for his consumption to rise. His consumption goes down.

d) Try asking an English major.

Although this solution is exactly what I'd expect from my students, I should add that there's one further consideration here: Very few people spend large fractions of their income on mutton kidneys. Therefore, when the price of kidneys goes up, very few people feel a whole lot poorer. That's a good reason to expect that the second factor in the solution to (b) is ordinarily quite small, which in turn is a good reason (though not a thoroughly compelling reason) to believe that only the first factor really matters. It is therefore extremely likely (though not definite) that Leopold's consumption falls in (b).

The extremely *un*likely (but still logically possible) scenario is that Leopold currently eats kidneys six days a week but splurges on steak every Sunday. When the price of kidneys rises, he feels quite a bit poorer (after all, he buys a *lot* of kidneys) and therefore gives up steak, eating kidneys seven days a week instead of six — and therefore consuming more than before, in defiance of the freshman economics textbooks that declare a price increase must always lead to a fall in consumption. (Sophomore-level textbooks have always acknowledged that this law might not be universal.)

Something very like this might have occurred in Leopold's home country of Ireland, in the years shortly before the Great Famine. On a typical day in 1844, the average adult male Irishman ate a staggering 13 pounds of potatoes. At 5 potatoes to the pound, that's 65 potatoes a day. The average for all men, women, and children was a more modest 9 pounds a day, or 45 potatoes. Foreign travelers in Ireland routinely wrote home about the seemingly superhuman Irish appetite (which was surely driven by a hard life of manual labor in the fields, burning a lot of calories that needed to be replenished). A typical extract from one of those letters observes that "the Englishman would find considerable difficulty in stowing away in his stomach this enormous quantity of vegetable food, and how an Irishman is able to manage it is beyond my ability to explain."

Economists have long suspected that a small rise in the price of potatoes could have had so devastating an effect on Irish families that they'd have cut back on their small and occasional extravagances and doubled down on potatoes. There is, alas, no reliable historical evidence to support this suspicion. There is, however, some evidence to suggest that something very similar does occur in parts of modern-day Asia, with potatoes replaced by rice and wheat.

If I had to guess, I'd say that the three most common prediction targets are sports, weather, and prices. I doubt I can do much to help you with the first two, but economists are at least pretty good at thinking about prices.

Following is a series of problems that will illustrate the economist's way of thinking.

8

The Price of Bread

Suppose the government imposes a price ceiling on wheat, so that instead of selling at the current price of, say, $4 per bushel, nobody is allowed to charge more than $3 a bushel. What happens to the price of bread?

SOLUTION: Well, you make bread out of wheat, and the price of wheat just fell, so bakers will want to supply more bread, which drives the price down, right?

Hold on. Let's start over. You make bread out of wheat, and the price of wheat just fell, so farmers will supply less wheat (either switching over to other crops or perhaps, eventually, selling their farms to developers). If there's less wheat, there's *got* to be less bread — which drives the price *up*, right?

The second argument is correct: the price of bread goes up.

What's wrong with the first argument? Bakers are indeed

happy that the price of wheat went down. But they're also quite *un*happy that wheat has become harder to find. They're paying less to the farmer but spending a lot more time scrounging around trying to find a farmer who's willing to sell to them. That takes much of the fun and profit out of making bread, so the statement "bakers will want to supply more" is wrong.

9

Cars and Bars

In a town with just one auto mechanic but several bars, a new law requires each business to contribute $20,000 a year toward the construction and maintenance of city parks. Which do you predict will rise more: the price of a car repair or the price of a drink?

SOLUTION: There's no reason on earth for the price of a car repair to change. Alfred, the lone auto mechanic, has long ago set prices that he believes will maximize his profits. He still wants to maximize his profits, so there's no reason to change those prices.

Needless to say, Alfred is unhappy about the new law, just as he'd be unhappy if he'd somehow misplaced a suitcase containing $20,000 in cash. But losing your suitcase is no reason to alter your business practices. If raising prices were a smart strategy, Alfred would have raised them long before he lost his suitcase, or long before the new obligation was imposed.

The only way Alfred can avoid this cost is to close up his shop, which he might or might not do. But as long as he stays in business, his price list remains unchanged.

In the short run, you can make exactly the same argument

about the bars. There's no reason any of their prices should change. But over time, we should expect some of those bars to close. After all, there are several of them—and with competition like that, they can't all be doing exceptionally well in the first place. Chances are excellent that in the face of an extra $20,000 expense, a few of them will simply give up.

That changes everything. Once a few bars close, customers migrate and the *demand* for drinks at the remaining bars increases. And as everyone knows, it makes sense to raise prices when the demand for your product goes up.

So, in the very short run, no prices change. Eventually, a few bars close and the remaining ones raise their prices. And after you crash your car on the way home from one of those bars, the auto repair will cost just as much as it always did.

10

Tickets at the Ballpark, Take One

A famous Chicago Cubs baseball player demands a $10 million raise, and the management accedes to his demand. What do you predict will happen to ticket prices at the ballpark?

SOLUTION: Paying your pitcher an extra $10 million a year is a lot like being forced to contribute an extra $20,000 a year to park maintenance—it's unpleasant, but once you've decided to keep the pitcher, there's no way to make it less painful.

Ticket prices are already set to maximize profit. If the Cubs' owner loses $10 million on an ill-advised stock market investment, he'd be even more ill advised to tamper with those prices. If he loses $10 million to a hard-bargaining pitcher, the story is exactly the same.

11

Tickets at the Ballpark, Take Two

The Chicago Cubs play at Wrigley Field, where the ushers have just demanded and received a substantial raise. What do you predict will happen to ticket prices at the ballpark?

SOLUTION: This problem is very different from the preceding one. Once you agree to give your star pitcher a raise, there's nothing you can do to lessen the pain of paying it. But if your ushers get a raise, you can lessen the pain by hiring fewer ushers. With fewer ushers, you might prefer to sell fewer tickets, as the ushers' primary job is to monitor the behavior of unruly fans. If you're willing to sell fewer tickets, you can get away with charging higher prices — so why shouldn't you?

Likewise, if the employees at Alfred's car repair shop successfully demand an increase in their hourly wage, or if the suppliers who provide him with auto parts raise their prices, I expect the price of a repair to rise. Unlike a $20,000 annual contribution to the parks department, these are costs he can reduce by choosing to repair fewer cars — whereupon he can afford to drive away a few customers by raising prices.

12

Trolls on a Bridge

If you have to pass through two tollbooths to get across a bridge, would you prefer the two booths to be owned by one troll or by two different trolls?

SOLUTION: One troll is better than two.

The only thing preventing the troll (or trolls) from setting astronomical fees is the fear of losing customers, who will find ways to avoid the bridge altogether.

For a troll who owns a tollbooth, a $1 price increase is punished by the loss of, say, 10 customers at that booth. For a troll who owns *both* tollbooths, a $1 price increase is punished by the loss of 10 customers at *both* booths. That's twice the punishment, and hence twice the incentive to keep prices down.

You might pay an exorbitant price in any event, but because of the double-incentive effect, the total cost of getting across the bridge will be less exorbitant with one troll than it is with two.

13

Software Pricing

Microsoft, a well-known monopolist, produces both the Windows operating system and the Office suite of software (including Word and Excel). To most customers, neither product is much use without the other.

As a consumer who plans to buy these products, would you prefer to see Microsoft broken up into two separate monopolies, one selling Windows and the other selling Office?

SOLUTION: One troll is still better than two.

The only thing preventing Microsoft from charging astronomical prices is the fear of losing customers.

For a hypothetical post-breakup company that makes just an operating system, a $1 price increase is punished by the loss of, say, 10 customers for that operating system. For a company (such as the current incarnation of Microsoft) that makes *both* operating systems *and* office software, a $1 price increase is punished by the loss of 10 customers for both the operating system *and* the office software. That's twice the punishment, hence twice the incentive to keep prices down.

You might pay an exorbitant price in any event, but because of the double-incentive effect, the total cost of Windows plus Office is less exorbitant today than it would be under the proposed breakup.

14

Merge Ahead, Take One

A monopoly tire company merges with a monopoly rubber company. As a potential car buyer, are you happy about this merger?

SOLUTION: You should welcome the merger. One troll is still better than two.

The only thing preventing the tire company from charging astronomical prices is the fear of losing customers.

For a company that makes just tires, a $1 price increase is punished by the loss of, say, 10 customers for that tire. For a company that makes both tires *and* rubber, a $1 price increase is punished by the loss of 10 customers for both the tire itself and the rubber that goes into the tire. That's twice the punishment, hence twice the incentive to keep the price down.

You might pay an exorbitant price in any event, but because of the double-incentive effect, the price of the tire will be less exorbitant with one monopolist than it is with two.

Do you hear an echo? The solutions to the three preceding problems are essentially identical. That's a cause for celebration. An insight is a precious resource, and the more times it can be recycled, the more precious it becomes.

15

Merge Ahead, Take Two

Three major computer manufacturers are seeking permission to merge into one giant company. A coalition of smaller manufacturers vocally opposes the merger, arguing that if it's allowed to take place, the new mega-company will exercise vast monopoly power. Do you agree with that prediction?

SOLUTION: It is certainly true in some cases that the merger of three large companies can lead to vast monopoly power. But this is not one of those cases.

I know this because a coalition of smaller companies is opposed to the merger. If the merger were likely to raise prices, the smaller companies would be applauding it. When the big guys raise their prices, the little guys can follow suit.

Instead, the smaller companies must fear that the merger will lead to *lower* prices, which means they believe the primary effect of the merger will be not greater monopoly power but greater efficiency.

As a general rule, firms welcome monopoly power *even when they're not part of the monopoly*. If anyone's prices rise, then everyone's prices can rise. So when one firm complains about another firm's monopoly power, you can be pretty sure they're dissembling.

If a coalition of well-informed consumers were vocally opposing the merger, it would be a fair guess that the merger is likely to raise prices by creating monopoly power. You can tell a lot about the probable effects of a policy by observing who's for it and who's against it.

Notice that the mergers in problems 14 and 15 are quite different. The first is a case of *vertical integration,* where a company merges with one or more of its suppliers (or one of its customers); the second is a case of *horizontal integration,* where a company merges with one or more of its competitors. For the reasons explained in the solutions, vertical integration is nearly always a boon to the consumer, while horizontal integration can go either way — but you can often tell which way things will go by observing the reaction of firms that are left out of the merger.

16

Life in Pullman

In the 1800s the Pullman Palace Car Company was famous for building luxurious railroad passenger cars. It was famous too for building the town of Pullman, Illinois, as a place for its employees to live and work. Pullman owned all the housing and rented it to the workers. It also owned grocery stores, where the workers shopped.

Elsewhere in Illinois, the demographically similar town of Pushman had many competing employers, many competing landlords, and many competing grocery stores.

Assuming the Pullman Company acts wisely in its own interests, where would you expect groceries to be more expensive — in Pushman or in Pullman?

(Incidentally, the story of Pullman is true. The town of Pushman was invented for this problem, but surely there were many towns very like it.)

SOLUTION: You should expect grocery prices to be the same in both towns.

To see why, imagine that the Pullman Grocery charges the same competitive prices as the groceries in Pushman, and try asking whether Pullman has any incentive to raise those prices.

The key is to note that Pullman, being a profit maximizer, presumably pays its workers just enough to keep them from moving to Pushman in search of a better life. So if prices go up at the Pullman grocery store, Pullman has to compensate the residents through higher wages, lower housing prices, or both.

To see how that plays out, take an example: Initially, the Pullman Grocery charges the competitive price of $10 for a week's worth of groceries. Suppose Pullman raises grocery prices by 50 percent. You might imagine that Pullmanites now pay $15 a week for their groceries. Not so. Probably they tighten their belts, eat a little less, and pay a grocery bill of, say, $14 a week.

To a Pullmanite, that's an extra $4 out of pocket *and* less food on the table. That's worse than just losing $4, so to keep that Pullmanite happy, the company must give back *more* than $4 in either higher wages or lower rents.

Bottom line: the company collects an extra $4 at the grocery store and loses *more* than $4 somewhere else. That's a losing proposition, and Pullman is presumably too smart to go for it.

This conclusion is perfectly general. Change the numbers in the example any way you like, and the end result is still the same — Pullman does best by keeping grocery prices as low as they are in Pushman.

I teach at a university whose administrators might have been able to learn a thing or two from the Pullman Company. We once had a lovely little on-campus restaurant where the faculty mingled at lunchtime. The restaurant lost money, so the administration shut it down. This struck some of us as shortsighted; anything that makes it easier to recruit and retain faculty can contribute to the larger enterprise in ways that the accountants might not immediately measure. Even if all you care about is the university's bottom line, losing $10,000 at the restaurant can be worth it if the alternative is to make the campus so unpleasant that you've got to start offering higher wages to keep people around.

In other words, insisting that campus restaurants make a profit is shortsighted in exactly the same way that it would be shortsighted for Pullman to insist on extracting monopoly profits from its grocery stores. It overlooks the fact that if you want to keep people around, and you do something that makes their lives worse, you've got to do something else — and possibly something more expensive — to make their lives better.*

By way of making this point, I posted a brief message to the all-faculty email list, observing that if we accept the logic that led to the restaurant closure — that each division is to be judged by its individual profits — then the first thing we should do is close the library. The outraged responses from faculty in other departments were unanimous in condemning those damned economists who want to close the library.

Who would have predicted that?

The one sure-fire way to make successful predictions is to predict every possible outcome. Predict both rain and sun for tomorrow, and you're sure to be right. (You're also sure to be wrong, but

---

* One difference between the university and Pullman: From the information given in the problem, we can deduce that it's *definitely* a bad idea to charge monopoly prices at the grocery stores. From the explanations given by the university, we can deduce only that it *might* be a bad idea to close the restaurant.

maybe you can learn not to care.) If you can get away with calling both "heads" and "tails" on the same coin toss, you're a winner every time.

There's a classic scam that runs along these lines: Pick a stock at random, tell 256 people its price is about to go up, and tell another 256 it's about to go down. After a week, when one of your forecasts has proved accurate, take the 256 people who got the accurate forecast, divide them into two groups of 128, tell one group that some other randomly chosen stock is about to go up and tell the other that the same stock is about to go down. After another week, you've provided 128 people with two accurate forecasts in a row. Divide them into two groups of 64, and repeat. Pretty soon you're down to 8 people who have heard you make six accurate forecasts in a row. Tell them that if they want your next forecast, they'll have to pay for it.

Making *honest* predictions is a lot more difficult, and sometimes a lot less lucrative. But it's definitely more satisfying.

CHAPTER 4

Explanations

S ome things cry out for explanation. Others appear entirely self-explanatory. But appearances can be deceiving. For example:

1

Ups and Downs

Why do people stand still on escalators but not on stairs?

To many people, the most puzzling thing about this puzzle is: Why would anyone call this a puzzle? Isn't the answer obvious? After all, if you stand still on stairs, you never get anywhere.

But that's true only if you stand still on the stairs forever. What about stopping for, say, a one-minute rest? People *do* stop to rest on the stairs, but they're far more likely to rest on the escalator. (If you doubt me, go have a look at the people on a real-world staircase and the people on a real-world escalator.) The question is why, and the answer just got at least a little less obvious.

Here's one guess: the sort of people who choose the escalator are, on average, less physically fit — and therefore more inclined to rest. So to avoid making this too easy, let's rule out that sort of explanation by focusing on a single person who takes *both* the stairs and the escalator.

2

Ups and Downs Again

Suppose you're in a department store where between floors 1 and 2 there is an escalator but no staircase, while between floors 2 and 3 there is a staircase but no escalator. You're traveling all the way from floor 1 to floor 3, and at some point along the way you're going to take a one-minute rest. Should you take your rest on the escalator or on the staircase? And why?

The problem, as I hope you're beginning to see, gets more vexing the harder you think about it.

The economist's hope is that any question about human behavior can be settled with an appeal to cost-benefit analysis. So let's look at the costs and benefits of putting one foot in front of the other.

First, the *cost* of taking a step is that you expend a certain amount of energy. That cost appears to be the same on the escalator as it is on the stairs.

Next, the *benefit* of taking a step is that you get one step closer to your goal. That, too, appears to be the same on the escalator as it is on the stairs.*

A step is worth taking if the benefit exceeds the cost. The costs and the benefits on the stairs are exactly the same as the costs and benefits on the escalator. Therefore, a person on an escalator is exactly as likely to be walking as a person on the stairs. We should see the same amount of walking — and the same amount of resting — in both venues.

But that's not what we actually see! What's gone wrong here?

Actually, the cost-benefit analysis I just gave you omits something important. But it's not so obvious where the omission lies. I've enjoyed watching some of the world's best economists and mathematicians grapple with this paradox over the years, sometimes filling multiple blackboards with graphs and equations, trying to figure out why the apparently correct cost-benefit analysis gives the wrong answer.

I'll let you ponder this for yourself awhile, and we'll come back to it at the end of the chapter. For now I'll skip right past the solution and point to the moral — a moral we seem to keep coming back to: sometimes the obvious is the enemy of the true. It is obvious to the casual observer that the reason people rest on escalators and not on stairs is that if you rest on stairs, you never get anywhere† — just as it is obvious to the untrained eye that the sun rises and sets every day because the sun orbits the earth. The more satisfied you are with that explanation, the less likely you are to look for a better one.

---

* On the stairs taking a step means that in the next second or so, I advance one step instead of zero. On the escalator taking a step means that in the next second or so I advance four steps instead of three. In either case, that's exactly one step's worth of additional progress.

† I want to stress that this can't be the answer to a question that pits a one-minute rest on the stairs against a one-minute rest on the escalator. If you take a one-minute rest on the stairs, you get where you're going just fine.

The puzzles in this chapter all concern familiar phenomena that cry out for explanations. Sometimes those cries are muffled by "obvious" solutions that mask a deeper truth. Why do coal miners have more political clout than fast food clerks? Why do banks sometimes offer mortgage deals that appear too good to be true? Why are black motorists more likely than white motorists to be stopped for random drug checks, even though the percentage found carrying drugs is the same for both groups? Why doesn't Sony want its TVs sold at a discount? Why, with all the phenomenal medical advances of the last two millennia, have maximum human lifespans not increased? Why do women's living standards go down after a divorce while men's living standards go up? Why don't Jews farm?

The diversity of these topics emphasizes the importance, always and everywhere, of digging beneath the surface. In each case the challenge is to go beyond the obvious — and sometimes to explain why the apparently obvious is not even true. In many cases a little logic is all you need; in a few cases you might need a few facts as well, which I will supply.

In every case, of course, the explanations I offer might be wrong — though I hope to convince you that they at least have a better chance of being right than some of the more "obvious" alternatives. If you think you can do better, I welcome your email.

3

Politico Economy

Matthew Nussbaum, of the online magazine *Politico,* tweets as follows:

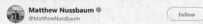

Matthew Nussbaum ●
@MatthewNussbaum   (Follow) ⌄

There are ~50,000 coal miners in US. There
are ~520,000 fast food cooks.
Coal miners seem to loom a lot larger in our
politics. Wonder why.
11:24 AM - 28 Mar 2017

Can you help him out?

SOLUTION: Many of Nussbaum's Twitter followers thought the answer was obvious — though they couldn't entirely agree on what the obvious answer was. Some pinned it on labor organizing, others on racism (coal miners are more likely than fast food clerks to be Caucasian), others on electoral politics or political corruption.

But Nussbaum's observation is in fact exactly what you should expect if you're aware that it's pretty hard to open a new coal mine and pretty easy to open a new fast food restaurant.

This gives coal companies a good reason to lobby for political favors (including favors for their employees, who, of course, they prefer to keep happy, especially if it's at someone else's expense). Whatever favors come their way are theirs to keep.

It also gives restaurant owners almost no incentive to lobby for political favors. If those favors are granted, new restaurants will sprout up to claim their share — and, in the process, are likely to compete all those gains away.

To take a stark example: If the government gives each coal mine a $50 tax break, then each coal mine gets a $50 tax break, and that's pretty much the end of the story. If the government gives each fast food joint a $50 tax break, new fast food joints crop up, the price of fast food gets bid down, profits fall, and the process continues until profits fall by about $50. (Up to that point, there's still an incentive for new entrants to keep flooding in.)

As a general rule, you should expect politicians to fawn not over the *largest* groups but over the groups that are *least able to grow.* Good farmland is much more limited than small tracts along the interstate, which is why farmers are showered with subsidies while motels fail all the time without anyone taking much notice. Any attempt to help those motels would just call forth more motels and more competition, leaving existing motel owners in the same dire straits they're in today. So why would they bother asking for help, and why would politicians bother to offer it?

This problem is a nice little reminder that a little bit of economic literacy goes a long way. Matthew Nussbaum is a pretty sophisticated observer, yet even he found the asymmetry between coal miners and fast food cooks mysterious, though pretty much anybody with a little economics training (or even just a little practice thinking about such puzzles) could have explained it to him in an instant.

4

An Amazing Deal?

If you've got a 30-year mortgage at 5 percent, many banks will allow you to make half your monthly payment every two weeks — in exchange for which, they will declare the mortgage paid off after about 25 years.

How can such a small change in the timing of your payments shave almost 5 years off the life of your mortgage?

SOLUTION: The obvious answer — the first one most people seem to think of — is that if you take the offer, you make half of each monthly payment two weeks early, and the bank earns an extra two weeks' interest on that payment. Over 30 years this can add up.

But it doesn't add up to very much. If you've got a $100,000 mortgage, and you make half the payments two weeks early, the bank earns two weeks' extra interest on $50,000. At an interest rate of 5 percent per year, that comes to a little less than $100 over the entire life of the mortgage.

Here's what's really happening (and what the bank is probably hoping you won't notice): most months are more than four weeks long, so if you pay every two weeks, you're paying *more* than twice a month. In fact, the number of two-week periods in a year is 26, so if you take the offer, you'll effectively make thirteen monthly payments every twelve months. At that rate, it takes well under 28 years to complete 30 years' worth of payments.

That accounts for two of the five years that get shaved off your payment schedule. The rest is accounted for by the fact that you're making a lot of these payments months or years ahead of time, not just two weeks early.

The ancient Greeks lived, on average, about 35 years, but many lived past 90 and a few (like the philosopher Gorgias) made it to about 108. Modern Americans and Europeans live, on average, about 80 years, but many live past 90 and occasionally someone makes it to 108. As far as we know, nobody in history has ever lived to be 125.

The dramatic improvement in average lifespans is a tribute to modern medicine, which has made great strides against infant mortality, infectious disease, and the big killers such as cancer and heart disease. But the longest lifespan you can reasonably hope for today is not substantially different from the longest lifespan you could have reasonably hoped for thousands of years ago.

5

The Limits of Medicine

If medicine is so effective at extending our lives on average, why is it so *in*effective at extending the upper limit?

SOLUTION: Because Nature is a good economist, in the tradition of the automotive pioneer Henry Ford. Legend has it that Ford once dispatched a team of engineers to the junkyard to see if there were any parts still in excellent condition on all the junked cars. When they identified a pin that was perfectly workable on every car in the junkyard, Ford instructed his engineers to conserve resources by cutting back on the quality of that overly durable pin.

In a well-designed car, everything starts to go wrong at about the same time. If the engine won't last past 100,000 miles, you don't need a transmission that will last for 500,000. (There's an exception to this rule for parts that are easily replaceable.) In a well-designed human body — and thanks to the pressures of natural selection, the human body is in many ways well "designed" — the vision, the hearing, the mental facilities, the physical strength, the arteries, and the resistance to cancer should all tend to deteriorate at about the time. If the lungs can't make it past 100, it would be pointless to have a stomach, a pancreas, or a liver that can make it to 120.

It would also be needlessly expensive, and here's why: Our organs require routine maintenance, and the intensity of that maintenance is part of the organ's "design." You can always make an organ last longer by maintaining it better, but you can never do that for free, because maintenance consumes energy that would otherwise be available for gathering food or fighting predators.

(A lot of maintenance consists of cell replacement, which is highly energy intensive.) If your stomach were designed to last 20 years longer than your lungs, your body would be well advised to conserve energy by taking less good care of your stomach — which means your stomach *won't* last 20 years longer than your lungs.

Because the human body tends to break down all at once, it's almost impossible to extend its lifespan. If your body contains 100 crucial organs, and if 98 spectacular medical breakthroughs render 98 of those organs impervious to disease, those breakthroughs will save a lot of lives (in cases where an organ would have broken down before it was supposed to) without having any appreciable effect on maximum lifespans. Two organ failures are just as deadly as a hundred.

This problem is a neat application of mainstream economic ideas to an issue outside the mainstream of economics. Economists have long understood that in a well-designed machine, all parts should wear out at the same time. So have poets, such as Oliver Wendell Holmes, who made this insight the basis of his charming poem "The Wonderful 'One-Hoss-Shay,'" which, because of its ideal design, broke down "all at once and nothing first, / Just as bubbles do when they burst." The insight that the same principle applies to organisms "designed" by natural selection appears in physiologist Jared Diamond's delightful book *The Third Chimpanzee*.

Many studies have shown that following a divorce, women's living standards tend to fall and men's living standards tend to rise. A number of commentators have leapt to the "obvious" conclusion that divorce is unfair to women. I'm not sure why they chose this over the equally "obvious" conclusion that marriage is unfair to men. After all, it appears that men who stay married are forced to sacrifice a substantial percentage of what they could achieve on their own.

But a little thought suggests that neither of these "obvious" conclusions holds water. What we observe (on average, of course, with no doubt a great many individual exceptions) is that men, much more than women, are willing to pay for the privilege of being married. They're getting something they value, and they're paying for it. Nothing unfair in that.

You might also be tempted to conclude that women, much more than men, are willing to pay for the privilege of being divorced. That's a sketchy argument, because not all divorces are voluntary on the woman's part. But here's a much stronger argument: husbands, in effect, pay their wives to stick around (by acquiescing to a lifestyle in which the husband consumes less, and the woman consumes more, than they would on their own). Why would you pay someone to be your wife unless you were pretty sure she considered marriage unpleasant?

So the data do suggest that, at least in marriages that are on the margin between success and failure, men prefer staying married and women prefer to divorce. Of course there are myriad exceptions to that rule. The moral is not that every man prefers marriage and every woman prefers divorce but that by some appropriate measure, marriage is on average better for men than it is for women.

The real question, then, is this:

6

Love and Marriage

Why are men, more than women, willing to pay to stay married?

SOLUTION: There's at least one good reason, rooted in both economics and biology, why we should have expected this all along. A thirty-year-old woman who wants a family is getting close to the point where she has to choose the best of her available suitors. A thirty-year-old man can always choose to wait another five or ten years till someone better comes along. In general, the longer you spend searching for something — be it a car, a house, or a life partner — the happier you're going to be with the one you end up with. So — again, with myriad exceptions — a woman's optimal strategy is to settle for an imperfect mate and then try to change him. A man's optimal strategy is to search until he finds someone close to perfect. It's therefore no surprise that women, more often than men, should end up feeling that their partners could use a little improvement.

In hindsight, it all makes sense. Once you realize that there's a biological clock, you should be able to predict that men (having searched long and hard for the perfect partner) would make financial sacrifices to preserve their marriages, and that women who stay married to imperfect partners would be kept in their marriages by financial rewards — or, to say the same thing another way, that women who leave their marriages would make financial sacrifices. (And you should also be able to make a lot of auxiliary predictions, such as this one: wives try harder to mold their husbands than husbands try to mold their wives — because husbands wait until they've found wives who need relatively little molding.) Fairness never had anything to do with it.

Have you shopped for a name-brand TV recently? If so, you've almost surely discovered that there's no reason to shop around. Except for a few extremely sketchy characters around the edges of the Internet (who are very unlikely to deliver the products they've promised), everyone charges the same price. That price is dictated by the manufacturer and enforced by a very simple policy: Sony has let it be known that if, say, Best Buy ever offers Sony

TVs at a discount, then Best Buy will no longer receive shipments of Sony TVs.* This inspires the next problem.

7

TV Shopping

Why doesn't Sony want its TVs sold at a discount?

SOLUTION: The "obvious" answer is that Sony wants its TVs to sell at a high price, which is good for Sony's profits. But *that answer makes no sense.* Sony doesn't care about the *retail* price of its TVs; it cares about the wholesale price — and the wholesale price is totally within Sony's control. As long as Best Buy hands $1,000 over to Sony, why should Sony care whether Best Buy collects $1,100 or $1,200 or $1,500 from the customer? In fact, it seems that Sony should *prefer* a lower retail price, which means more TVs will get sold.

Here, though, is what Sony is really worried about: If retailers are free to set their own prices, you'll walk into Best Buy, latch onto a salesperson, ask questions for an hour, spend another hour playing your favorite YouTube videos on all the different display models, ask a bunch more questions, and then go home and order from Amazon, where the price is lower. Best Buy will soon enough get tired of this and either stop carrying Sonys altogether or stop displaying them and answering questions about them. This means fewer sales and, of course, lower profits for Sony.

It's not just Amazon, of course. Sony also has to worry that

---

* This practice is usually called *resale price maintenance* by economists and *universal pricing policy* by businesspeople.

you'll avail yourself of all Best Buy's services and then buy from the brick-and-mortar discounter down the street. How does Sony combat this threat? By prohibiting all discounts, period.

Incidentally, the net effect of this is that consumers pay higher prices but get better service. Is that on balance a good thing or a bad thing for consumers? With a bit of economic theory (at a level that's appropriate for a textbook but not, alas, here), one can show that under reasonable assumptions, the extra service is worth more to consumers than what they're implicitly paying for it; in other words, Sony's policy ends up being good for its customers as well as for its shareholders.

In the 1890s, my eastern European Jewish ancestors emigrated to an American Jewish farming community in Woodbine, New Jersey, where the millionaire philanthropist Baron de Hirsch provided land, tools, and training at the nation's first agricultural high school. But within a generation the family had settled in Philadelphia, where they became accountants, tailors, merchants, and, eventually, lawyers and college professors.

De Hirsch had a vision of American Jews achieving economic liberation by working the land. If he'd had a better sense of history, he would have built not an agricultural college but a medical school, because for well over a millennium prior to the settlement of Woodbine, Jews had not been farmers — not in Palestine, not in the Muslim empire, not in western Europe, not in eastern Europe, not anywhere in the world.

You have to go back almost two thousand years to find a time when Jews, like virtually every other identifiable group, were primarily an agricultural people. Around AD 200, Jews began to quit the land. By the seventh century, Jews had left their farms in large numbers to become craftsmen, artisans, merchants, and moneylenders — they were the only group to have given up on agriculture. Jewish participation in farming fell to about 10 percent through most of the world; even in Palestine it was only about 25 percent. Every other group stayed on the farms.

Even in the modern state of Israel, where agriculture has been an important component of the economy, it's been a peculiarly capital-intensive form of agriculture, one that employed well under a quarter of the population at the height of the kibbutz movement, and less than 3 percent of the population today.

This brings up the following puzzle.

8

Why Don't Jews Farm?

Why did Jews and only Jews take up urban occupations, and why did it happen so dramatically throughout the world?

SOLUTION: To anyone familiar with the history of the Jews, the obvious guess is to see this as a side effect of persecution or discrimination. But two economic historians — Maristella Botticini (of Boston University and the University of Torino) and Zvi Eckstein (of Tel Aviv University and the University of Minnesota) — have given this one a lot of thought, and they are skeptical of that guess.

First, say Botticini and Eckstein, the exodus from farms to towns was probably not a response to discrimination. It's true that in the Middle Ages, Jews were often prohibited from owning land. But the transition to urban occupations and urban living occurred long before anybody ever thought of those restrictions. In the Muslim world Jews faced no limits on occupation, land ownership, or anything else that might have been relevant to the choice of whether to farm. Moreover, a prohibition on land ownership is not a prohibition on farming — other groups facing similar restrictions (such as Samaritans) went right on working other people's land.*

Nor, despite an influential thesis by the economic historian Simon Kuznets, can you explain the urbanization of the Jews as an internal attempt to forge and maintain a unique group identity. Samaritans and Christians maintained unique group identities without leaving the land. The Amish maintain a unique group identity to this day, and they've done it without giving up their farms.

So, what's different about the Jews? First, Botticini and Eckstein explain why other groups *didn't* leave the land. The temptation was certainly there — skilled urban jobs have always paid better than farming, and that's been true since the time of Christ. But those jobs require literacy, which requires education — and for hundreds of years, education was so expensive that it proved a poor investment despite those higher wages. (Botticini and Eckstein have data on ancient teachers' salaries to back this up.) So, rational economic calculus dictated that pretty much everyone should have stayed on the farms.

But the Jews (like everyone else) were beholden not just to economic rationalism but also to the dictates of their religion. And the Jewish religion, unique among religions of the early Middle Ages, imposed an obligation to be literate. To be a good Jew you had to read the Torah four times a week at services: twice on the Sabbath and once every Monday and Thursday

---

* Another version of the discrimination hypothesis says that Jews chose not to invest in land for the very rational reason that they were often forced to migrate, and land is not portable. I once heard a Nobel Prize–winning economist dismiss this explanation because "it doesn't really answer the question; it only reduces it to a different question, namely: Why are Jews not Christians?" Botticini and Eckstein dismiss the same explanation for a very different reason: the urbanization of Jews was under way long before the forced migrations started.

morning. And to be a good Jewish parent you had to educate your children so that they could do the same.

The literacy obligation had two effects. First, it meant that Jews were uniquely qualified to enter higher-paying urban occupations. Of course, anyone else who wanted to could have gone to school and become a moneylender, but school was so expensive that it made no sense. Jews, who had to go to school anyway for religious reasons, naturally sought to earn at least some return on their investment. Only many centuries later did education start to make sense economically, and by then the Jews had become well established in banking, trade, and so forth.

The second effect of the literacy obligation was to drive a lot of Jews away from their religion. Botticini and Eckstein admit that they have little direct evidence for this conclusion, but there's a lot of indirect evidence. First, it makes sense: people do tend to run away from expensive obligations. Second, we can look at population trends: while the world population increased from 50 million in the sixth century to 285 million in the eighteenth, the population of Jews remained almost fixed at just a little over a million. Why were the Jews not expanding when everyone else was? We don't know for sure, but a reasonable guess is that a lot of Jews were becoming Christians and Muslims.

So, which Jews stuck with Judaism? Presumably those with a particularly strong attachment to their religion and/or a particularly strong attachment to education for education's sake. (The burden of acquiring an education is, after all, less of a burden for those who enjoy being educated.) The result: Over time, you're left with a population of people who enjoy education, are required by their religion to be educated, and are particularly attached to their religion. Naturally, these people tend to become educated. And once they're educated, they leave the farms.

Of course there are always exceptions. My great-grandfather raised chickens. But he did it in the basement of his row house in North Philadelphia.

In a recent five-year period on the Maryland stretch of I-95, a black motorist was three times as likely as a white motorist to be stopped and searched for drugs. Black motorists were found to be *carrying* drugs at pretty much exactly the same rate as whites. (A staggeringly high one-third of stopped blacks and the same staggeringly high one-third of stopped whites were caught with drugs in their cars.)

This was widely reported in the news media as clear-cut evidence of racial discrimination. After all, if blacks and whites are equally likely to be caught carrying, shouldn't they be equally likely to be stopped? And if blacks are in fact stopped three times as often, isn't that best explained by racial animus on the part of the police?

The news organizations that posed these questions treated them as rhetorical and acted as if the answers were obvious. Unfortunately, the "obvious" answers make absolutely no sense. So let's take the questions seriously.

9

What Do Police Officers Want?

A. Given what you've just read, who would you say was more inclined to carry drugs?

a) Black motorists
b) White motorists
c) Black and white motorists about equally

B. Which of the following could plausibly explain the way police decided who to stop?

a) Racial prejudice
b) A desire to maximize arrests
c) A desire to deter drug traffic

SOLUTION:

A. The key observation here is that blacks carry drugs just as frequently as whites do *even though they are three times as likely to get caught.* If you believe that people respond to incentives, then you must believe that if blacks were stopped at the same lower rate that whites were, more of them would have carried drugs.

In other words, in that time and that place and for whatever reason, blacks were certainly more inclined to carry drugs than whites were.

B. Only choice (b) fits the facts.

To see why, think about how the police would behave if they *were* single-mindedly out to maximize arrests. They'd start by focusing their attention on the group that's most inclined to carry drugs — in this case, blacks (as we saw in part A).

That makes it easier for whites to slip through the net, and harder for blacks. Because people respond to incentives, whites start carrying more drugs and blacks start carrying fewer.

If blacks are *still* carrying more drugs than whites, the police shift even more of their focus to blacks, leading the gap to close a bit more. This continues until whites and blacks are carrying drugs in equal proportions.

At that point (which could have been reached long before the data were collected) there's no particular reason to crack down on blacks any further, but no particular reason to ease up on them either. (And any temporary easing would quickly lead to a discrepancy between black and white arrest rates and a return to the equilibrium.)

So when the police are out to maximize arrests, the incentive structure leads blacks and whites to carry drugs in equal proportions, which is exactly what we observe.

In other words, choice (b) fits the facts. Now what about choices (a) and (c)?

Choice (a) is "racial prejudice." If this means anything, it must mean cracking down on blacks *beyond the point where it serves any objective purpose*—that is, beyond the point where blacks and whites carry drugs in equal proportions. That additional crackdown would serve as an additional deterrent to blacks, who would then be *less* likely than whites to carry drugs.* But that's not what we see, so choice (a) is wrong.

Choice (c) is "maximize deterrence." But if you want to maximize deterrence, you'll concentrate more on stopping whites, because there are more whites in the population to deter.

Searching mostly blacks can be a good way to make a lot of drug arrests, but it's a lousy way to deter drug traffic. It advertises to whites that they have little to fear from the police, which emboldens more whites to carry drugs. And because there are a lot more white people than black people, this effect can be quite large.

So if the police were focused on deterrence, they'd focus more on stopping whites, which would deter more whites from carrying drugs—and then the average white motorist would

---

* By that standard, it's not blacks but Hispanics who have cause for complaint. Stopped Hispanics, over the same period, were only about one-third as likely to be carrying drugs as stopped blacks or whites. Why would the police stop a Hispanic with a one-ninth chance of carrying drugs instead of a black or a white with a one-third chance? Arguably, it's because they have something against Hispanics.

carry fewer drugs than the average black. Again, that's not what we see, so choice (c) is wrong too.

In summary:

- If the police are out to maximize drug arrests, they'll reallocate their resources until blacks and whites carry drugs at about the same rate.
- If the police are out to harass blacks, they'll allocate additional resources to stopping blacks, causing blacks to carry drugs at a lower rate than whites.
- If the police are out to deter drug traffic, they'll allocate more resources to stopping whites, causing blacks to carry drugs at a higher rate than whites.

What we actually see is blacks and whites carrying drugs in equal numbers. The only theory that fits is that the police are trying to maximize drug arrests.

An auxiliary question is: How should you feel about what the police are doing? It depends, surely, on how you feel about the drug war. If you're a committed drug warrior, you'll be rooting for maximum deterrence, and you'll be unhappy that the police are choosing to maximize arrests instead. If you're a committed libertarian on this issue, you'll of course be unhappy to see *any* resources devoted to stopping drug traffic — but you might well think that a policy that maximizes arrests is the worst of all possible policies. It seems that pretty much the only person who might opt for the existing policy is a police officer angling for a promotion.

The next problem is one I *can't* explain.

10

Why Aren't All Buildings
the Same Height?

Okay, I understand why not *all* buildings are the same height. I understand, for example, why my house is not 40 stories high. I don't want that much space, and I prefer not to share my house with strangers. I even understand why my house is not as tall as my next-door neighbor's: I prefer a ranch and he prefers a colonial.

I understand too why my house is not the same size as my supermarket. They serve different purposes. But why is the Empire State Building so much taller than any other office building in midtown Manhattan? If it was a good idea to make one building 102 stories high, why wasn't it a good idea to make the neighboring buildings — at least those that were being built around the same time and for the same purpose — 102 stories high as well?

Presumably the optimal height of an office building depends on things like land prices, the cost of adding more stories, and the nature of the rental market. How could that calculation have turned out so differently for one office building than for another being constructed in the same neighborhood in the same year?

Taller buildings cost more per story than shorter buildings. So if Jack plans to put up a 40-story building while Jill plans to put up a 60-story building across the street, here's how they can both get richer: Jack builds 50 stories instead of 40, Jill builds 50 stories instead of 60, and Jill buys the top 10 stories of Jack's building. It's cheaper for Jill to put her top 10 stories on Jack's building than on her own, and they can negotiate a price that lets them share the savings. So why don't they do it? Why doesn't that kind of bargaining cause all buildings (or all buildings constructed around the same time and place) to be the same height?

You could try making the same argument with houses: instead of my 1-story house and my neighbor's 3-story house, we could have two 2-story houses, and my neighbor could own my top floor. Well, that's clearly no good because I don't want strangers — or even acquaintances — traipsing through my house. But in a large office building, you're sharing with hundreds of strangers anyway, so the objection washes away.

It's no use arguing that some builders can't raise enough capital to build more than, say, 40 stories. That only raises the question of why those builders aren't driven out of the market by those who can raise more capital — or why they don't raise the capital by preselling those top 10 floors to the builder next door who wants to own 60 stories altogether.

Maybe it all comes down to this: some tenants are willing to pay a premium for either the exclusivity of a short building or the extra amenities (newsstands, restaurants, health clubs) of a tall one. This could make it profitable to put up a few of these unusually sized buildings, even if their heights fail to minimize construction costs. But this explanation seems to fall short when it comes to the coexistence of 40- and 60-story buildings. It's hard for me to believe that a 40-story building really feels that much more exclusive or intimate than one with 50 or 60 stories.

So on this one, color me stumped. Email me if you think you can help.

Now I'm ready to tell you why people stand still on escalators but not on stairs.

Remember why this is a problem: The *benefit* of taking a step — namely, one step's worth of progress toward your goal — is the same in both places. The *energy cost* of lifting your foot and moving it forward is also the same in both places. If the benefit exceeds the cost in one place, how can the benefit not exceed the cost in the other?

Here's the solution: It's true that the *immediate* costs and benefits of a step on the stairs are the same as the immediate costs and benefits of a step on the escalator. But a step on the escalator has a hidden additional cost: For every step you take on the escalator, you eventually get off the escalator a little sooner. That means you're throwing away the tail end of a free ride. A free ride is a valuable asset. Discarding that asset — or even just its tail end — is very much a cost, which needs to be added to the energy cost. So a step taken on the escalator really is costlier than a step taken on the stairs, and it's perfectly rational to take fewer steps in a place where steps are costlier.

If you meet someone who thinks that the answer to the escalator problem is immediately obvious, try posing the following variant.

11

Sprinting Uphill

You travel from floor 1 to floor 2 by escalator and from floor 2 to floor 3 by stairs. You have exactly enough energy to make one 10-second sprint at any stage along your journey. Should you make your sprint on the stairs or on the escalator?

SOLUTION: As with resting, the immediate costs and benefits of sprinting are the same in both places. But sprinting on the escalator has one additional effect: it gets you off the escalator sooner and therefore discards the tail end of your free ride. Therefore it's a mistake to choose the escalator.

In my experience, there are people who insist that the answers to problems 1 and 2 are so obvious that they're not worth thinking about — yet many of those same people have to stop and think for a while before answering problem 11. Since this is exactly the same problem in reverse, and has exactly the same solution, I think we can be pretty sure those people are missing something.

Personally, I often stand still on escalators but almost never on stairs, though there was a time when I wouldn't have been able to defend that choice. Often we instinctively get things right without being conscious of why — but it's comforting to figure it out eventually. Solving this problem had absolutely no effect on my behavior, but it did make me feel a lot better about it.

CHAPTER 5

Strategy

O n the British TV game show with the unfortunate name *Golden Balls,* two contestants vie for a single jackpot of, say, $10,000.

Each contestant makes a secret choice to *split* or *steal.* If both split, they share the prize. If one steals while the other splits, the stealer wins it all. If both steal, nobody gets anything.

On the face of it, then, you should certainly steal. After all, if the other guy steals, you're going home empty-handed no matter what you do — but if he splits, you've got a chance to steal the entire jackpot. In other words, stealing can't hurt you but might help you.

So as long as everyone is perfectly rational, everyone figures this out, everyone steals, and everyone goes home empty-handed. If that strikes you as paradoxical, it's only because you're making the manifestly false assumption that rational behavior must lead to good outcomes. You'd know better if you'd ever been to a ballpark, where, every time something exciting happens, everyone (perfectly rationally) stands up to see better, and as a result nobody sees any better.

But on *Golden Balls,* there's an extra twist to the game. The contestants have a few minutes to negotiate and make promises, in front of a national audience. In principle, the negotiation should make no difference. No matter what anyone says, in the end, everyone should realize that stealing can only help them, and therefore everyone should steal—unless, of course, they care what's being said about them the next day over water coolers throughout the United Kingdom.

Therefore, contestants routinely take the opportunity to swear that they plan to split, and beg their counterparts to do the same. Typically, they lead with passionate paeans to their own honesty. ("I'm the sort of person who would never, never, lie about a thing like this . . .")

Nick Corrigan was not a typical contestant. His opponent, Ibrahim Hussein, led off predictably:

> IBRAHIM: If I give you my word . . . now let me tell you what my word means. My father once said to me, "A man who doesn't keep his word is not a man. He's not worth nothing. He's not worth a dollar" . . . If I gave you my word that I was gonna split, I would split . . .

Ibrahim, who admitted afterward that he'd planned all along to steal, had in fact never met his father.

But Nick stunned his opponent, the host, and the audience with this astonishing gambit:

> NICK: Ibrahim, I want you to trust me one hundred percent. I'm going to pick the steal ball.

After Ibrahim's double take, Nick continued:

NICK: I'm going to choose the steal ball. I want you to do split, and I promise you that I will split the money with you.

IBRAHIM: After you take the steal ball?

NICK: Yeah.

IBRAHIM (clearly not sure he's heard this right): So you're gonna take steal . . .

NICK: Yeah.

IBRAHIM: And I'm gonna take split . . .

NICK: Yeah.

IBRAHIM: So you take the money . . .

NICK: Yeah. And I will split it with you . . .

IBRAHIM: After the show?

NICK: Yeah.

[Delighted laughter from the audience]

NICK: Ibrahim, I promise you I will do that. If you take steal, we will both walk away with nothing. I'm telling you, one hundred percent, I'm gonna do that.

IBRAHIM: Well, I appreciate that. But I'll give you another alternative. Why don't we both pick split?

NICK: I'm not gonna pick split. I'm gonna steal. Honestly, one hundred percent, I'm gonna steal . . . I'm honest, and that's why I'm telling you I'm gonna steal. If you do split, then I will split the money with you . . . I know that I am a decent guy and I will split the money with you.

IBRAHIM: Well then, we should both do split then.

NICK: No, I'm gonna do steal.

Here's why this ploy is so brilliant: If Nick keeps his promise to steal, then split becomes a no-lose strategy for Ibrahim. He has no chance of winning any money directly but at least some chance that Nick will keep his subsidiary promise and split after the show.

Moreover, the pressure on Nick to keep that subsidiary promise might be considerably greater than the pressure on Nick to split in the first place. Contestants on this show break promises to split all the time, and Nick would have been just another in that long line. But a broken promise to split *after the show* would be a particularly *memorable* broken promise and would have made Nick a national villain.

Ibrahim went for it. He chose to split. As a matter of fact, so did Nick. Of course, they split the jackpot.

Nick Corrigan was, at least on this occasion, a brilliant strategist. The puzzles in this section will give you a chance to demonstrate your own strategic prowess, and will lead up to the most profound moral in all of economics.

1

The Prisoner's Dilemma

You and a fellow named Jeter have both been arrested and charged with a crime. The prosecutor puts each of you in a separate room and presents you with a menu of options: If you both confess, you'll each serve 5 years in jail. If neither confesses, the prosecutor will still have enough evidence to convict you on a lesser charge, and you'll each serve 2 years in jail. If you confess and Jeter doesn't, the prosecutor will reward you with a 1-year sentence while Jeter will have to serve 10. If Jeter confesses and you don't, Jeter gets the 1-year sentence and you get the 10.

Should you confess?

SOLUTION: Of course you should confess! (Unless, perhaps, you care about Jeter, or worry that he'll take revenge on you.) Confessing is a no-lose strategy. Here's why:

- If Jeter confesses, you can get a 5-year sentence by confessing or a 10-year sentence by not confessing. Obviously it's better to confess.
- If Jeter doesn't confess, you can get a 1-year sentence by confessing or a 2-year sentence by not confessing. Obviously it's better to confess.
- If you're not sure what Jeter's doing, you can at least be sure that either he's confessing or he's not. Either way, it's still better to confess.

This makes confessing a no-brainer.

When I teach the Prisoner's Dilemma to my college freshmen, I find that many have encountered it before, most of those are quite sure they've fully understood it, and a great many of those have in fact missed the point entirely. That is, many of them think you confess *because you're afraid that Jeter will confess.*

But that's not the point at all. It's true that if you believe Jeter is confessing, you'll want to confess. But it's equally true that *even if you are sure Jeter is not confessing, you'll still want to confess.*

Jeter, of course, reasons exactly the same way. You each confess, and you each serve 5 years. The irony is that if you'd each been too stupid to figure this out, you might each have not confessed and served only 2 years each.

The Prisoner's Dilemma is closely but imperfectly analogous to the game of *Golden Balls.* In either game, you can "play nice" (by splitting or by not confessing) or you can "play tough" (by stealing or by confessing). Then the logic of the two games goes like this:

GOLDEN BALLS	PRISONER'S DILEMMA
If he plays tough, I lose no matter what.	If he plays tough, I win by playing tough.
If he plays nice, I win by playing tough.	If he plays nice, I win by playing tough.
So playing tough can't hurt me and might help me.	So playing tough is sure to help me.
So I'll play tough.	So I'll play tough.

(Here I've used the word *win* to mean "do the best you can possibly do, given what the other guy is doing.")

In both cases, the bottom line is the same: as long as everyone is self-interested and rational, everyone plays tough, leading to an unfortunate outcome.

You might be tempted to conclude that it pays to be stupid (or at least irrational). That's not quite right. The real lesson is that it pays to have an *opponent* who's stupid or irrational — and that the advantage of having an irrational opponent can outweigh the handicap of being irrational yourself.

Economists love the Prisoner's Dilemma because it illustrates a key idea in economics:

In general, **rational behavior need not lead to good outcomes.**

Arms races are rational (I'm always better off armed, whether you're armed or not, so of course I should arm), but they can impoverish everyone. The war against cancer is unlikely to be won by voluntary contributions, because no matter how much you care about beating cancer, it's perfectly rational to observe that the outcome probably won't hinge on your personal $50 donation.*

---

* On the other hand, there are charities to which the Prisoner's Dilemma does not apply. If a million children are starving and you feed one of them, you've done some good, and the good you've done is quite independent of whether the other

Shared pastureland tends to be overgrazed; communal fishing grounds tend to be overfished. After a while, the grass is gone and the fish have vanished. Economists call this phenomenon the *tragedy of the commons,* but it's really just another manifestation of the Prisoner's Dilemma. If others are overusing the communal resource, the rational response is to grab your own share before it's gone. If others are *not* overusing the communal resource, the rational response is to grab an outsize share for yourself, confident that everyone else's good stewardship will leave plenty for you to grab in the future.

Here's a quick application:

2

Dirty Beaches

You are the president of a small country with two public beaches. Diamond Beach is gorgeous, with sparkling white sand, clear blue water, spectacular rock formations, and shelter from the wind. Everyone loves it just about as much as everyone else does. Zircon Beach is quite ordinary. Some people think it's fairly nice; most don't care for it at all.

A substantial oil deposit runs under both beaches. If you're determined to get at the oil, is it better to allow drilling at Diamond Beach or at Zircon Beach?

SOLUTION: Because everyone agrees that Diamond Beach is gorgeous, it's probably overrun and ruined by the crowds. That's

---

999,999 also get fed — so your decision to give should be largely independent of whether others are also giving.

where I'd start drilling. This preserves Zircon Beach for the relatively few people who will at least get some enjoyment out of it.

There's a general moral here: a freely available public resource has social value only insofar as people *differ* about its value.

Because everyone appreciates Diamond Beach pretty much equally, the crowd size must grow until an afternoon at the beach is no more appealing than an afternoon at home. After all, if the beach were more appealing than home, more people would head to the beach, adding to the congestion and subtracting from the appeal. And this continues until all of the beach's value is whittled away.

That's a classic tragedy of the commons, and there are only a few ways to avoid it. It's avoidable if Diamond Beach is so large that crowds are not an issue. It's avoidable if there's an admission charge to keep the crowd size down.* And it's at least partly avoidable if some people like Diamond Beach substantially more than others do, and can therefore still enjoy it even after the crowds have grown big enough to deter others from entering. (This also works if some people don't much mind the crowds.)

But as long as Diamond Beach is small enough to get crowded, free to enter, and equally desirable to everyone, it's certainly the beach you'll want to sacrifice.

You might be thinking that this is all well and good as the solution to a stylized brain teaser but has little to do with the real world, where no beach is equally desirable to everyone. Pick a beach. Ask your friends about it. It's a pretty sure bet that some will like it more than others.

That's true, and that's why real-world beaches retain some so-

---

* Even with an admission charge, Diamond Beach is no more appealing than the backyard, but now at least the beach delivers value in the form of admission fees, which can presumably be spent to provide something useful to someone.

cial value. But the *extent* of that value continues to depend not on how much people like the beach but on how much they disagree. If a very large number of people all have roughly (but not exactly) the same opinion of the beach at Atlantic City, then the value of the beach at Atlantic City will be largely (but not entirely) whittled away by overcrowding—regardless of whether that shared opinion is enthusiastically positive or just sort of "meh."

The logic of strategic interaction has a few additional surprises in store. Here are some to think about:

3

The Two-Sided Card Game

We start with a deck of 100 cards. Each card has a number on each side. There's a card with 0 and 1 on the sides, another with 1 and 2, another with 2 and 3, and so on, all the way to 100.

A referee chooses a card at random and holds it up so that you can see one side and I can see the other. We each then choose (by pushing a hidden button) to either pass or play.

If either of us passes, the card is returned to the deck, the deck is reshuffled, and no money changes hands.

If we both play, the person facing the higher number wins $200, the person facing the lower number loses $100, the card is returned to the deck, and the deck is reshuffled.

A card has been chosen. On your side is the number 65. Do you pass or play?

SOLUTION: Let's start with an easier question: On your side is the number 0. Do you pass or play? A moment's thought should convince you to pass. If you see a 0, I must see a 1. You can't win this round. So you should always pass when you see a 0. So should I. And because we're smart enough to understand that, we will.

Next: What should you do if you see a 1? This time there are two possibilities. Either I see a 0, in which case I'm sure to pass and it doesn't matter what you do — or I see a 2, in which case you're sure to lose. You have no hope of winning, so you'd better pass.

Again, we're both smart enough to understand that. So we both always pass when we see a 1.

What if you see a 2? Then either I see a 1, in which case I pass and it doesn't matter what you do, or I see a 3, in which case you can only lose. So you should pass on seeing 2.

By the same reasoning, you should pass on seeing 3, 4, or 5, or (after you've gone through this reasoning several dozen more times) on seeing 65, or, for that matter, on seeing 99.

Even if you see 100, there's no particular reason to play. It's true that you can't lose, but you can't win either, because I always pass on 99.

So at least one of us passes on every round. We never lose anything, but we never win anything either.

Meanwhile, our considerably less intelligent cousins are playing the same game next door. Their strategy is to always play. Each of them wins $200 about half the time, loses $100 about half the time, and goes home rich.

Shades of the Prisoner's Dilemma! The moral is the same: In a strategic situation, your own rationality always works to your advantage. Your opponent's rationality can work against you. Sometimes it's better for neither of you to be rational than for both to be.

4

Deep Pockets

When I was in high school, my English teacher (who must have had a free period at the time) would show up briefly every day at the beginning of my math class. He and my math teacher would empty all the cash out of their pockets onto the desk. Whoever had brought the most claimed the entire pile. (In case of a tie, they both kept what they'd brought.)

What's your strategy in that game?

Should you carry lots of money to increase your chance of winning? Should you carry less to minimize your losses? Obviously it pays to be unpredictable, so you don't want to carry, say, $5 every day. But exactly how often should you carry, say, exactly $47?

(To make things simpler, assume that you must carry a whole number of dollars.)

SOLUTION: Let's think through a few scenarios.

If you bring $0, you're sure not to lose anything, and you're equally sure not to win anything.

If you bring exactly $1, you might win, but only if your opponent shows up with empty pockets, in which case your prize is $0. On the other hand, you might lose your dollar. So there's nothing to be gained and a dollar to be lost. Therefore, being a rational creature, you will never bring exactly $1. Neither will your rational opponent.

If you bring exactly $2, you still can't win any money, because we know your opponent never brings exactly $1. On the other hand, you might lose. So there's nothing to be gained and $2 to be lost. Therefore you never bring exactly $2, and neither does the other guy.

If you bring exactly $3, you still can't win any money, because we now know your opponent never brings either $1 or $2. Therefore you never bring exactly $3, and neither does he.

And so on down the line. If you're both rational, the only amount you can possibly bring every day is $0.*

But my math and English teachers did not ever, in my memory, show up with $0 in their pockets. What should I conclude about the quality of my high school education?

5

Deeper Pockets

Suppose you're playing the Deep Pockets game with magical money that always doubles its value when it changes hands. So, for example, if you bring $5 and your opponent brings $3, she loses her $3 and you gain $6. How does this affect your strategy?

SOLUTION: The argument from the preceding problem works just as well for this one, and shows that fully rational adversaries always bring $0 to the table.

Of course if you and your opponent are both irrational enough to ignore this good advice and each spin a roulette wheel to de-

---

* Actually, I've assumed a bit more than rationality—I've assumed also that you and your opponent are *aware* of each other's rationality, and aware of your awareness of each other's rationality, and aware of your awareness of your awareness of each other's rationality, and so on. Economists express this by saying that your rationality is *common knowledge*. We'll have a bit more to say about this in chapter 10.

cide what to carry every day, then in the long run you'll each win twice as much as you lose.

The games of Deep Pockets and Deeper Pockets have the flavor of an auction. Of course any auction is a game of strategy and an opportunity to test your strategic skills, as you decide when to bid, how much to bid, and when to quit. The next several problems will give those skills a workout.

6

Art at Auction

You're participating in a sealed-bid auction for a one-of-a-kind painting, for which you'd be happy to pay $100 but not a penny more. You place your bid in an envelope, all the envelopes are opened, and the high bidder buys the painting for the amount of her own bid. What number should you put in your envelope?

SOLUTION: How much do you expect your opponents to bid? How comfortable are you with risk? Without that information, the only specific advice I can give you is, don't bid more than $100. But you probably didn't need me to tell you that.

7

Art at Auction, Take Two

You're participating in another sealed-bid auction for another one-of-a-kind painting, for which you'd once again be happy to pay $100 but not a penny more. However, this time the rules are slightly different: you place your bid in an envelope, all the envelopes are opened, and the high bidder buys the painting for the amount of the *second*-highest bid. Now what number should you put in your envelope?

SOLUTION: As you go through life, almost every decision you make has the potential to look bad in hindsight. Sometimes I carry an umbrella, only to look foolish when the sun comes out. Sometimes I don't, only to look both foolish and wet when the rain starts.

Only rarely do we get the opportunity to make a choice we can't possibly regret. This is one of those rare occasions. You should bid exactly $100, because *there is no conceivable circumstance in which you might regret that bid.*

Suppose, for example, that the envelopes are opened and you learn that the highest of the other bids is $80. Congratulations! Your $100 bid just won the auction, you'll be paying $80, and no other bid could have turned out better.

Or suppose, for a different example, that the envelopes are opened and you learn that the highest of the other bids is $120. Congratulations! Your $100 bid just lost the auction, you avoided outbidding the other guy and paying $120 for an item you don't think is worth that much, and no other choice could have turned out better.

Any other choice could turn out badly. If you bid $70 and the highest of the other bids is $80, you'll kick yourself for losing. If you bid $130 and the highest of the other bids is $120, you'll kick yourself for winning. We all spend enough time kicking ourselves as it is; why risk it when you don't have to? Bid the $100, and no matter how things turn out, you'll be patting yourself on the back.

If you frequent online auction sites such as eBay, this is often all you need to know. In many eBay auctions, you submit a "maximum bid" and then, if you win the auction, you pay not your own maximum bid but the second-highest (or the second-highest plus some very small amount). If that ceramic rabbit is worth exactly $100 to you and not a penny more, your best strategy is to submit a bid for $100 and not give the matter another thought until the auction results are revealed.

Occasionally the problem is complicated by your not *knowing* what the rabbit is worth to you until you find out how many others are after it — something like "I'd pay a hundred dollars for that rabbit if I were the only bidder, but I'd pay two hundred if twenty others are bidding." This makes no sense if you're buying the rabbit strictly for your own enjoyment, but could make excellent sense if you're buying it either for its resale value or for its likely ability to impress your friends. In those cases, you might want to check back now and then and increase your bid if (and only if) you've got a lot of competitors. But of course, those competitors would be well advised to hold off bidding until the very last minute, hoping it will be too late for you to react (and you'd be well advised to do the same), so "bid once and don't think about it" might still be about the best you can do.

8

The Hundred-Dollar Auction

A hundred-dollar bill has been put up for auction. You and one other bidder have shown up. The rules of the auction are that the high bidder gets the hundred-dollar bill, but *both* bidders pay the amount of the highest bid. Otherwise, this is an ordinary English-style auction where the auctioneer asks, "Who will give me five dollars?" "Who will give me six dollars?" and so forth. What's your bidding strategy?

SOLUTION: Your mistake was showing up in the first place.

If you bid, say, $5, then your opponent has a choice: drop out (and owe $5), or raise the bid to $6 and win the hundred-dollar bill. So the bidding is sure to go a lot higher than that.

What happens if you've just bid, say, $99? Then your opponent has a choice: drop out and owe $99, or raise the bid to $100, hoping to win the hundred-dollar bill and break even. Of course, the latter is the better choice, so he bids $100.

But we're not finished. Now *you've* got a choice: drop out and owe $100, or raise the bid to $101, hoping to win the hundred-dollar bill and take a net loss of only $1. Of course, you bid the $101.

Your opponent can now either drop out and lose $101 or raise the bid to $102, aiming for a $2 net loss. The bid goes up, and the arms race continues, either forever or until the bidding gets so high that the auctioneer is no longer willing to extend you any credit. Depending on how long the auction is allowed to continue, you can lose thousands, tens of thousands, or millions.

The point is that once you're in, there's never a right time to drop out. Whenever you're behind, you can always do better by raising the bid a dollar. Ditto for your opponent. So the auction can't end until you're bankrupt. Stay home.

This might serve as a cautionary metaphor for politicians. Imagine a congressional race where the biggest campaign spender is sure to win. That's essentially an auction for a congressional seat, where both bidders pay the amount of the highest bid. Once you're in that race, there's no right time to quit spending until at least one of the candidates is completely tapped out — possibly long after they've both spent more than the seat was ever worth to them.

• • •

Earlier in this chapter, I promised you a series of strategy problems leading up to the most profound moral in all of economics.
The time for that has come. Here's the first of those problems. If
you don't see anything profound about it, bear with me. I promise
this is leading up to something big.

9

The Chicken and the Eggs

Name two ways to get a chicken to lay more eggs.

Hint: Unlike many problems in this book, you can't solve this
one with pure logic. It requires some specialized knowledge. In
fact, it's probably completely unfair of me to include it here. I also
don't plan to tell you the answer for a little while. I just want you
to stop for a moment, digest the question, and think about how
you'd answer it. Then proceed to the next problem, which you *can*
solve with pure logic.

10

Card Golf

Each of ten people holds a stack of cards. On each card is a
number, which the holder can see but you cannot. Everyone's
stack is different. Some stacks might have several cards with the
same number. In other stacks all the numbers might be different. Perhaps one person holds a 3, a 5, a 7, and a 9, while another
holds a 1, a 4, an 8, and a 12. Your task is to collect fifty cards.

Your score is the total of all the numbers on the cards you collect. As in golf, your goal is to minimize your score. What's your strategy?

SOLUTION: You *could* ask all ten people to hand over their five lowest cards. But that might not work out very well. One person's lowest card might be 100, while someone else is holding twenty cards with single digits.

Here's a much better idea: First ask everyone to hand over all of their 1 cards. Then ask everyone to hand over all of their 2 cards. Then ask everyone to hand over all of their 3 cards. Stop when you've got fifty cards. (If you go over fifty, you can always discard a few of the most recently collected.)

You can now be quite sure you've got the lowest possible score. After all, the only way to *change* your score would be to swap at least one of the cards in your collection basket for some other card that's *not* in your basket. But that can't possibly drive down your score, because *every single card outside the basket is worse—or at least not better—than any single card inside the basket.* So your score must already be as low as possible.

Now try this slight variant:

11

The Czar's Dilemma

The president of Slobbovia has just appointed you as his czar of agriculture. In Slobbovia, there are ten wheat farmers, each of whom can produce various quantities of wheat at various costs. Perhaps Farmer Nichols can produce one bushel for $3, a second bushel for an additional $5, a third for an additional $7, and a fourth for an additional $9, while Farmer Littlefield can produce one bushel for $1, a second for an additional $4, a third for an additional $8, and a fourth for an additional $12. All the farmers know their own costs, but you don't know any of them. Your task is to arrange for the production of 50 bushels of wheat. Your goal is to conserve resources by minimizing production costs.

What's your strategy?

SOLUTION: You *could* order each of ten farmers to produce 5 bushels of wheat as cheaply as possible.

But that might not turn out very well. One farmer's first bushel might cost $100, while another farmer can produce 20 bushels all at costs in the single digits.

Here's a much better idea: First direct each farmer to produce as many bushels as possible at a cost of $1 per bushel or less. Then direct them to produce as many as possible at $2 or less. Then $3, $4, and so on, until you've got 50 bushels. You can now be quite sure you've minimized the production cost for 50 bushels of wheat. After all, the only way to *change* the production cost would be to "swap" at least one of the bushels you've ordered up for some other bushel you did *not* order up—telling, say, Farmer Littlefield to produce one less bushel and Farmer Nichols to produce one more. But that can't possibly drive down the total cost, because *every single bushel that Farmer Nichols—or anyone else—didn't produce is more expensive—or at least no cheaper—than any single bushel that Farmer Littlefield—or anyone else—did produce.* So the production cost must already be as low as possible.

We're closing in on the profound moral I've been promising you. First, just one more puzzle, building on the previous one.

12

The Czar's Problem Gets a Little Harder

You're still serving as the Slobbovian czar of agriculture, and you're attempting to implement the solution to the preceding problem so you can get 50 bushels of wheat at the lowest possible cost. You start by directing every farmer to produce as many bushels as possible at a cost of $1 per bushel. Unfortunately, the farmers see no reason to take directions from you. And you have no way of punishing disobedience, because you have no idea what the production costs are on any given farm, so you don't know who's disobeying.

Now what's your strategy?

SOLUTION: Try this. First announce that you'll pay $1 a bushel for wheat. You'll discover that every farmer who can produce a bushel for less than $1 will choose to do so. If that doesn't produce 50 bushels, announce that you'll pay $2 a bushel for wheat. Now every possible $2-or-less bushel will be produced. Continue until you have your 50 bushels.

That works! It also renders you, as czar, obsolete — because in the absence of a czar, the price system automatically implements exactly the same solution. Demanders offer, say, $1 a bushel for wheat. Those suppliers who can produce wheat for less than $1 per bushel are happy to respond. If that doesn't meet demand, the price gets bid higher and farmers step up to supply additional bushels. And so on, until demand is met.

Now at last we have our moral:

The price system does the best possible job of producing any given quantity of wheat (or anything else) at the lowest pos-

sible cost. No czar, no planning board, and no other mechanism can do better.

That matters profoundly. It matters because costs are measures of resource consumption. To say that it costs $100 to produce a particular bushel of wheat is to say that $100 worth of resources — land, labor, pesticides, fuel, and more — is exhausted in the process. In the long run, societies prosper by husbanding their resources. That is, societies prosper by minimizing production costs. A system of prices and individual choices accomplishes exactly that.

In other words, these puzzles, simple as they are, get to the heart of why *a functioning price system must lie at the heart of any successful economy.* If you want to know why Americans prosper while North Koreans starve, you must start by understanding the idea behind the last few puzzles.

That's true even though there are important differences between the puzzle world and the world we actually inhabit. Here are two:

In the puzzle you know in advance that you want farms to produce exactly 50 bushels of wheat. In the real world, the price-adjustment process affects not just the amount of wheat produced on each farm but also the amount of wheat demanded by each household. But it's still true that whatever quantity we end up with, it's been produced in the cheapest possible way.

In the puzzle there are 10 farms. In the United States of America there are more than 2 million farms. So if you're imagining some alternative solution that involves collecting all the cost data from all the farms, your solution is surely irrelevant to the real world — especially because the cost of producing, say, bushel number 8 on farm number 1,471,206 is *constantly changing,* not just from day to day but from hour to hour. Costs change with local weather conditions; they change when a reaping machine breaks down or a farm animal gets sick and needs attention; they change when a fertilizer or pesticide delivery fails to arrive as scheduled; they change whenever a farm hand fails to show up for work or hurts his back in the middle of the workday.

Those constant changes are mostly invisible to the czar but are acutely visible to individual farmers. That's why the problem of cost minimization can't in practice be solved — even approximately — by any mechanism other than the price system. Only under the price system are production decisions left to those people who have access to the most crucial information.

The moral of the Prisoner's Dilemma, and of many of the other problems we've met in this chapter, is that rational behavior can lead to quite terrible outcomes. The moral of the Czar's Dilemma is that rational behavior — in this case the rational behavior of farmers seeking to maximize their profits — can lead to the *very best possible outcome,* provided the czar himself is both civic-minded and rational enough to step aside and let the price system do its work.

There is no a priori reason to believe that a bunch of self-interested, profit-maximizing farmers would fulfill the social demand for wheat at the lowest possible cost, conserving as many resources as possible for other uses in both the present and the future. Indeed, the more familiar you are with the Prisoner's Dilemma, the more you should instinctively doubt that *any* rational self-interested action is likely to turn out very well. This makes it all the more remarkable that it's possible for rational action to solve the Czar's Dilemma not just pretty well but astoundingly well — as well as it could be solved if all of the little bits of information held by hundreds of millions of people could be gathered in one place, digested, and instantly deployed.

To drive the point home, let's look at a related puzzle about the necessity of using price signals if you want to allocate resources efficiently.

13

The Czar's Other Dilemma

Now that you've stepped down as agriculture czar, the Slobbovian government has appointed you to the newly created position of energy czar, tasked, among other things, with allocating the limited supply of natural gas to the various businesses that are clamoring to get their hands on it—mostly chicken farms and steel mills, as it happens.

Fortunately, your job is pretty easy—the natural gas supply is 20 cubic feet a day (nobody's pretending that these numbers are realistic), chicken farms have traditionally used about 10, and steel mills have traditionally used about 10. So your plan is to continue that tradition.

Unfortunately, you've learned that because of an earthquake, the natural gas supply is about to be cut in half, and likely to remain at half for the foreseeable future. Now that the daily supply is only 10 cubic feet, how much should you allocate to the steel mills and how much to the chicken farms?

SOLUTION: Well, let's see. Based on their traditional consumption, it seems that chicken farms and steel mills need roughly equal quantities of natural gas, right? So now that the total supply is down to 10 cubic feet, maybe you should allocate 5 cubic feet to chicken farms and 5 to steel mills. Share the pain equally.

Bad idea. As it happens, the steel mills can't operate without natural gas. But the chicken farms can quite easily dispense with it. That's because there are two ways to get a chicken to lay more eggs. One is to turn up the heat in the henhouse (using heaters that are usually powered by natural gas), and the other is to feed them a little more.* Deprive the chicken farmers of natural gas and they'll grumble a little, but they'll buy more chicken feed and the egg supply will go on pretty much uninterrupted. So you should let the steel mills have all the natural gas.

Does it feel like there was something unfair about that problem? The only way to get the solution was to have a rather obscure bit of knowledge about chickens — which most people don't have. (That's why you probably failed to solve problem 9.) But that's the whole point. Almost *nobody* has that obscure bit of knowledge, except for chicken farmers, students who have taken my economics course (where I sometimes use this example), and Dan Gressel, the economist and hedge fund manager whose family was in the egg business and who suggested the example to me in the first place.

You might think that we could also add energy czars to the list of people who know such things, but don't be so sure. First of all, the puzzle posited that *you* had been appointed czar. If you didn't know the answer to problem 9, why would you expect more of any other appointee?

More to the point, natural gas in the real world is not allocated just to steel mills and chicken farms; it is allocated across hundreds of thousands of industries, and it is hopeless to imagine that anyone in the world is acquainted with all the quirky ways in which various industries might or might not deal with a natural gas cutback. In fact, it's even worse: you're not just allocating across industries; you're allocating across individual firms. Any individual steel mill might or might not be running equipment that can easily be converted from natural gas to some other fuel.

So the key point here is that no czar is likely to be able to solve

---

* Chickens use calories from food to produce both eggs and body warmth. A chicken in a heated henhouse can divert more calories to egg production. So can a chicken who's better fed.

problem 13, either in the stylized version I've presented here or in the far more complex real-world version of the problem. The czar's best strategy, then, is once again to step out of the way and let the price system do its work. A shortage develops; the price of natural gas starts to rise; and pretty soon the chicken farmers (along with everyone else who has good substitutes available) decide all on their own to switch from natural gas to chicken feed. The reallocation takes care of itself, in the most efficient possible way.

The chief merit of the price system is that it makes effective use of information that is not available to any single decision maker. When the price system is overridden, information is discarded. When information is discarded, resources are misallocated. When resources are misallocated, prosperity suffers. If you're trying to make people prosperous, relying on prices is your best strategy.

Does that mean we never want to override the price system? Of course not. I expect, for example, that most of us would want to shut down the market for professional hit men, even when it operates with admirable efficiency. But it does mean that prices serve a function that nothing else can serve, and when we ignore them — as when a politician or a bureaucrat tells firms what to produce or how to produce it — we do so at our peril.

CHAPTER 6

How Irrational Are You?

W hich would be worse — a world without Bach or a world without clean sheets? What's better — a dog or a cat? Should toilet paper unwind over the roll or under?

These questions are eternal. They will never be put to rest because there are no objectively right or wrong answers. You can be sure of your opinions, I can be sure of mine, and we can both respect our differences.

Which would you prefer — $1 million, or a 50–50 shot at $5 million? Once again, there's no right answer. If you prefer the sure thing and I prefer the gamble, we can agree to disagree.

Beware, then, of people who try to "prove" that your choice is wrong. Someday someone is going to explain to you that "of course" you should take the 50–50 shot, because (obviously) half of $5 million is more than $1 million. Maybe that person will even try to show off her college education by dressing up the argument with fancy jargon about "maximizing your expected value." But fancy jargon can't change the fact that the argument is silly to begin with. You're not, after all, choosing between a sure $1 million and a sure half of $5 million; you're choosing between a sure $1 million and a *chance* of $5 million. A preference for a sure thing is no less rational than a preference for chocolate ice cream, just as a preference for a shot at $5 million is no less rational than a preference for vanilla. Let a thousand flowers bloom.

It's hard to qualify as irrational in the eyes of an economist. We'll endorse almost any choice you make, and if your choice seems odd, we'll shrug our shoulders and say, "Well, there's no accounting for tastes."

But though it's hard to qualify as irrational, it's not impossible. The philosopher Sidney Morgenbesser once ordered pie in a restaurant. The waitress offered a choice of apple, blueberry, or cherry. Morgenbesser chose apple. Then the waitress remembered that the restaurant was out of blueberry. "In that case," said Morgenbesser, "I'll have the cherry."

Now, Sidney Morgenbesser was a well-known scamp who was always looking for a way to rattle his dinner companions. But if he'd been serious, even the most tolerant economist would have called him irrational.

Better yet, we could have taken his money.

"Hey, Sidney, I've got three slices of pie here—apple, blueberry, and cherry. Which one do you want?"

"I'll take the apple."

"Here you go. Incidentally, I just gave away the blueberry to my cousin Jeter, so that's not available anymore."

"In that case, I'll take the cherry."

"Well, you can trade the apple in for the cherry, but I've got to charge you a ten-cent restocking fee."

"No problem. I really want the cherry."

"Okay, here you go. Incidentally, Jeter sent the blueberry back, so it's available again. Oh, now you prefer the apple? Well, you can

trade the cherry in for the apple, but I've got to charge you another ten-cent restocking fee."

"Okay, that sounds worth it."

"Here we go, then. By the way, Jeter took the blueberry after
all. Oh, you want the cherry now? That'll be ten cents, please."

"Ummm . . . sure."

"Huh. Jeter sure is fickle. He returned the blueberry again, so
it's available now. Would you like the apple?"

After a thousand rounds of this, I've collected $100 of Sidney's
money, leaving me with a pure profit of $80 after paying Jeter his
20 percent commission.

There are plenty of other ways for a person to be irrational,
and plenty of ways to get rich off those people. In fact, that's a
good *definition* of irrationality — you're irrational if your preferences allow me to bleed you dry.

So if you prefer a sure million to a sure $5 million, I'll cheer-
fully label you irrational — and I'll suggest we make a trade. Or if
you don't have $5 million on you, I'll at least offer you a one-dollar
bill for a five.

Or if you prefer a 50 percent chance of $1 million to a 60 per-
cent chance of $1 million, I'll call that irrational — and I'll suggest
we play a game. Let's throw a ten-sided die. If the number that
comes up is 5 or less, I'll give you a cool million; if it's 6 or less,
you give *me* a million. That way you get your 50 percent chance at
$1 million, and all you're giving up in return is a mere 60 percent
chance at $1 million, which you claim to value less.

What I really like about that game is that I *cannot lose.* Either
we break even or (if the die comes up 6) I walk away with a million
of your dollars. Bets like that are called *Dutch books,* and whenever you have an irrational preference, you're vulnerable to some
version of a Dutch book.

I've devised a little quiz to determine how irrational you are.
It's important to know upfront that *most of these questions have*

no right or wrong answers; in other words, you can answer them any way at all without being labeled irrational. So don't worry about trying to find the "right" answers; just do your best to answer honestly.

Many of the questions ask you to imagine yourself in some pretty unusual situations — being offered a choice between two fabulous prizes, or being forced to play Russian roulette. The quiz will work best if you take a few minutes to fully imagine yourself into these situations as best you can — thinking about what it would be like if you really faced these choices and making your best forecast of how you'd behave.

Here we go.

The Irrationality Quiz

1. Which would you rather have:
   A. An 11 percent chance to win $1 million
   B. A 10 percent chance to win $5 million

2. Which would you rather have:
   A. $1 million for certain
   B. A lottery ticket that gives you:
      an 89 percent chance to win $1 million
      a 10 percent chance to win $5 million
      a 1 percent chance to win $0

3. Which would you rather have:
   A. $1 million for certain
   B. A 98 percent chance to win $5 million

4. Which would you rather have:
   A. A 1 percent chance to win $1 million
   B. A 0.98 percent chance to win $5 million

5. You're forced to play a game of Russian roulette with a six-shooter containing two bullets, like so:

What's the maximum amount you'd be willing to pay to remove both those bullets before the game starts? (Here *willing* means "willing and able," so the highest answer you're allowed to give is "All I've got.") Answer assuming that you don't care what happens to your money after you're dead.

6. You're forced to play a game of Russian roulette with a six-shooter containing four bullets, exactly one of which is for sale, like so:

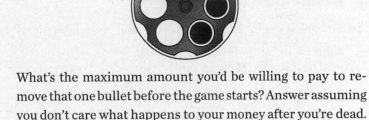

What's the maximum amount you'd be willing to pay to remove that one bullet before the game starts? Answer assuming you don't care what happens to your money after you're dead.

7. In front of you are three urns, each containing two thousand balls. Most of the balls are labeled "loser," but a few have dollar amounts written on them. You can reach into the urn of your choice and win the prize (if any) on the ball you draw. Which urn would you rather draw from?

    A. Urn A, with two $1,000 balls (and the rest losers)

    B. Urn B, with twenty $100 balls (and the rest losers)

    C. Urn C, with one $1,000 ball, ten $100 balls (and the rest losers)

    D. They all sound equally good

8. An urn contains thirty red balls and sixty blue balls. Some of the blue balls are light blue and some are dark blue, but I'm not going to tell you how many of each. You get to reach into the urn and pull out a ball. Which would you prefer?

    A. To win $1,000 if the ball is red

    B. To win $1,000 if the ball is light blue

    C. A and B sound equally good

9. Just as in problem 8, an urn contains thirty red balls and sixty blue balls. Once again, some of the blue balls are light blue and some are dark blue, but I'm not going to tell you which. You get to reach into the urn and pull out a ball. Which would you prefer?

    A. To win $1,000 if the ball is either red or dark blue

    B. To win $1,000 if the ball is blue

    C. A and B sound equally good

10. You are asked to make a prediction, and you win $1,000 if you get it right. Which do you prefer to predict?

    A. The outcome of an upcoming two-person congressional race to which you've paid absolutely no attention

    B. The outcome of a coin toss

    C. I like both options equally

Scoring

1. There is no irrational answer to question 1. No matter what you answered, your score for this problem is 0.

2. Score 1 irrationality point if your answer differed from

your answer to question 1 (that is, give yourself 1 point if you answered A to question 1 and B to question 2, or vice versa).

3. There is no irrational answer to question 3. No matter what you answered, your score for this problem is 0.

4. Score 1 point if your answer differed from your answer to question 3.

5. There is no irrational answer to question 5. No matter what you answered, your score for this question is 0.

6. Score 1 point if your answer to question 6 differed from your answer to question 5.

7. Score 1 point if you answered C.

8. There is no irrational answer to question 8. No matter what you answered, your score for this problem is 0.

9. Score 1 point if your answer differed from your answer to question 8.

10. Score 1 point if you answered B.

Interpreting Your Score

0: Perfectly rational. Career choice: ambassador to the planet Vulcan.

1: Almost perfectly rational. Career choice: economist.

2: More rational than most. Career choice: life coach.

3: You think like a human. Career choice: psychologist.

4: You're on the edge. Career choice: performance artist.

5: Unstable. Career choice: standing on lawn in bathrobe, shaking fist at passing cars.

6: Flakier than a pie crust. Career choice: random-number generator.

Understanding Your Score

Did your score surprise you? Did it hurt your feelings? Are you annoyed with the test? Are you sure there must be a mistake somewhere? If so, add 1 point to your irrationality score!

No, on second thought, don't. Irrationality, as economists define it, isn't about *feelings;* it's about *actions.* Whether you glide through life in the knowledge that all is for the best in this best of all possible worlds or stockpile canned goods against the imminent apocalypse; whether you fall asleep counting your blessings or your grudges, we're willing to call you rational. But not if your quiz answers were wrong. Because in every case, if your quiz answers were wrong, I can think of a way to take all your money.

Your Answers to Questions 1 and 2

I know, I know, I promised you that most of these questions have no right or wrong answers. That's true, but there are still wrong (or at least irrational) *patterns* of answers. If you gave opposite answers to questions 1 and 2, you fell into one of those irrational patterns.

To see why that pattern is irrational, forget all about questions 1 and 2 for a moment and think about three new questions instead. I've labeled these P, Q, and R so they don't get confused with the various As, Bs, and Cs that are floating around.

P. I'm going to give you a gift. Would you prefer that gift to be a cat or a dog?

Q. I *might* give you a gift. If I do, would you prefer that gift to be a cat or a dog?

R. My uncle Harry might give you a cat. If he doesn't, I'll give you a gift. Would you prefer that gift to be a cat or a dog?

One key element in the economist's definition of rationality is that you should give the same answer to all three questions. It's fine to prefer cats to dogs and fine to prefer dogs to cats, but if you prefer cats to dogs, you'd better also prefer a *possible* cat to a *possible* dog.

Now let's replace the cat and the dog with a different set of gifts.

A MILLION DOLLARS FOR SURE

A LOTTERY TICKET THAT MIGHT BE WORTH FIVE MILLION DOLLARS

And let's start over.

P. I'm going to give you a gift. Would you prefer that gift to be the million dollars or the lottery ticket?

Q. I *might* give you a gift. If I do, would you prefer that gift to be the $1 million or the lottery ticket?

R. My uncle Harry might give you a million dollars. If he doesn't, I'll give you a gift. Would you prefer that gift to be the $1 million bill or the lottery ticket?

Once again, if you're rational, you'll give the same answer to all three questions. Some people prefer the sure million, some people prefer the chance at something better, and all can be rational, as long as they're consistent.

Now, here's the relevance:

In question Q (where I *might* give you a gift), I plan to reach into an urn with 89 black balls and 11 white balls. You'll get your gift if the ball comes up white. If you chose the $1 million, you've got an 11 percent chance to win that $1 million. If you chose the lottery ticket, you've got an 11 percent chance to win that ticket, which is the same thing as a 10 percent chance at $5 million.*

In other words, the choice you made in question Q is exactly the same as the choice you made in problem 1 of the irrationality quiz.

In question R (where my uncle Harry might give you $1 million and otherwise I'll give you a gift), I plan to reach into the same urn. If the ball comes up black, you'll get your $1 million from Uncle Harry, and if it comes up white, you'll get your gift from me. If you chose the $1 million, you're sure to walk away with $1 million (maybe from Harry, maybe from me). If you chose the lottery ticket, you've got an 89 percent chance to walk away with $1 million (from Harry), a 10 percent chance to walk away with a winning lottery ticket worth $5 million, and a 1 percent chance to walk away with a losing lottery ticket worth $0.

In other words, the choice you made in question R is exactly the same as the choice you made in problem 2 of the irrationality quiz.

We've agreed that if you're rational, you must answer both Q and R the same way you answered P. But Q and R are the same as questions 1 and 2 of the irrationality test. Therefore, if you're behaving rationally, you answered both questions the same way.

And that's why, if you answered the two questions differently, you earned an irrationality point.†

My cousin Jeter is unconvinced by that reasoning. Like most people (including me the first time I saw these questions), he answered B to question 1 — that is, he took the 10 percent chance

---

* There's an 11% chance you'll get the lottery ticket and a $10/11$ chance the ticket is a winner. I multiplied these chances to get the 10% chance that you'll get the ticket *and* it's a winner.

† In case that went by too fast, I've included an alternative and slightly longer explanation in the appendix.

of $5 million over the 11 percent chance of $1 million — and answered A to question 2 — taking the sure million over the chance at $5 million. And like many people, he persists in defending his choices.

"Question two offers me the option of a sure thing," says Jeter. "I hate uncertainty, so I take the sure thing when it's available. That's choice A. In question one, there's no sure thing available, so I take a shot at the bigger prize. That's choice B."

There are several problems with that defense. First, it makes absolutely no sense. In question 1, 89 percent of the time Jeter gets nothing no matter what he's chosen. The other 11 percent of the time he can have either a *sure* million by choosing A or a $10/11$ chance at $5 million by choosing B. If he likes sure things so much, why wouldn't he prefer an 11 percent chance of a sure thing over an 11 percent chance of a gamble?

Jeter's other problem is that if he stands by his choices, I can take away all his money.

Here's how: all I need is an urn with 89 black balls, 10 white balls, and 1 gray ball:

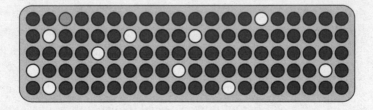

Then I say: Okay, Jeter. Let's play a game where we pull out a ball and give each other prizes depending on its color. In fact, here are four different games we might play; I'll call them games 1A, 1B, 2A, and 2B:

	BLACK (89 balls)	WHITE (10 balls)	GRAY (1 ball)
1A	$0	$1 million	$1 million
1B	$0	$5 million	$0
2A	$1 million	$1 million	$1 million
2B	$1 million	$5 million	$0

Then I make Jeter this offer:

"You've told me that you prefer game 1B to 1A. So let's draw a ball, I'll give you the 1B payoff, and all I ask in return is that you give me the 1A payoff. That should make you happy!"

Before Jeter has time to object that he doesn't have that kind of cash lying around, I sweeten the pot with another trade in his favor:

"You've also told me that you prefer game 2A (the sure million) to 2B. So I'll *also* give you the 2A payoff, and all I ask in return is the 2B payoff. That should make you even happier!"

The cool thing about this pair of trades is that we're absolutely certain to break even no matter what ball we draw. If it's white, I give Jeter $5 million and he gives me $1 million, then I give him $1 million and he gives me $5 million. That's break-even. You can check that we also break even if the ball we draw is either black or gray.

That's pretty cool indeed. It means that it doesn't matter whether we've got the millions we need to meet our obligations, because our debts to each other exactly cancel every time we play.

But remember that according to Jeter's stated preferences, this game is rigged entirely in his favor. If he's serious about that, he should be willing to pay for the privilege of playing. I charge him $10, we play, we break even, I charge him $10 to play again, we play again, we break even, and I charge him $10 to play again. I've turned him into a money pump.

Surely you don't want to be a money pump. So it pays to be more rational than Jeter.

Your Answers to Questions 3 and 4

In question 4, there's a 99 percent chance you'll win nothing no matter what you choose. The other 1 percent of the time, you'll either win a sure million (if you chose A) or have a 98 percent chance to win $5 million (if you chose B). In other words, 99 percent of the time your choice doesn't matter, and the other 1 percent of the time you're making the same choice you made in question 3. Surely, then, you should have made the same choice both times. If you didn't, you earned an irrationality point.

To say this another way:

- If you prefer dogs to cats, then you should prefer a 1 percent chance of a dog to a 1 percent chance of a cat.
- If you prefer cats to dogs, you should prefer a 1 percent chance of a cat to a 1 percent chance of a dog.
- If you prefer a sure million to a 98 percent chance at $5 million (that is, if your answer to question 3 was A), then you should prefer a 1 percent chance of a sure million to a 1 percent chance of a 98 percent chance at $5 million (that is, your answer to question 4 should be A).
- If you prefer a 98 percent chance at $5 million to a sure million (that is, if your answer to question 3 was B), then you should prefer a 1 percent chance of a 98 percent chance at $5 million to a 1 percent chance of a sure million (that is, your answer to question 4 should be B).
- So it's perfectly rational to answer A to both questions, and it's perfectly rational to answer B to both questions. But it can't be rational to answer A to one and B to the other.

Your Answers to Questions 5 and 6

Question 5 asks what you'd pay to remove both bullets from this six-shooter just before playing Russian roulette.

What, in other words, would you pay to avoid a one-third chance of death? There's no right answer to that question. Some people would pay everything they own. Others would rather take their chances with a pair of bullets than face certain financial ruin.

Now consider a new question: Suppose you have a weak heart, so there's a fair chance you'll die of a heart attack before the Russian roulette game gets under way. Does that change your answer to question 5?

Answer: If you're rational, it shouldn't. If your heart gives out, it gives out, and then it doesn't matter what you've paid. If you manage to avoid the heart attack, then you're right back in exactly the same Russian roulette game, presumably willing to pay exactly the same amount to avoid exactly the same one-third chance of death. So when you're making your decision, you should assume the game will actually take place.

Question 6 asks what you'd pay to remove one bullet out of four from this six-shooter:

The sad truth about this game is that three times out of six, one of those not-for-sale bullets is going to kill you, *whether or not* you've bought the fourth bullet. In other words, three times out of six, it makes not a whit of difference whether you did or didn't pay to remove a bullet. *Having a not-for-sale bullet come up is exactly like dying of a heart attack* — you can't do anything about it. If it happens, you're dead, and if it doesn't, you're right back to playing Russian roulette. So when you're making your decision, you might as well concentrate on the *other* three times out of six. In other words, you might as well assume you're playing with a three-shooter containing a single bullet, which is for sale.

The question, then, is, What would you pay to avoid a one-third chance of death? I hope you gave the same answer that you gave to question 5. If not, give yourself an irrationality point.

That's the whole argument. If you buy it, you can move on to the discussion of question 7. But in case you thought it went by too fast, let me break it down into pieces.

Here are five questions for a Russian roulette player:

Question A: How much would you pay to remove both bullets from this six-shooter immediately before playing Russian roulette?

Question B: How much would you pay to remove the single bullet from this three-shooter immediately before playing Russian roulette?

Question C: How much would you pay to remove the single bullet from the same three-shooter if you'd been warned that an anvil might fall on your head and kill you before the Russian roulette game gets under way?

Question D: Suppose you're going to play Russian roulette with one of these 2 three-shooters, with the gun in question to be chosen by a coin flip.

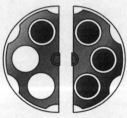

Immediately prior to the coin flip, how much would you pay to remove the single bullet from the left-hand gun?

Question E: How much would you pay to remove the single for-sale bullet from the following six-shooter immediately before playing Russian roulette?

I claim that questions A and B should have the same answer, because both come down to the question "What would you pay to avoid a one-third chance of death?"

I claim that questions B and C should have the same answer, because a falling anvil is quite irrelevant to the risks you're willing to take in Russian roulette. If the anvil kills you, it kills you and there's nothing you can do about it. So you concentrate on the case where your decision *does* matter, and ignore the anvil.

I claim that questions C and D should have the same answer, because playing Russian roulette with the right-hand gun is tantamount to being hit by an anvil.

I claim that questions D and E should have the same answer, because the six-shooter in question E is *the same thing* as the pair of three-shooters in question D.

Now, question A is the same as quiz question 5, and question E is the same as quiz question 6. Therefore those questions should have the same answer — assuming, of course, that you're rational.

"Wait a minute!" you might object. "You say we can ignore the cases where a not-for-sale bullet comes up because in those cases I die anyway and my choice doesn't matter. Why can't I just as well ignore the cases where an *empty* chamber comes up, because in those cases I live anyway, and my choice doesn't matter?"

The answer is that if an empty chamber comes up, your choice *does* matter, because it affects how much money you'll have left to live on. So that argument won't work.

For that matter, if you care about your heirs, then *my* argument won't work, because your choice affects their inheritance, which matters to you even if you die. That's why I was careful to include the assumption that you don't care what happens to your money after you're dead.

Your Answer to Question 7

Which would you prefer: a cat, a dog, or a pet (cat or dog) to be determined by a coin flip? If you prefer the cat to the dog, you must (assuming you're rational) prefer the cat to the coin flip. Why risk getting your second choice when your first choice is available? Likewise, if you prefer the dog to the cat, you'll also prefer the dog to the coin flip.

It's possible that you like cats and dogs equally. In that case, the cat, the dog, and the coin flip are all equally good.

That exhausts all the possibilities! You prefer the cat to the dog, or you prefer the dog to the cat, or you like them both equally. In *none* of these cases will you *prefer* the coin flip.

With that in mind, which 2,000-ball urn would you rather draw from?

A. Urn A, with two $1,000 balls (and the rest losers)
B. Urn B, with twenty $100 balls (and the rest losers)
X. I'd rather flip a coin to decide

Just as with the dog and the cat, choice X is irrational. Let's try again.

A. Urn A, with two $1,000 balls (and the rest losers)
B. Urn B, with twenty $100 balls (and the rest losers)
X. The great big urn X into which all the contents of urns A and B have been poured

If you choose X, there's a 50-50 chance you'll draw a ball that came from A and a 50-50 chance you'll draw a ball that came from B — just as if you'd flipped a coin. So if preferring to flip a coin is irrational (and it is), so is preferring to draw from X.

But urn X contains four thousand balls, of which two say $1,000 and twenty say $100. That's exactly the same as two copies of urn

C from the original problem, all mixed together — giving exactly the same odds of winning any given prize that you could have gotten from urn C.

So if preferring X is irrational (and we've already agreed that it is), then so is preferring C. If you did prefer C, you picked up an irrationality point.

Your Answers to Questions 8 and 9

Remember that you're drawing from an urn with thirty red balls and sixty blue balls. Some of the blue balls are light blue and some are dark blue, but I haven't told you how many.

Now I want you to reach into that urn and draw a ball. If that ball is dark blue, I'm going to give you the envelope I'm holding. If it *doesn't* come up dark blue, which would you prefer?

A. To win $1,000 if the ball is red
B. To win $1,000 if the ball is light blue
C. A and B sound equally good

A rational person can answer this question without knowing what's in the envelope. After all, you either will or will not draw a dark blue ball. If you do, your choice won't matter anyway. And if you don't, it doesn't matter what's in the envelope. So there's no circumstance where the contents of the envelope should affect your choice.

Now let me reveal that the envelope is empty. That makes this choice identical to question 8.

Oh, wait — I was mistaken. Actually, the envelope contains $1,000. That makes this choice identical to question 9.

Did changing the contents of the envelope change your answer? In other words, did you give different answers to questions 8 and 9? If so, you earned both an irrationality point and an invitation to lunch. I'd very much like to sit down with you and offer a deal: We'll draw a ball from that urn. If (like many people) you chose 8A over 8B and 9B over 9A, we can make these trades: I'll give you the prize from 8A, and all I ask in return is the prize from 8B. To sweeten the pot, I'll give you 9B, and all I ask in return is the prize from 9A. As you can see, no matter what ball we draw, we'll give each other $1,000 and break even.

	RED	LIGHT BLUE	DARK BLUE
8A	$1,000	$0	$0
8B	$0	$1,000	$0
9A	$1,000	$0	$1,000
9B	$0	$1,000	$1,000

Because this game caters entirely to your preferences, I assume you'll be glad to pick up the lunch tab — and then keep paying me for the privilege of playing again and again.

Your Answer to Question 10

Would you rather bet on a coin toss or on the outcome of a congressional race you know little about?

I claim that no rational person can *prefer* the coin toss. Here's why: You can always toss a coin to decide which congressional candidate to bet on — which means you're betting on a coin toss either way. (Notice that if you choose your candidate via a coin toss, you have exactly the same 50-50 chance of winning as if you'd bet on the coin toss directly.) So the election bet can't be worse than a coin-toss bet.

If you think you know something about politics, you might prefer to bet on the election. If you think you know nothing at all about politics, you might be *just as happy* betting on the coin toss. But if you *preferred* the coin toss, you earned an irrationality point.

So You're Irrational. Now What?

If you scored higher than 0 — and almost everyone does — you've got room for improvement. You are, of course, perfectly entitled to be cheerfully irrational. But if you can learn to make more rational decisions, you really will be happier in the long run, in the sense that you'll be more likely to get more of the things you want, whatever those things might be.

Consider, for example, the sixty University of Chicago students who reported to researchers that they'd be willing to pay more for a $50 gift certificate than for a lottery ticket where the *worst* possible outcome is the same $50 gift certificate! (You win either the $50 certificate or a $100 certificate, depending on a coin flip.) Surely these students could benefit from a little guidance.

If your irrationality is a problem for you, it might be an even bigger problem for economists, who like to build theories around the assumption that everyone is always perfectly rational. Economic theory predicts that everyone will score 0 on the irrationality test. That prediction is wrong. This leaves the economists with a variety of possible responses, each with some merit but all of them highly imperfect:

1. Give up. Admit that the rationality assumption is false, throw much of economics out the window, and start over.

2. Find a creative interpretation. Behavior that looks irrational in one light might look perfectly rational in another. Perhaps people are (rationally) pursuing goals we haven't fully considered. For example, in quiz question 1, the people who choose option B risk walking away empty-handed and regretting their choice — whereas in quiz question 2, those who choose option B and walk away empty-handed can always tell themselves, "Eh, I probably would have lost no matter *what* I'd chosen." (Of course, there's a sense in which you'll be lying to yourself. In question 2, exactly as

in question 1, there's exactly a 1 percent chance that choosing B can convert you from a winner to a loser.) Some economists have argued that the rational pursuit of *regret avoidance* can explain away a lot of so-called irrationality.

3. Deny the results. Why should we believe what quiz takers tell us they would do in highly fanciful situations they've never actually been in? And indeed, there's some evidence that the more realistic we make these questions, the more rational the answers get.

4. Deny the relevance of the results. Take people's word for how they'd behave in Russian roulette games, but take solace in knowing that economists are rarely called upon to predict behavior in Russian roulette games. As long as our theories work pretty well in most everyday situations, who cares very much if they go haywire in situations that almost never arise?

5. Rejoice. People are irrational. That means we have something useful to teach them! Get the word out: Take an economics class, and you'll learn to make better decisions. Or at the very least, study this book!

CHAPTER 7

Law School Admissions Test

S o you want to go to law school? Or to win arguments with people who went to law school? Then you'll need to think clearly about how to assess evidence.

Economists can help, because we assess evidence all the time. How sure are you that a proposed economic policy can accomplish its goals? Sure enough to recommend the policy? How sure are you that a defendant is guilty? Sure enough to convict? These questions have a lot in common.

Start here.

1

Reasonable Doubt

Here I have a couple of urns. The one on the left contains 70 white balls and 30 black. The one on the right contains 30 white and 70 black.

While you weren't looking, I reached into one of these urns and randomly drew out a dozen balls. (I flipped a fair coin to choose the urn.) As you can see, 4 of those balls were white and 8 were black.

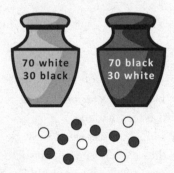

If you had to guess, which urn would you guess I drew from?
a) What's your estimate of the probability you're right?
b) Do you think you're right beyond a reasonable doubt?

SOLUTION: It's roughly 98 percent probable that I drew from the right urn. To make that a little more graphic, suppose you had the opportunity, on the first of every month, to place a bet that's as close to a sure thing as this one is. Then you'd lose your bet only about once every four years or so. By the standards that are ordinarily employed in courtrooms, that's quite comfortably beyond a reasonable doubt.

The decision theorist Howard Raiffa once posed this problem (with some minor changes) to a group of lawyers at a cocktail party and was surprised when one of them exclaimed, "I bet you drew from the left-hand urn." Another lawyer was quick to correct him: "No, you got confused. The drawing was eight blacks and four whites, not the other way around."

"I know," said the first lawyer, "but in my experience at the bar, *life is just plain perverse, so I would bet on the left-hand urn!* But I am not really a betting man."

The other lawyers all agreed that this was not a very rational thing to do — that the evidence was in favor of the right-hand urn.

But by how much? They discussed it for a while and decided that the evidence was pretty meager — the odds might have gone up from 50-50 to about 55-45. They also agreed that because lawyers should cultivate the habit of being skeptical, they'd be inclined to slant their judgments downward and act as if the odds were roughly 50-50.

But as I've told you, the correct answer is about 98 percent, so that the balls were drawn from the right-hand urn beyond a reasonable doubt. As Raiffa observed, this story points out that most people vastly underestimate the power of a small sample. The lawyers described above had an extreme reaction, but even statistics students tend to cluster their guesses around 70 percent.

Is 98 percent really beyond a reasonable doubt? That's ultimately a subjective question, but given a reasonable interpretation of what *reasonable* means, my own subjective answer is a pretty emphatic yes. There's not much in life that we can be more than 98 percent sure of.

A world in which the reasonable-doubt cutoff is set at 98 percent is a world where it's almost impossible to convict anyone for anything, and consequently a world with a lot of crime. On the other hand, a world in which the reasonable-doubt cutoff is only, say, 50 percent is a world with a lot of false convictions. I would not want to take the risk of living in either of those worlds. Somewhere in between is, if not a comfortable medium, then at least the most comfortable of all possible mediums.

So if I were on trial for the crime of drawing from the right urn, I hope this evidence would be strong enough to convict me. If you're unwilling to convict on this evidence, then you're ipso facto willing to free forty-nine guilty men before you'll convict a single innocent. According to the frequently cited eighteenth-century legal scholar William Blackstone, it's better that ten guilty men escape than that one innocent suffer. To let forty-nine guilty men escape is to go far above and beyond this standard.*

In fact, empirical evidence suggests that for real-world juries, the cutoff for reasonable doubt is somewhere around 74 percent. (That is, juries tend to convict in cases where independent observers, seeing the same evidence the jury saw, estimate the subjective probability of guilt to be anything more than about 74 percent, or perhaps a bit less.)

I think I'd be pretty comfortable with a 74 percent standard if I thought I lived in a world where all police and prosecutors could be counted on not to take advantage of that standard to falsify evidence against people they don't like. In the world I actually inhabit, I think I'd prefer to set the bar a little higher, though certainly not as high as 98 percent. To my knowledge, no serious scholar has *ever* defended a bar that high. So once again I think we can safely say that 98 percent counts as well beyond a reasonable doubt.

With those preliminaries out of the way, let's enter the courtroom.

---

* While "ten guilty men" is something like the industry standard, the legal scholar Alexander Volokh has documented a long tradition encompassing a wide range of numbers, some as high as one hundred or more. But it's difficult for me to believe that the largest of these numbers was ever meant to be taken seriously.

2

The Boy with Purple Hair

One Tuesday afternoon a particularly heinous murder is committed in Manhattan, and police seal off all the bridges and tunnels to ensure that the culprit remains on the island. Based on an incontrovertible combination of DNA evidence and eyewitness testimony, officers are told to be on the lookout for a suspect with naturally purple hair. An hour or so later, a police officer notices a purple-haired man named Nathan standing at a bus stop and detains him. Tests soon prove that Nathan's hair is, indeed, naturally purple, and solely on this basis he is held for trial. At the trial, expert testimony establishes that naturally purple hair is extremely rare—in fact the odds against it are a million to one.

a) Based on these facts, is Nathan guilty beyond a reasonable doubt?
b) Oops. Did I say the odds against naturally purple hair are a million to one? I meant to say a *billion* to one. *Now* is Nathan guilty beyond a reasonable doubt?

SOLUTION:

a) On a weekday afternoon, there are about 4 million people in Manhattan. If the odds against naturally purple hair are a million to one, then about 4 of those people will have naturally purple hair. Any of them is as likely as Nathan to be the culprit, which means there's about a 25 percent chance he's guilty. You should let him go free (though you might want to keep an eye on him).
b) If the odds against naturally purple hair are a *billion* to one, then the probability that there's even one possible culprit besides Nathan is about 4 million divided by a billion, or

about ⁴⁄₁₀ of 1 percent. That makes it at least 99.6 percent certain that Nathan is the murderer. (It's actually more than that, because even in the highly unlikely event that Nathan *does* have a purple-haired doppelganger, he could still be guilty.) That's damned near certain.

The moral of this problem is that *you cannot assess evidence without weighing it against relevant background information.* (In this case, the relevant background information is that there are 4 million people in Manhattan.) This is a moral that runs at large: it applies in the courtroom, it applies when you're analyzing economic data, and it applies in the doctor's office.

3

The HIV Test

Your employer requires you to take an HIV test, and you've just gotten the results. The bad news is that according to the test, you're infected. The good news is that regardless of the patient's HIV status, every test result has a 5% chance of being wrong. So there's a 5 percent chance you're okay, right?

SOLUTION: Wrong. The relevant background information is that most people — let's say 99 percent of your demographic group — are uninfected. So you're probably uninfected too. Even though the test is wrong only 5 percent of the time, odds are that this is one of those times.

In fact, the probability that you're uninfected is about 84 percent. Why 84 percent? In a population of 100,000 people, we've assumed that just 1 percent — that is, 1,000 — are infected. Of the 1,000 who are infected, 95 percent get accurate (and grim) test results. Of the 99,000 who are uninfected, 5 percent, or 4,950, get *in*accurate results that say they're infected. That makes 950 + 4,950 = 5,900 people who got bad news, and of those 5,900, only 950, or 16 percent, are actually infected. The other 84 percent are just fine.

It's all a matter of weighing the evidence. The test result is evidence that you're infected. But the fact that most people are uninfected is evidence that you are too. Both bits of evidence are relevant, and it would be wrong to ignore either of them.

If you're skeptical, try a starker example: Suppose you know you have a rare gene that renders you absolutely immune to viruses. Then surely you are entitled to laugh off the results of the HIV test, no matter how dire they appear. The test cannot trump the background information that you're uninfected. And similarly, no test can completely trump *any* background information, including the background information that most people are not HIV positive.

For that matter, if you ever have your IQ tested and manage to score 300, you're probably smart enough to know that it's extremely unlikely that the test is accurate, because you've got enough background knowledge to know that mis-scored IQ tests are a lot more common than IQs of 300.

Now back to the courtroom.

4

The Accused Soldier

At the tail end of a great battle, a foot soldier is seen lobbing a grenade toward the tent that serves as headquarters for his commanding officer. Sometime later, parts of the officer's body are found scattered around the area.

In his defense, the soldier is able to prove that the grenade in question was the notorious M16.5, which explodes only half the time. Besides, a lot of other grenades went off around that tent, and the officer might have been dead long before the incident.

But the prosecution is able to prove that *if* the grenade went off, then there's a 90 percent chance that it killed the officer.

How likely is the soldier to be guilty of murder? That is, how likely is it that his grenade went off and killed the officer?

SOLUTION: Well, let's see. There's a 50 percent chance that the grenade went off, and *if* it went off, there's a 90 percent chance that it killed the officer. So the chance that it went off *and* killed the officer is 50 percent times 90 percent, or 45 percent, right?

Wrong. Yet again, you can't assess evidence without accounting for relevant background information. In this case, the relevant background information is that *the officer is dead.* Although the grenade goes off only half the time, the officer's being dead makes it particularly likely that this is one of those times. The naive calculation fails to account for that.

So we have to approach this a different way. Start by observing that there are three ways the officer could have died:

a) The soldier's grenade went off and killed the officer.
b) First another grenade killed the officer, then the soldier's grenade went off.
c) First another grenade killed the officer, then the soldier's grenade failed to go off.

We're told that the soldier's grenade goes off exactly half the time. That makes (b) and (c) equally likely. We're also told that *if* the soldier's grenade went off, it's 90 percent likely to have killed the officer. In other words, (a) is 9 times as likely as (b).

So out of 11 similar cases, we should expect scenario (a) to occur 9 times, scenario (b) once, and scenario (c) once. The defendant is guilty with probability 9/11. Call it about 82 percent.

5

The Four Suspects

A murder has been committed. There are four suspects: Bob, Carol, and Ted, who smoke, and Alice, a nonsmoker.

Bob   **Carol**   **Ted**   **Alice**

You're quite sure that one (and only one) of these is the culprit but have no reason to suspect one more than another. So you call in your two crack investigators, Agents 86 and 99, explain the situation, and send them out separately to investigate further.

Agent 86 reports back that, based on the evidence he's discovered, the odds are two to one that the culprit is a smoker. Agent 99 reports back that based on the separate evidence *she's* discovered, the culprit is definitely female. Unfortunately, that's all they can conclude.

You have complete confidence in your investigators. Who's your main suspect, and how sure are you?

SOLUTION: We know that the culprit is female, so it can only be Carol or Alice. And we know the odds are two to one for a smoker, so it looks like Carol—the smoker—is the most probable culprit, right?

Wrong. It's probably Alice. You should be 60 percent sure of that.

Here's why: When you first sent Agent 86 out into the field, all four suspects looked equally likely. Because three of the four suspects are smokers, 86 started out believing the odds were three to one that the culprit smokes. But along the way, something must have convinced him that the odds were only *two* to one. So whatever evidence he discovered must have tended to exonerate the smokers. That already leaves Alice as the chief suspect.

Indeed, based on Agent 86's report alone, there's a ⅓ chance that Alice is guilty and a ⅔ chance that one of the smokers is guilty. Spreading that ⅔ out equally over the three smoking suspects, the probabilities are

Bob ⅔   Carol ⅔   Ted ⅔   Alice ⅓

So Alice is half again as likely as Carol to be the culprit (because ⅓ is 50 percent more than ⅔).

Now Agent 99 arrives, to eliminate Bob and Ted from consideration. But this doesn't change the fact that Alice is half again as likely as Carol to be the culprit. That makes the probabilities 40 percent for Carol and 60 percent for Alice.

Solving crimes is all about assessing evidence. Often that means thinking about statistics, as in the past few problems. But sometimes the evidence is of a very different kind.

6

Theft on the Moon

You have a sealed lockbox about a cubic yard in volume, containing $100,000 in $100 bills. Your balance scale tells you that the box (with the money inside) weighs 50 kilograms. You give the box to your friend Al, who flies it to the moon, while you, along with your balance scale, follow in a separate vehicle. Upon arrival, you set up your balance scale on the moon's surface, retrieve the sealed box, and verify that it still weighs 50 kilograms. You then give the box to your friend Barb, who loads it into her all-terrain vehicle and drives it to your moonbase, with you following along, again in a separate vehicle. When you get to the moonbase, Barb returns your lockbox. You open it and it's empty.

Who stole your money, Al or Barb?

SOLUTION: On earth, the left half of your balance scale, supporting a 50-kilogram metal ballast, just balances against the right half, supporting your sealed lockbox.

Actually, that's not quite right. The left half of your balance scale supports a 50-kilogram metal ballast *plus the invisible column of air above it* (shown in gray), while the right half supports your sealed lockbox *plus a column of air with a lockbox-size hole in it:*

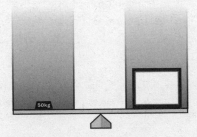

On the moon both columns of air are removed. That lightens the left half more than it lightens the right half, so the scale should now tip to the right. If it doesn't — if the scale still balances — the lockbox must have gotten lighter. Its contents must be gone. Al took your cash.

By way of a reality check: On earth, $100,000 in $100 bills weighs about 2 pounds. So does a cubic yard of air. So the weight of the missing money on the right does indeed cancel the weight of the extra missing air on the left, which explains why the scale still balances on the moon.*

There's more to the law than resolving individual cases. There's also the problem of designing more effective legal institutions. Here's one to think about:

7

Medieval Justice

Professor Peter Leeson of George Mason University reports on a form of medieval justice:

> For four hundred years the most sophisticated persons in Europe decided difficult criminal cases by asking the defendant to thrust his arm into a cauldron of boiling water and fish out a ring. If his arm was unharmed, he was exonerated. If not, he was convicted.

---

* There's one additional relevant difference between the earth and the moon: on the moon, the air underneath the balance pans, which helps to support them, is no longer present. But that affects both sides of the balance equally, so it's safe to ignore it.

Could this be an effective way to sort out the guilty from the innocent?

SOLUTION: Professor Leeson believes the answer is yes.

As long as defendants believe (superstitiously) that ordeals yield accurate verdicts, guilty defendants always confess to avoid the ordeal. At the same time, innocent defendants always opt for the ordeal — and are always acquitted, provided the priests cheat by (for example) substituting tepid for boiling water, or "sprinkling" a few gallons of cold holy water over the cauldron, or liberally redefining what counts as "unharmed."

Not only does the system work but it's continually reinforced. Even the superstitious masses are smart enough to figure out that their equally superstitious neighbors opt for ordeals only when innocent; therefore they expect all ordeals to yield acquittals, and their expectations are always confirmed.

If not everyone is perfectly superstitious, then the story is a little more complicated. Still, as long as there's a healthy amount of superstition floating around, and as long as the priests are eager to convict the guilty and acquit the innocent, you'd expect most ordeals to yield acquittals, and you'd expect nonbelievers to be denied the ordeal option. (After all, the system works only as long as the participants believe it's rigged not by the priests but by God.)

And indeed there's at least some historical evidence for this theory. First, a great many trials by ordeal ended in acquittals, which at least shows that they were not designed to convict everyone. Second, nonbelievers were generally exempt from trials by ordeal, which would make sense if the whole arrangement depended on beliefs. And third, ordeals were generally administered by clerics (which would have been necessary to reinforce the needed superstitions) and in fact died out when clerics stopped administering them.

Professor Leeson's conclusion is that "no one longs for the return of ordeals, but if the necessary belief structure existed to support them, perhaps they should."

Finally, because every well-trained lawyer should know something about civil as well as criminal law:

8

Settling Lawsuits

In 1914 the British government passed a law to control rents. It defines the "standard rent" on a house to be the rent in 1914, unless that is less than the ratable value, in which case it is equal to the ratable value. (No, I do not know what a "ratable value" is, but that won't matter here.) It then declares that a house is covered by the law "if either the standard rent or the ratable value is less than 105 pounds."

Thanks to the obscurity of the language, there was a great deal of confusion about which houses were and were not covered, resulting in a considerable number of lawsuits.

Can you settle all of those lawsuits in one stroke by restating the criterion for coverage in (much) simpler terms?

SOLUTION: A house is subject to the law if and only if the ratable value is less than 105 pounds. (Think about it!)

CHAPTER 8

Are You Smarter Than Google?

*I*n the years I've been blogging at TheBigQuestions.com, I haven't shied away from controversy. Religion, politics, and manners are standard fare, though I try not to post unless I have something at least a bit novel to say. As a result, I'm usually not preaching to any particular choir, which means I risk offending every variety of knee jerker.

I've gotten used to being called a radical socialist, a mindless liberal, a heartless conservative, and a reactionary mooncalf. But in all my years of blogging, no post has inspired more vitriol than one titled "Are You Smarter Than Google?"

In fact, it's not even close. This post generated many thousands of responses, on both my own blog and others', a great many of them demanding that I be fired, publicly humiliated, and/or banned from the Internet. I don't delete comments, even when they're very strongly worded, unless they're extremely abusive and/or quite thoroughly devoid of intellectual content. In this case, I deleted many hundreds.

What was the content of this post? It was the following brain teaser.

1

Are You Smarter Than Google?

There's a certain country where everybody wants to have a son. Therefore, each couple keeps having children until they have a boy, then they stop. What fraction of the population is female?

Well, of course you can't know for sure, because maybe, by some extraordinary coincidence, the last 100,000 couples in a row have gotten boys on the first try, or maybe, by an even more extraordinary coincidence, the last 100,000 couples have had to try eight times before succeeding.

Therefore (as I told my readers in the original blog post), the question is meant to be answered *in expectation,* which means this: If there are a great many countries just like this one, what fraction of the population is female in the average country?

This problem has been around, in many forms, for at least half a century, but it keeps finding new life. I found it in a children's puzzle book when I was about ten years old, and (much more recently) Google has used it to screen job candidates. The official answer — that is, the answer I found in the back of that puzzle book, and the answer Google reportedly expected from its job candidates — is simple, clear, and wrong.

And no, it's not wrong because of small real-world discrepancies between the number of male and female births, or because of anything else that's extraneous to the spirit of the problem. It's just wrong. The correct answer, unlike the expected one, is not so simple.

So are you smarter than the folks at Google? Before you read ahead, what's your answer?

I'll wait . . .

Ready now?

Okay, let's continue.

The answer Google seems to have expected is the same answer I gave when I first saw this problem long, long ago. It goes like this:

SOLUTION: Each birth has a 50 percent chance of producing a girl. Nothing the parents do can change that. So each individual child is equally likely to be male or female, and therefore, in expectation, half of all the children are girls.

I'll give you another chance to take a break. Before you read ahead, what's wrong with that reasoning?

Ready?

Okay then:

Actually, most of it is right. Each birth has a 50 percent chance of producing a girl — check! Nothing the parents do can change that — check! So, each individual child is equally likely to be male or female — check!

But it does not follow — and in fact is not true! — that in expectation, half of all children are girls.

What *does* follow is that, in expectation, the number of boys and the number of girls are equal. But that's not at all the same thing.

To see why not, try this much easier problem:

2

Eggs and Pancakes

Every day I flip a coin to decide what to have for breakfast. If the coin comes up heads, I have two eggs and one pancake. If it comes up tails, I have two eggs and three pancakes. On average, what fraction of my breakfast items are pancakes?

THE WRONG SOLUTION: On the average day (in fact each and every day) I have exactly two eggs.

On the average day, I also have two pancakes (two being the average of one and three). So on average, the number of pancakes is equal to the number of eggs.

Therefore, on average, half my breakfast items are pancakes.

Except for the final sentence, all of that is true but most of it is irrelevant. I do in fact have two pancakes on the average day, but that has nothing to do with the question. Here's the right answer:

THE RIGHT SOLUTION: Whenever I flip heads, ⅓ of my breakfast items are pancakes. Whenever I flip tails, ⅗ of my breakfast items are pancakes. The average of those two numbers is ⁷⁄₁₅. The answer to the question, then, is that on the average day ⁷⁄₁₅ of my breakfast items are pancakes.

Here's the analogy:

Imagine many breakfasts	Imagine many countries
At the average breakfast, the number of pancakes is equal to the number of eggs (TRUE!)	In the average country, the number of girls is equal to the number of boys (TRUE!)
Therefore at the average breakfast, the fraction of items that are pancakes is ½ (FALSE!)	Therefore in the average country, the fraction of children that are girls is ½ (FALSE!)

Moral: Two things (be they eggs and pancakes or boys and girls) can be equal in expectation,* but that tells you nothing about their expected ratio.

The gist of that moral is that the official answer to the Google problem is wrong. But we still have to figure out what's right.

It turns out that the correct answer depends on the size of the country. This is easiest to think about when the country is so tiny that it has just one family. Let's solve that case first, then we'll move on to bigger countries.†

Here are some possible configurations for that one family:

Probability	Configuration	Ratio
½	B	0
¼	GB	½
⅛	GGB	⅔
¹⁄₁₆	GGGB	¾

From this, we can see that the number of boys is always exactly 1.

---

* Remember that "in expectation" means the same thing as "on average."

† If you — like many of my blog readers — are prepared to object that the one-family assumption is contrary to the spirit of the problem, let me assure you that I agree with you. I'm solving this case first not because it's the most important case but because it's the easiest. I hope that you, unlike some of my more impatient blog readers, will bear with me.

The number of girls, of course, can be anything at all, but we want to know what it is on average. For that, we take each possible number, multiply it by the corresponding probability, and add up, as follows:

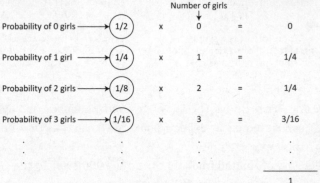

Number of girls

Probability of 0 girls	1/2	x	0	=	0
Probability of 1 girl	1/4	x	1	=	1/4
Probability of 2 girls	1/8	x	2	=	1/4
Probability of 3 girls	1/16	x	3	=	3/16
.	.		.		.
.	.		.		.
.	.		.		.
					1

The numbers in the infinitely long column on the right add up to 1. (If you don't believe me, try adding several terms and you'll see them approaching closer and closer to 1.) That is, the expected number of girls is equal to the expected number of boys — just as we knew it must be.

But to get the expected *fraction* of girls, we need to do the same calculation with fractions of girls instead of numbers of girls. And it comes out like this:

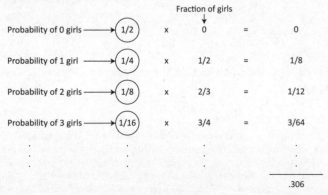

Fraction of girls

Probability of 0 girls	1/2	x	0	=	0
Probability of 1 girl	1/4	x	1/2	=	1/8
Probability of 2 girls	1/8	x	2/3	=	1/12
Probability of 3 girls	1/16	x	3/4	=	3/64
.	.		.		.
.	.		.		.
.	.		.		.
					.306

The numbers in the right-hand column add up to just about 0.306, or 30.6 percent.*

Now again — that calculation is only correct for a country with just one family. For a country with two families, a similar but more complicated calculation gives an expected fraction of about 38.63 percent. If you want to see that calculation, you can in the appendix.

For a country with 10 families, the expected fraction is about 47.51 percent. For a country with 100 families, it's about 49.75 percent. For a country with 1,000 families, it's about 49.98 percent. For a country with 5,000 families, it's about 49.995 percent. For a country comparable to the United States, with about 100 million families, the expected fraction is about 49.999999975 percent.

You might be tempted to say, "Aha! Surely there's no important difference between 49.995 percent and 50 percent. So the official reasoning is correct after all!"

Hold on there! First of all, even if the correct answer was *exactly* 50 percent, the official reasoning would still be entirely wrong. We don't generally give full credit (or even partial credit) for bad reasoning that just happens to get the right answer.

Besides, who says there's no important difference between 49.995 percent and 50 percent? Try telling that to Al Gore, who got 49.995 percent of the Bush/Gore vote in Florida in the year 2000 and thereby lost the presidency of the United States.

Or if that doesn't convince you, try this variation, where the official reasoning will lead you neither slightly astray nor moderately astray or even hugely astray, but *infinitely* astray:

---

* Where did the 30.6 percent come from? It takes a bit of work. If you remember your calculus, you might be able to show that the sum of the infinite series is actually $\log(2)-1$, which is just about 30.6 percent. If you don't remember your calculus, I hope you'll take my word for this.

3

The Google Problem Redux

There's a certain country where everybody wants to have a son. Therefore each couple keeps having children until they have a boy, then they stop. What is the ratio of boys to girls?

This differs from the original Google Problem by asking about the ratio of boys to girls, rather than the fraction of girls in the population.

Again, the answer in any one country could of course be just about anything, so we need to specify that the question is to be answered *in expectation* or, in simpler words, *on average* over many such countries.

SOLUTION: There's always some chance—perhaps a tiny chance, but still some chance—that every single family has a boy on the first try. If that happens, there are no girls, so the ratio of boys to girls is infinite.

To get the *expected* ratio, we have to average over all possible ratios, including infinity. That average is infinity.

If you said that the answer was ½, you were infinitely wrong.

It turns out that a lot of people — and especially, I suppose, the sort of people who like to solve brain teasers on the Internet — have seen some version of this problem before and have had the (correct) insight that in expectation the number of boys and the number of girls must be equal. Some of them tend to feel pretty proud of that insight, which makes them exceptionally reluctant to admit that it fails to solve the problem.

I'd intended to blog twice on the subject — once to pose the puzzle and once to reveal the answer. Instead, the discussion ended up stretching over six blog posts. You can find links to all of them at www.TheBigQuestions.com/google.html.

A lot of readers fell into the trap. A lot of those defended their answers vigorously, then gradually saw the light as I and other commenters pointed out their errors. Those people learned something, and many of them were delighted. That delighted me, too.

Others brought up interesting and valid new twists. Here are a few examples:

- My analysis assumes that all families have finished reproducing. What if we take a snapshot *before* the last family gets its son? (Answer: It depends on when you take the snapshot. But in no case is the expected fraction of girls equal to $1/2$.)
- What if you count the parents and not just the kids? (The answer changes, but it's still not $1/2$.)
- What if the country's population is literally infinite? (Answer: Then there are infinitely many girls and infinitely many boys, giving a fraction of infinity over infinity, which is not a number at all, and certainly not $1/2$. Besides, who ever heard of a country with an infinite population?)*

But others kept returning to the comments section to defend the wrong answer, while a great many others jumped into the fray to help point out their errors — help that was not always appreciated.

The whole thing might have died down in a few days had it not caught the attention of an Internet phenomenon named Luboŝ

---

* In a delightfully ironic twist, many of the readers who insisted on assuming that the population was literally infinite were the same readers who excoriated me for working through the case of a single-family country, even for illustration, on the grounds that a single-family country is "unrealistic."

Motl. It's been said of Luboŝ that he's hard to ignore, but it's always worth the effort. I eventually took this advice to heart, but not before we had several rounds of increasingly bizarre correspondence.

Luboŝ is a physicist by training and a crank by choice. He appears to haunt the Internet twenty-four hours a day from his home in the Czech Republic. When he blogs about physics, he's often clear, accurate, and generous with his explanations. The rest of the time he burnishes his reputation as a nut.

That's what he was doing when he announced on his blog that the only acceptable answer to the Google problem is 50 percent, and that you (or in this case I) would have to be a complete idiot to believe otherwise. He gave absolutely no argument to support this position, and repeatedly asserted that no argument was necessary. Those who know him will recognize this as classic crankmode Luboŝ.

Because Luboŝ was quite insusceptible to reason (completely ignoring, for example, a series of simple numerical examples that proved him wrong, and refusing ever to state the secret additional assumptions that he claimed would support his 50 percent answer), I went a different route and publicly offered to bet him up to $15,000 (and anyone else up to $5,000) that a computer simulation (for a country with four families reproducing for 30 generations) — with disputes over interpretation to be settled by a panel of randomly chosen statistics professors from top departments — would prove me right.

At first a dozen readers (not including Luboŝ) stepped up to get in on this bet, but they all soon either changed their minds or mysteriously stopped responding to emails.

Then I screwed up.

A reader named Larry suggested a slightly different bet, which I accepted without carefully reading his terms. This bet turned out to be stacked against me.

I knew that in a country with four families, the expected fraction of girls is about 44 percent. I therefore agreed to Larry's bet that a series of simulations would show it to be less than 46.5 percent, leaving a little room for statistical anomalies. But I overlooked Larry's stipulation that we include the parents in the count. This turns out to drive the expected ratio up over 46.5 percent (though it's still less than 50 percent).

Having rashly accepted Larry's challenge, I was legitimately on the hook for a $5,000 bet I was almost sure to lose. I'd have paid up if necessary, but Larry most graciously suggested that he'd settle for some autographed books.

Hundreds of others refused to take the bet but continued to defend the wrong answer. A happy exception was a reader known to me only as Tom, who started out as a serial repeater of false and tired pro–50 percent arguments. I (and others) tried patiently pointing out his errors, but he seemed hell-bent on ignoring everything we said — to the point where I eventually lost my patience and said, "I'm sorry, but it appears that you are too stupid to think about this brain teaser." To his great credit, Tom responded not by digging his heels in further but by taking a little time to think — and then returning a few days later with a beautifully reasoned essay that not only explained the right answer but offered a whole new (and completely correct) explanation of why the answer cannot possibly be 50 percent. He graciously allowed me to share his essay with my readers as a guest poster, and I know from my email that it helped a lot of people see the light.

That happy experience aside, I remain astonished that so many became so emotionally invested in defending the wrong answer to a simple brain teaser. Clearly, the right answer comes as a surprise to many people. It came as a surprise to me at first! But I still don't quite get why so many people are so resistant to being surprised. Or more to the point: How does someone get so emotionally invested in a simple brain teaser that he is willing to make the same false arguments over and over and over and over and over and over and over again but not care enough to read and digest the right answer? Perhaps that would be a good puzzle for a book called *Can You Outsmart a Psychologist?*

Over many years of teaching, one thing I've learned is that when students don't see the point of pure theory, you can usually snag their attention with an application to sports. (Interestingly, this works best with students who are inclined to dismiss pure theory as "just a game.")

Let us, then, turn to the age-old issue of "hot hands" in basketball. The question is whether basketball players experience good and bad streaks beyond what you'd expect from pure chance. Of course we've got a lot of data on this, but historically a great many people have misinterpreted those data — precisely because they didn't understand the issues in the great Google problem controversy.

I'll tell you that story in a moment. But first let me show you how to make some money.

We'll play a game: One of us flips a coin four times in a row to get three pairs of consecutive Hs and Ts. For example, if you flip HHTH, your three pairs are HH, HT, and TH. If you flip THTT, your pairs are TH, HT, and TT.

Now I'll give you a dollar for each HH, and you give me a dollar for each HT. This is a perfectly fair game, because HH and HT are equally likely. If you doubt me, try writing down all sixteen possible outcomes, then count all the HHs and all the HTs. There are exactly twelve of each.

	Number of HH	Number of HT
HHHH	3	0
HHHT	2	1
HHTH	1	1
HHTT	1	1
HTHH	1	1
HTHT	0	2
HTTH	0	1
HTTT	0	1
THHH	2	0
THHT	1	1
THTH	0	1
THTT	0	1
TTHH	1	0
TTHT	0	1
TTTH	0	0
TTTT	0	0
	TOTAL: 12	TOTAL: 12

If you play this game against an experienced gambler, she will quickly realize that it's fair. First, experienced gamblers have a very good sense of facts such as "HH and HT are equally likely." Second, if you play long enough, you'll probably both come pretty close to breaking even on average, which tells you that the game is probably fair.

Now try a variation:

4

Wanna Play?

Once again, we'll flip four times to get three sequences. We'll count the HHs and the HTs. I'll give you a number of dollars equal to the *percentage* of those sequences that are HH, and you give me a number of dollars equal to the percentage that are HT. Does that game strike you as fair?

SOLUTION: If you think like so many of my blog commenters, you'll say, "Well, HH and HT are equally likely, so on average half of all the HH and HT flips will be HH and the other half will be HT. This is another fair game."

If you do think that way, please contact me. I'd like to play this game against you. Because here are the relevant percentages:

	Number of HH	Number of HT	Percentage of HH
HHHH	3	0	100
HHHT	2	1	67
HHTH	1	1	50
HHTT	1	1	50
HTHH	1	1	50
HTHT	0	2	0
HTTH	0	1	0
HTTT	0	1	0
THHH	2	0	100
THHT	1	1	50
THTH	0	1	0
THTT	0	1	0
TTHH	1	0	100
TTHT	0	1	0
TTTH	0	0	–
TTTT	0	0	–
	TOTAL: 12	TOTAL: 12	AVERAGE: 40.5

In each row the percentage shown is the percentage of all pairs starting with H that are HH. (In the last two rows, there are no pairs starting with HH, so the ratio can't be computed. If our flips produce either of those patterns, no money changes hands.)

The average of all the percentages is 40.5 percent, which is definitely not at all the same thing as 50 percent. On the average play of this game, I will pay you $40.50 and you will pay me $59.50. In the long run I make an average of $19 each time we play.

The moral? Two things (in this case, HH and HT) can be equal in expectation — that is, they occur equally often — but that tells you nothing about their expected *ratio*. Perhaps that moral rings a bell by now.

Now back to the hot hands. Take a ballplayer. Put him at a distance from the basket where he makes just about half his free throws. (This distance will be different for different players.)

Have him take four shots. Write down an H for each success and a T for each miss. Repeat with many different players.

If there are no hot hands, then HH and HT should occur about equally often. (That is, after a successful shot, a second success should be no more likely than a miss.) So a good test of the hot-hands theory would be to count the HHs and the HTs for all the players and see whether the totals are roughly equal.

In 1985 a group of researchers (let's call them GVT, because those were their initials) set out to analyze exactly this experiment. Unfortunately, they kept track of the wrong statistic. Instead of asking whether, on average, there are equal numbers of HH and HT, they figured they might as well ask whether, on average, there are equal *fractions* of HH and HT. After all, equal numbers should be the same thing as equal fractions, right? At least that's what so many of my blog commenters thought — and GVT made exactly the same mistake.

So they counted pairs and computed fractions. And coinciden-tally, they discovered that on the average throw, among all pairs that start with H, the fraction that are HH is just about ½.

Here's what they figured: The percentages for HH and HT are about fifty-fifty. That's just what you'd expect from a series of coin flips. So foul shots are like coin flips. There are no hot hands.

Here's what they should have figured: The percentages for HH and HT are about fifty-fifty. If these were coin flips, we'd expect them to be about 40.5 and 59.5. We're getting a *much* bigger frac-tion of HHs on the basketball court than we'd get from a coin flip. The hot hands must be real.

It took almost twenty years before another group of research-ers noticed this mistake. Meanwhile, GVT had fooled not only themselves but a substantial fraction of the economics profes-sion into believing that their study had rejected the hot-hands hypothesis, when in fact it had confirmed it.*

Once again, the obvious can be the enemy of the true. It's "ob-vious" that if boys and girls are equally likely to be born, then on average the fraction of girls should be ½. It's equally obvious that if you're equally likely to flip HH and HT, then on average, the fraction of HHs should be ½. Neither of those things is true. If you insist on believing them, you're an easy mark for coin-flip-ping con men.

---

* This doesn't necessarily mean that the hot-hands hypothesis is *true* — it means only that this particular bit of evidence points in that direction. There is other important evidence in both directions, some of it collected (and correctly inter-preted) by the same GVT team.

CHAPTER 9

Backward Reasoning

*O*nce upon a time there was a city where people considered it extremely important to be thought of as rich — or at least as rich as possible. Some of them were indeed very rich, with bank balances as high as the legal maximum of 100 kalooties. (Kalooties were the local unit of account, and were quite valuable. Any wealth over 100 kalooties was automatically confiscated by the state.) Others had literally no savings at all, and people occupied every rung in between.

To impress the neighbors with your wealth, there were two strategies. One was to talk a good game and perhaps throw enough money around to create the impression that you had plenty to spare. The other was to post your financial records on your front door. These records had recently become quite impossible to counterfeit.

Of course, everyone with 100 kalooties posted those records. Without posting, the best you could hope for was that others would think you *might* have 100 kalooties; by posting you remove all doubt.

This was very tough on people like my friend Mirabella, who was worth 99 kalooties. Prior to the financial-posting craze, some of the neighbors had suspected she might be worth 100. Now they knew better; if she *did* have 100 kalooties, she'd have posted. She therefore had nothing to lose and something to gain by posting her financial records, so that's what she did, raising others' perceptions of her wealth from "at most 99" to "exactly 99."

Everyone else with 99 kalooties did the same thing. This was very tough on people like my friend Jeter, who was worth 98 kalooties. By not posting, he'd been revealed as having *at most* 98 kalooties. To raise others' perceptions from "at most 98" to "exactly 98," he posted too. So, of course, did everyone else with 98 kalooties.

This led everyone with 97 kalooties to post, which led everyone with 96 kalooties to post, and so on, until everyone with 1 kalooty posted. That left only the people with 0 kalooties. They generally didn't post, but it didn't matter: their zero bank balances were already evident to everyone. If they'd had even 1 kalooty, they'd have posted by now.

At the outset of this story, you might have guessed that only the very rich would reveal their financial records, while those in the middle would continue to put up false fronts. Not so. The impetus to reveal one's wealth cascades from the very richest down to the next richest and doesn't stop until it's swept up the entire population.

Economists call that sort of reasoning a *backward induction* (though, for the record, a mathematician would just call it an *induction*). If you've been reading this book in order, you've already seen some examples of backward induction (in the solutions to the Two-Sided Card Game and Deep Pockets in the "Strategy" chapter). It will play a key role in future chapters too.

Following are some of my favorite backward-induction problems:

1

The Hungry Lions

You and nine of your fellow lions have cornered a plump and tasty-looking Christian and are contemplating dinner. The lions have formed an orderly queue, and you are in first place, which means the Christian is yours if you want him. Unfortunately, if you eat the Christian, you will immediately *turn into* a Christian, at which point the lion in second place will have the option of eating *you,* and so forth down the line. Your alternative is to walk away hungry, in which case all of the other lions are required to do the same.

Assuming that lions prefer hunger to death, should you eat the Christian?

SOLUTION: Start with a simpler problem: What do you do if you are the only lion? You eat the Christian, of course.

Now what do you do if you're the first of two lions? Eating the Christian puts us in the world of just one lion, where the Christian (that is, you!) gets eaten. You should walk away, which means the Christian survives.

Now what do you do if you're the first of three lions? Eating the Christian puts us in the world of two lions, where the Christian survives. So enjoy your meal.

And what if you're the first of four lions? Eating the Christian puts us in the world of three lions, where the Christian gets eaten. Walk away.

And so forth. If the number of lions is odd, you should eat. If the number of lions is even, you should walk away. Ten is an even number. The Christian survives. Hallelujah!

2

Selling Snake Oil

You are a thoroughly unscrupulous traveling snake-oil sales-man, with no qualms about substituting cheap water for genu-ine snake oil. You figure it will take the customers about a week to discover the ruse, but by then you'll be long gone.

Unfortunately, everybody's on to you. There's no way to tell snake oil from water on the day of purchase, and people realize they have no reason to trust you. So you've never made a sale.

The solution, clearly, is to sell an honest product and to settle down in one place so that people know you stand behind that product. To that end, you sign a one-year lease on a storefront and announce that you'll be selling snake oil from that storefront on every one of the next 365 days. You've even paid a full year's rent in advance to prove that you plan to stick around.

Obviously, your business depends on your reputation, and your reputation depends on your honesty, and the customers can see all that. So now you should finally make some sales.

How's that strategy working out for you?

SOLUTION: Nice try, but your strategy won't work.

Your lease runs 365 days. On day 365 — your last day in town — there's no future to care about and therefore no reason to pro-vide an honest product. Potential customers, who can easily fig-ure all this out, won't buy anything that day.

Now: Why would you provide an honest product on day 364? Only to preserve your reputation for day 365. But since nobody's buying on day 365 anyway, that reputation is worth nothing. So you might as well sell water on day 364. Potential customers, who can easily figure that out, won't buy anything that day.

And why would you provide an honest product on day 363? To preserve your reputation for day 364, when nobody's buying anything anyway? There's no point in that, so you sell water on day 363. Potential customers, who can easily figure that out, won't buy anything that day.

Can you see where this is going?

The bottom line, of course, is that even on day 1, nobody will trust you because they realize there's no point in preserving your reputation for day 2, because on day 2 nobody will trust you because they realize that there's no point in preserving your reputation for day 3, because on day 3 nobody will trust you because . . .

Therefore, you might as well not bother trying to earn anyone's trust in the first place.

Of course in the real world, real businesses do in fact provide quality merchandise in order to earn the trust of their customers, and it often seems to work. The interesting question for an economist, then, is in what relevant ways the real world differs from the world of this problem.*

One important difference is that unlike the snake-oil salesman, who announces that he'll be around exactly 365 days, most businesses plan to be around indefinitely (or at least claim to). If we don't know the end date, we can't get this argument started in the first place.

That's not an entirely satisfying answer, though, because if this is the entire story, then if Sears, Roebuck were to give us an end date by announcing that it plans to close all its stores exactly four

---

* One possible factor is that people who buy your snake oil on day 1 and discover that it doesn't work on day 2 can come back and cause trouble for you on day 3. That won't work, though, for products that take more than a year to prove their worth — or for customers who aren't sure you'll still be there on day 3.

thousand years from today, we'd all stop trusting their merchandise immediately. This does not seem plausible.

Economists have struggled to find a better answer. Many of those answers run something along these lines: Some snake-oil salesmen are constitutionally unable to cheat, or at least find cheating very difficult. This makes it worthwhile for even the natural cheaters to provide quality products, at least for a while, in hopes of being mistaken for one of the naturally honest dealers.

I'm not thrilled with that solution. I suspect the real resolution comes down to the tendency of your reputation to follow you from one situation to another, so that, for example, an honest retailer might be viewed as a better marriage prospect. In other words, strategic encounters are not quite so isolated as economists sometimes pretend.

Yes, it can be optimal to cheat your customers in an artificial situation where, once you've closed your shop, you'll never have to worry about running into those same customers again. In truth, you never know who might cross your path again unexpectedly. (This is the wisdom incorporated in the old adage "Be nice to people on your way up, because you might run into them again on your way down.") Even if the game at hand ends on a fixed date, life itself proceeds uncertainly, and it can be useful to have a reputation for trustworthiness that follows you into your next career (and for that matter, into all your other human relationships).

Ted Castronova is a professor of telecommunications at Indiana University and is generally recognized as the world's foremost authority on the economics of the synthetic worlds that are the settings for computer games such as World of Warcraft, where players earn, hoard, steal, and trade all sorts of imaginary lucre. In an earlier incarnation Ted was a professor of political science at the university where I teach, with an office directly below mine.

His course Force and Desire was the most popular in the history of the university.

A significant fraction of your grade in this course depended on the outcome of a great many repetitions of the Prisoner's Dilemma game, which you could play online against your fellow students at your leisure.* (With several hundred students enrolled in the class, there was always someone to play against.) As you'll recall from chapter 5, the "rational" strategy in the Prisoner's Dilemma is always to confess. You and your opponent might agree to not confess, but it's always in your interest (and your opponent's!) to violate that agreement. Still, if there were a way to enforce the agreement, both players would benefit.

In Ted's class, each "year in jail" translated into a small reduction in the points that counted toward your course grade, so it really paid to enforce agreements. And students found ways to do that. We heard stories of fistfights erupting over broken agreements, a violent response to today's cheating being a good way to minimize tomorrow's. We heard stories of students trading sex for good behavior. We heard stories of cliques whose members played only against one another, with social ostracism the penalty for choosing "confess." As Ted pointed out in his final lecture to the class, there is no such thing as an isolated game. These little Prisoner's Dilemma encounters had long-run effects on reputations and on personal relationships, all of which create strong incentives for good behavior.

So if you're bothered by the conclusion of the snake-oil problem, I don't think you should blame backward induction. You should instead blame the artificiality of the problem, which is set up to ignore all the long-run consequences of being tarred with

---

* This is the same Prisoner's Dilemma game that we met in chapter 5, problem 1.

dishonesty. As long as it's properly applied, backward induction remains a perfectly valid and valuable technique.

But there are still skeptics who are convinced that backward induction itself is some kind of flimflam, and they enjoy making their point by concocting new puzzles where backward induction seems to give nonsensical answers. Here's one they love:

3

The Surprise Quiz

You're taking a class that meets every weekday. One Friday afternoon your teacher announces that there will be a surprise quiz sometime in the next week. You'll find out the exact date when she hands out the quizzes but not a moment before.

It occurs to you that if the quiz is on Friday, you'll know it as soon as Thursday's class is over — because at that point Friday will be the only remaining possibility. But the professor has promised that you won't know the date in advance. So the quiz cannot be on Friday.

It occurs to you a little later that if the quiz is on Thursday, you'll know it as soon as Wednesday's class is over — because at that point, having ruled out Friday, you'll know that Thursday is the only remaining possibility. But the professor has promised that you won't know the date in advance. So the quiz cannot be on Thursday.

It occurs to you also that, with Thursday and Friday both ruled out, the quiz cannot be on Wednesday, because if it is, you'll know it at the end of Tuesday's class. And with Wednesday ruled out, the quiz cannot be on Tuesday.

That leaves Monday. But now that you know the quiz must be on Monday, the quiz *can't* be on Monday, because then it won't be a surprise. You conclude that there will be no quiz af-ter all.

The following Wednesday, however, the professor fulfills her promise by handing out a quiz. You are very surprised.

Where did your reasoning go wrong?

Philosophers have had a lot to say about this puzzle, and they don't all agree about how to resolve it. Some have contended that because the paradox arises from the technique of backward in-duction, we are forced to consider all backward-induction argu-ments fundamentally untrustworthy.

But that is arrant nonsense. It is arrant nonsense because *the backward induction has absolutely nothing to do with the paradox*. It is, in fact, pure misdirection, and serves no purpose but to di-vert your attention from the real source of the difficulty.

I say that because it's easy to eliminate the backward induction entirely while leaving the paradox intact:

4

The Surprise Quiz
(Stripped-Down Version)

One Friday afternoon your professor announces, most oddly, that there will be a surprise quiz next Monday — and that you'll learn the exact date when she hands out the quizzes but not a moment before.

It occurs to you that because you've been told the quiz will be on Monday, the quiz *can't* be on Monday, because then it won't be a surprise. You conclude that there will be no quiz after all.

Come Monday, however, the professor fulfills her promise by handing out a quiz. You are very surprised.

Where did your reasoning go wrong?

In this form, the problem looks pretty silly. That's because the backward-induction part, which was there only to mask the basic silliness, has been eliminated. But there are many ways to mask silliness. I could have given a different version of the problem in which your attention is directed away from the silliness by a digression about a circus troupe. It would not follow that all arguments involving circus troupes are fundamentally untrustworthy.

As far as resolving the stripped-down version of the problem, it seems to me that we need only say this: the professor tells you both that there will be a quiz on Monday and that the date of this quiz will surprise you. You don't see how this can be true. Therefore you conclude that she's lying, and there will be no quiz on Monday. This enables her to administer a surprise quiz on Monday, which means she was actually telling the truth.

But if you consider that a paradox, then there are even simpler versions:

5

The Incredible Teacher

Your teacher says, "You do not believe what I'm saying right now." You realize that if you believe this is true, it must be false. Therefore you believe it's false, and therefore it's true. Having figured this out, you now believe it's true. But then it must be false . . .

It seems to me that if there's any mystery about the Surprise Quiz paradox, the same mystery remains fully alive in the Incredible

Teacher paradox.* But there are no backward inductions in the Incredible Teacher paradox, and so, even if you think that some deep logical problem remains, there is no reason to implicate backward induction in that difficulty.

There is nothing wrong with backward induction.

Of course, like any other technique in economics or physics or philosophy or math or medicine, backward induction can be misapplied. It would be a misapplication, for example, to read the story at the beginning of this chapter, mistake it for a description of the real world, and conclude that real-world humans always reveal their incomes. That's a misapplication because the story is loaded with specific assumptions that don't hold in the real world. (You might enjoy counting them.) But if we abandoned every logical technique that had ever been misapplied, we'd be left with nothing.

We're not yet finished with backward induction. It will serve us well in the next couple of chapters.

---

* It also seems to me that there is, in fact, no mystery — just a bit of wordplay. But that's beside the point.

CHAPTER 10

Knowledge

*T*he prominent logician Joel David Hamkins tells this story about the frustrations of parenting:

My wife and I have a standing agreement where I pick up our son Horatio from school and she picks up our daughter Hypatia.

One day, because I knew I would be near Hypatia's school, it was convenient to swap duties. I emailed her a message, "I'll pick up Hypatia today, and you get Horatio. Please confirm; otherwise it is as usual." She texted me back, "Let's do it. Let me know if you get this message, so that I know we're really on." I left her a voicemail, "OK, we're definitely on for the swap! . . . as long as I know you get this message." She emailed me back, "Got the message. We're on! But let me know that you get this message so I can count on you." You see, without confirmation she couldn't be sure that I knew she had gotten my earlier confirmation of her acknowledgment of my first message, and she may have worried that the plan to swap was consequently off.

And so on ad infinitum . . .

How truly frustrating it was for us that at no stage of our conversation could we seem to know for certain that the other person had all the necessary information to ensure that the plan would be implemented! The result, of course, since we had time to exchange only at most a finite number of messages, was that the only rational course of action was for us each to abandon the plan to swap: we both independently decided just to pick up the usual child.

The moral of the story is that you and I can both know something, but that's not the same as both knowing that we both know, and that in turn is not the same thing as both knowing that we both know that we both know, and that in turn is not the same thing as our having *common knowledge,* which means that we both know that we both know that we both know that we both know . . . and that this remains the case no matter how many times you repeat the phrase "that we both know."

In fact, no matter how many times Hamkins and his wife exchange messages, their plans never become common knowledge. As Hamkins observes, this distinction has a lot of practical consequences. When two computers are trying to coordinate a file transfer, it's not always enough for each computer to know that they're both ready. They might also need to know that they both know that they're both ready, and need to know that they both know that they both know that they're both ready — and there can be no end to this. Because the computers, just like Hamkins and his wife, are limited to a finite amount of communication, they can never be sure that the file transfer is going to work.

There's a difference between *shared knowledge* (the things we all know) and *common knowledge* (the things we all know that we all know that we all know . . .). As the Hamkins family unhappily discovered, the distinction can make a great deal of difference.

The problems in this chapter will highlight that distinction, along with other subtleties about how we gather and process knowledge — knowledge that's shared, knowledge that's unshared, knowledge that's common, and knowledge that's deliberately concealed.

1

The Obedient Prisoners

Littlewood Penitentiary is designed for exceptionally obedient prisoners. The doors are always left wide open, but nobody leaves, because they've been told not to.

Of course, each prisoner's penchant for obedience must be tested. Therefore there are a lot of arbitrary rules. For example, there are no mirrors allowed. For another, every prisoner has a colored dot permanently attached to his forehead, but it is forbidden ever to talk about these dots. Therefore, no prisoner knows the color of his own dot, although of course they can all easily see the colors of everyone else's.

As a matter of fact, exactly 25 of the 40 prisoners have red dots, though of course none of the prisoners knows this exact number.

There's also a rule that anyone who is *sure* that his own dot is red is permitted to leave the prison but must do so exactly at the stroke of midnight. But nobody has ever figured out his dot color, and nobody has ever left.

The prisoners really are perfectly obedient, and none of them would ever think of violating any of these rules.

Every morning all 40 of them meet for breakfast at a great circular table, where the warden says a few words to them. One bright Thanksgiving morning the warden says, "It's another colorful morning here at Littlewood Penitentiary. I think it would be boring if all your forehead dots were the same color. I'm thankful that there's at least one blue and at least one red."

a) How many prisoners show up for breakfast the next morning?
b) How many show up for breakfast the following Thursday?
c) How many show up for breakfast on Christmas Day?

SOLUTION: Everybody shows up for breakfast the next morning, and everybody shows up for breakfast the following Thursday. But only the 15 prisoners with blue dots show up for breakfast on Christmas Day. The remaining 25 have all left the prison on the twenty-fifth day after Thanksgiving.

To see why, let's work through a sequence of similar problems:*

Problem A: Instead of assuming there are 25 red dots, assume there's only 1. It belongs to a prisoner named Al.

At first, of course, Al has no idea what color his dot is. But he does know that all the others are blue.

So when the warden lets it slip that there's at least one red dot, Al knows it must belong to him. He leaves that night.

Problem AB: This time assume there are just two red dots. They belong to Al and Bob.

At first Bob has no idea what color his dot is. But he does know that Al's is red and all the rest are blue. So when the warden reveals that there's at least one red dot, Bob is not surprised, and learns nothing about what's on his own forehead—at least not yet.

But Bob can reason thus: "If my dot is blue, then Al has the

---

* This sequence of similar problems is a good example of the backward-induction technique we met in the preceding chapter—but the good news, if you're reading chapters out of order, is that you can solve the problem perfectly well without knowing the name of the technique you're using.

only red dot. That's exactly the setup for problem A. And I know from the solution to that problem that Al will leave tonight."

When midnight comes and goes and Al is still around, Bob can conclude that Al *doesn't* have the only red dot — in other words, Bob's own dot must be red. Al, of course, reasons exactly the same way. Therefore, at the *next* midnight, they both leave.

Problem ABC: Now assume that there are exactly three red dots, on the foreheads of Al, Bob, and Carl.

When the warden makes his statement, Carl can reason thus: "If my dot is blue, then Al and Bob have the only red dots. That's exactly the setup for problem AB. And I know from the solution to that problem that Al and Bob will both leave two nights from now."

When Al and Bob *don't* leave on the second night, Carl knows that Al and Bob *don't* have the only red dots, so Carl's own dot must be red. So, by the same logic, do Al and Bob. They all leave on the third night.

Problem ABCD: Now assume that there are exactly four red dots, on the foreheads of Al, Bob, Carl, and Donald.

When the warden makes his announcement, Donald reasons thus: "If my dot is blue, then Al, Bob, and Carl have the only red dots, which is the setup for problem ABC, and I know from the solution to that problem that they will leave on the third night."

When that doesn't happen, Donald knows his own dot is red. So do Al, Bob, and Carl. They all leave on the fourth night.

And so on, all the way up to problem ABCDEFGHIJKLM-NOPQRSTUVWXY, which is the problem at hand. All 25 red-dot prisoners, from Al all the way up to Yancy, leave on the twenty-fifth night.

That's a perfectly correct solution, yet it leaves many people feeling like they must have been hoodwinked. Here's what troubles them: the warden hasn't told the prisoners anything they don't already know. They can see for themselves that some dots are red and others are blue. If that's all the warden tells them, how can it cause anything to happen that wouldn't have happened anyway?

Indeed, that reasoning would be exactly correct if the warden, instead of announcing to the crowd that some dots are red and others are blue, had whispered exactly the same words to each prisoner individually. In that case the prisoners would learn nothing and none of them would leave.

But the public announcement reveals more than the whispered secrets do. After the warden's announcement, the prisoners know not just that some dots are red and others are blue, but that *everybody knows* that some dots are red and others are blue, and that *everybody knows that everybody knows* that some dots are red and others are blue, and so on. In other words, the warden's announcement converts the fact that there is at least one red dot from *something everyone knows* to *common knowledge*.

Think about problem AB, where Al and Bob have the only red dots. Before the warden speaks, Bob, who can see Al's forehead, knows that there's at least one red dot. But he doesn't know that *Al knows that there's at least one red dot*. After the warden speaks, Bob knows this, and uses it to deduce that if Bob's own dot is blue, then Al will leave tonight.

In problem ABC, the logic relies on Carl knowing that Bob knows that Al knows that there's at least one red dot. And so on, all the way up to the problem at hand, problem ABCDEFGHI-JKLMNOPQRSTUVWXY, where the logic relies on Yancy knowing that Xavier knows that Wilbur knows that . . . that Al knows that there's at least one red dot. Once again, *that* is the key piece of new information that the prisoners get from the warden.

2

Elk or Moose?

Ed and Marsha live in separate apartments overlooking the same garden. They generally communicate only via brief text messages. Here's this morning's transcript:

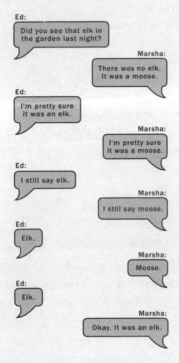

Now, you should know that Marsha is not at all a go-along-to-get-along sort of gal. She only speaks what she believes is true. You should also know that while she was conversing with Ed, she wasn't communicating with anyone else, wasn't Googling, wasn't consulting any sort of reference materials, and wasn't looking out the window.

So what changed her mind?

SOLUTION: You might be tempted to think that between Ed's first message and his last, Marsha learns nothing new. On the contrary, each message from Ed tells her something she didn't know before.

Ed's first message tells her this:

> Ed thinks it was an elk. He must have a reason for that.

That, by itself, is enough to shake Marsha's confidence, at least a bit. After all, why should she trust her own reasons any more than she trusts Ed's?

In fact, if Marsha's own reason for believing the moose theory is not terribly strong, she might change her mind on the spot.*

Likewise for Ed. If his reason isn't very strong, he might change his mind as soon as he hears Marsha say, "It's a moose."

But he *doesn't* change his mind. Instead he comes back with "I'm pretty sure it was an elk." Now Marsha knows that

> Ed still thinks it was an elk even though he knows I think it was a moose. He must have a fairly good reason for that.

That's news—and all the more reason for Marsha to change her mind! And when Marsha comes back with "I'm pretty sure it was a moose," Ed learns the same about Marsha, and has all the more reason to change *his* mind.

When nobody's mind changes, Ed and Marsha reveal that their own reasons are better than just fairly good—let's say they're at least *quite* good. That is, Marsha now knows that

---

* I do this all the time. I'll have some vague, ill-informed opinion about some issue in medieval history or foreign policy or particle physics, and I'll discover that someone disagrees with me. If my own opinion is sufficiently ill informed, I'll figure the other guy is probably right. Why, after all, should I trust my own opinion over his when mine is ill informed and his might not be?

Ed still thinks it was an elk even though he knows I think it was a moose even though I know he thinks it was an elk even though he knows I think it was a moose. He must have a quite good reason for that.

That's even more news—and an even stronger reason than before for Marsha to change her mind. And likewise, of course, for Ed.

With each round of texts, Ed's stubbornness reveals a little more about the quality of his reason, and Marsha's stubbornness reveals a little more about hers. With each exchange, Ed has a little more confidence in Marsha's reason (even without knowing what it is!) and Marsha has a little more confidence in Ed's.

To put this another way, suppose you're Marsha. Then:

- On the first round, you dismiss Ed's opinion.
- On the second round, you dismiss Ed's opinion, even though you've learned he holds his opinion strongly enough to dismiss yours.
- On the third round, you dismiss Ed's opinion, even though you've learned that he holds his opinion strongly enough to dismiss yours even though he's learned you hold your opinion strongly enough to dismiss his even though you've learned that he holds his opinion strongly enough to dismiss yours.

And so forth.

These dismissals become increasingly difficult, as your awareness of Ed's confidence becomes increasingly great. Ed, of course, faces the same dilemma.

Eventually, one or the other (presumably the one who started out slightly less confident) has to cave. This time it was Marsha.

We are all Ed and Marsha, in the sense that virtually none of our opinions are perfectly well informed. We have reasons for our opinions, and some of those reasons are better than others.

When others disagree with us, it's presumably because they've got reasons of their own. That should be enough to make us doubt our own opinions, *even if we don't know what those countervailing reasons are.*

Of course my disagreeing with you might not prove much — it proves only that I have a possibly not very good reason for my contrary opinion. But if I continue to disagree with you *even though I know you disagree with me,* then you can infer that my reason must be at least a little better than you'd thought, and if I continue to disagree with you *even though I know you disagree with me even though you know I disagree with you,* then my reason must be at least even a little better still, and so on. As this information is revealed, we learn a lot about the quality of each other's reasons. Eventually, if my reason is, say, a 6 on a scale of 10, while yours is a 7, we're going to discover that, and I — at least if I'm honest — will change my mind. If we're honest, and if we come to doubt our opinions enough, we abandon them.

It can, of course, be constructive to have conversations where we all share our reasoning and try to pick it apart. But the argument here is that *even without those conversations* — that is, *even if we never learn the reasons for one another's opinions* — we should all, like Ed and Marsha, come quickly to agreement about pretty much everything.

The conclusion, then, is that it's quite impossible for fully honest people ever to disagree with each other for very long. Unfortunately, people in the real world disagree with one another all the time. The uncomfortable conclusion seems to be that in the real world there are no honest truth seekers. Perhaps Ed (and all of his real-world counterparts) would rather win an argument than learn the truth. Or perhaps there's something missing in the analysis — but nobody has quite pinpointed what that something might be.

This has a striking implication for financial markets. Suppose I believe that the stock of Consolidated Amalgamation is due for an upswing. I therefore want to buy that stock. I learn that you're willing to sell it to me. Suddenly I have to reconsider: What might *you* know that I don't know? Maybe I don't want to buy after all.

Or — if I have a *very good reason* to expect that upswing — I might still want to complete the transaction. But now it's *you* who has to worry about what *I* might know. And if you're still willing to sell despite that worry, then I've learned that *your* reasons for selling are better than I might have guessed, so now it's I who might want to back out. If I don't back out, you've learned even more about the quality of my reasons, and if you still don't back out, I've learned even more about yours. Eventually, one or the other of us walks away from the deal.

Why, then, are stocks ever traded? Here's one answer: if I own a sunscreen company and am worried that my income will vanish in the event of a rainy summer, I might want to invest in a raincoat company as a hedge. What the argument seems to suggest is that all financial trades should be related to that kind of hedging behavior, never to pure speculation.

But then what about horse races? Horse races, unlike the stock market, *are* pure speculation — that is, they are driven entirely by differences of opinion. So why are there horse races? I go to place a bet. I learn that someone is willing to take that bet. Right then and there, I should question what that person knows that I don't, and he should do the same about me. The longer we both maintain our willingness to bet, the more we should respect each other's opinions and doubt our own. The conclusion, apparently, is that horse races cannot exist.

A determined and confident theorist might be tempted to trumpet this surprising discovery and conclude that if horse races *appear* to exist, they must be illusory. For that matter, anyone who disagrees must be illusory also. I am glad to say that I have not yet met that theorist. I think it's both a good thing that many theorists are determined and a good thing that their determination and confidence have some limits.

So far, in this chapter, the denizens of our problems have been trying to share their knowledge. But sometimes the goal is to prove you know something without revealing what you know. Mathematicians and computer scientists call this the problem of finding *zero-knowledge proofs*.

For example:

3

Password Protection

Alice and Bob are Lower Slobbovian spies meeting for the first time in the hostile territory of Upper Slobbovia. To confirm each other's identities, they've both been given the same secret numerical password, which happens to be 782384270271. Alice and Bob are pretty sure they've found each other, but neither wants to reveal the password in case the other is an Upper Slobbovian agent.

Fortunately, a stranger nearby has offered to be helpful, but of course it's important that the stranger not learn the password.

How do Alice and Bob, with the stranger's help, confirm their identities to each other?

SOLUTION: Here's one solution; maybe you can come up with others. The stranger thinks of a secret number (say, 345,919,100,191) and whispers it to Alice. Alice mentally adds the secret number to the password (Lower Slobbovian spies receive intense training in mental arithmetic) and gets a total of 1,128,303,370,462, which she whispers to Bob. Bob mentally subtracts the password and whispers the result to the stranger. The stranger confirms that his own number has come back to him, so that the number Bob subtracted must be the same as the number Alice added.

In the absence of a friendly stranger, Alice might try privately typing the password, 782384270271, into Google and then telling Bob what she got for the first hit. Bob can then do the same and make sure he gets the same first hit Alice does. Or maybe not—I just tried this and learned that "782384270271 did not match any documents."

4

The Sudoku Dilemma

The Sunday paper has arrived, and you've completed the sudoku puzzle in record time (after making a copy so your friend Bosco can do the same puzzle later). You want to prove to Bosco that you know how to solve the puzzle—but without showing him any part of the solution. How do you manage that?

SOLUTION: Here's one way.

Start with 27 scraps of paper labeled 1, another 27 labeled 2, and so on up to 9.

On the untouched puzzle grid, cover each printed digit with three scraps of paper showing that digit. Put three 1s on each 1, three 2s on each 2, and so on. Place them face up so Bosco can see you're not cheating.

On each blank square, place 3 scraps of paper showing the digit from your solution. Place them facedown so Bosco learns nothing from them.

Now allow Bosco to choose a column and take 1 scrap of paper from each square in that column. Have him turn the face-up scraps facedown, and thoroughly shuffle the entire pack of nine scraps. Now turn them face up. If your solution is legitimate, each digit should appear once.

Repeat with each column, each row, and each 3-by-3 grid.

You could in principle cheat by placing 3 scraps with different numbers on a single square. If you do this cleverly enough, on well-chosen squares, there's at least a chance that by some amazing coincidence you'll pass all of Bosco's tests. But I wouldn't count on it.

CHAPTER 11

Now Are You Smarter Than Google?

I want to share a very cool puzzle that combines several ideas from the past few chapters and adds a twist.

I'm not sure where this puzzle originated. I heard it first from Professor John Conley of Vanderbilt University, and I've often assigned it to my classes. Google has used it to weed out job candidates. The answer that Google expects is the same answer I gave John Conley and the answer I usually get from my best students. But it turns out there's more to be said.

Oh, by the way — although this is the first problem of the chapter, I'm calling it problem 10, not problem 1. Don't worry for now about why.

10

The Ferocious Pirates

Ten ferocious pirates have come into possession of 100 gold coins, which they must divide among themselves. The procedure for dividing them is as follows:

1. The most ferocious pirate proposes a division (such as "I'll take fifty, the second-most-ferocious pirate gets ten, and everyone else gets five apiece").
2. The pirates vote on whether to accept the division. As long as half or more of the pirates vote yes, the division is accepted, the coins are divided, and the game is over.
3. If, instead, fewer than half the pirates vote yes, the most ferocious pirate is thrown overboard. The second-most-ferocious pirate now becomes the most ferocious pirate and we return to step 1.

Each pirate's first priority is to avoid being thrown overboard; his second priority is to amass as many coins as possible, and his third priority is to have the pleasure of seeing other pirates thrown overboard.

The pirates are assumed to be perfectly rational and fully aware of one another's strategies.

What happens?

SOLUTION: This is a perfect opportunity to apply the backward induction technique that we first met in chapter 9. We'll start with some simpler problems:

Problem 1: Suppose there's just one ferocious pirate. Call him James. Obviously, James allocates 100 coins to himself, votes for his own plan, and wins.

Problem 2: Suppose there are two ferocious pirates—Igor and James, with Igor the most ferocious. Now Igor has half the votes and can therefore impose any plan he wants to. He therefore allocates 100 coins to himself, votes for his own plan, and wins. James gets nothing.

Problem 3 adds a third pirate—Howard, who is more ferocious even than Igor. If Howard wants to avoid being thrown overboard, he needs at least two votes for his plan. He's got his own vote, so he's got to buy a vote from either Igor or James —both of whom realize that if Harold goes overboard, they'll be playing the game from problem 2. Igor likes that game so much that he can't be bought. James, on the other hand, foresees that if we end up in problem 2, he'll get 0—and can therefore be bought for a single coin. So Howard's proposal is 99 for Howard, 0 for Igor, 1 for James. Howard and James vote yes and the plan is approved.

Problem 4: Now let's add a fourth pirate, the even more ferocious George. To pass a plan, George needs two votes—his own and someone else's. If his plan fails, we'll be in the world of problem 3, where Howard gets 99 coins, Igor gets 0, and James gets 1. Therefore it would take 100 coins to buy Howard's vote, it would take 1 coin to buy Igor's, and it would take 2 coins to buy James's. Igor's vote is the cheapest, so that's the one George buys. George's proposal, then, is 99 for George, 0 for Howard, 1 for Igor, 0 for James. George and Igor vote yes, and the plan is approved.

Problem 5: If there's a fifth and even more ferocious pirate —call him Freddy—then Freddy needs three out of five votes to pass his plan. In addition to his own vote, he'll buy the two cheapest votes available. In view of what happens in problem 4, George's price is 100, Howard's is 1, Igor's is 2, and James's is 1. Therefore Freddy buys Howard's and James's votes for 1 coin each. Freddy gets 98, George gets 0, Howard gets 1, Igor gets 0, James gets 1.

And so on (you can fill in problems 6, 7, 8, and 9 yourself!) until we reach

Problem 10 (the original problem!): With 10 pirates, Arlo (the most ferocious) gets 96, Bob gets 0, Charlie gets 1, Dave gets 0, Eeyore gets 1, Freddy gets 0, George gets 1, Howard gets 0, Igor gets 1, and James gets 0. Charlie, Eeyore, George, and Igor all join Arlo in voting yes, because if they vote no, Bob will propose a division in which they get nothing.

Conclusion: The only possible outcome is 96-0-1-0-1-0-1-0-1-0.

I want to repeat that:

Main Conclusion: 96-0-1-0-1-0-1-0-1-0 is the only possible outcome.

That's the solution I've always wanted from my students and apparently the solution that Google has always wanted from its job candidates. Unfortunately, there's a fly in the ointment: the main conclusion is false. There are plenty of other solutions. Here's one:

ANOTHER SOLUTION: The most ferocious pirate proposes to take all the coins, leaving everyone else with nothing. The other nine all want this proposal to fail. Nevertheless, they all vote yes and the proposal is accepted.

Wait a minute! What happened to the rationality assumption? Why, for example, would Bob — the second-most-ferocious pirate — ever vote in favor of a division that leaves him with 0 coins?

The answer is that Bob, being perfectly rational, is aware that his vote doesn't matter. As long as everyone else votes yes, the proposal is sure to pass. So his yes vote, which doesn't change the outcome, is perfectly rational. (A no vote would be equally rational.)*

Another possible solution is that one of the pirates (perhaps even the most ferocious pirate!) votes no, while the rest vote yes. Or three vote no while seven vote yes.

In each of these cases no single voter can change the outcome, so there's no particular reason for anyone to change his vote. In other words, everyone is being perfectly rational, taking as given the choices made by everyone else.†

To highlight the point, here's one more problem:

11

Who Wins the Election?

The 2040 US presidential election has come down to Justin Bieber versus Miley Cyrus.‡ It happens that every single voter prefers Cyrus, and all voters are perfectly rational. Who wins?

SOLUTION: It's quite impossible to say. Bieber could quite plausibly get 100 percent of the votes. After all, if you're aware that everyone else is voting for Bieber anyway, then you know Bieber is sure to win. In that case, your vote can't change the outcome,

---

* How can Bob be absolutely sure that his vote doesn't matter? Because it was an *assumption of the problem* that all pirates are fully aware of one another's strategies — and therefore, in particular, Bob knows for certain how the other pirates are voting. If you don't like that assumption, read on. We'll address this issue.

† In the jargon of economics, any of these solutions is a perfectly good *Nash equilibrium.*

‡ The Canadian-born Bieber is eligible thanks to the 2030 annexation of Canada by the United States.

so you might as well vote for Bieber along with everyone else. (You also, of course, might as well vote for Cyrus.) There is nothing irrational about voting for the candidate you hate, provided you're quite sure your vote won't change the outcome.

Of course this solution depends very heavily on the additional assumption that voters are fully aware of one another's intentions, and hence fully aware that no voter can change the outcome. But it *is* a solution to the problem as stated, which certainly does not rule out this additional assumption.

Back to the pirates now. We have a problem here.

Our main conclusion tells us that the only possible outcome is 96-0-1-0-1-0-1-0-1-0, with all of the odd-numbered pirates voting yes. But that's not true! We've in fact discovered a great many additional outcomes.

So we're forced to ask the following question:

12

What Went Wrong?

Where is the mistake in the solution to The Ferocious Pirates?

SOLUTION: That solution (as you'll see if you flip back a couple of pages and reread it carefully) makes this implicit (and quite unwarranted) assumption:

Pirates always vote for their preferred outcomes.

Given that assumption, the argument really is airtight and the main conclusion is correct.

But we have nothing to justify that assumption. From the statement of the problem, we can't predict anything about how pirates behave in cases where their votes don't matter. And that's a lot of cases, leading to a lot of additional solutions.

If you want to rule out the weird extra solutions, you've got to change the statement of the problem in order to give the pirates a *reason* to vote for the outcomes they want. That's easy. Instead of assuming that pirates always know one another's strategies, let's allow them a little doubt. If Bob the pirate is not sure how the others are voting, it's always possible he's got the deciding vote — which makes voting for his preferred outcome the only rational choice.

Why might Bob be unsure of how the others are voting? One possibility: maybe he's not 100 percent sure they're all rational. Or maybe he's not 100 percent sure that they all *know* they're all rational. Or maybe he's not 100 percent sure they all know that they all know that they all know that they're not rational. If rationality is not *common knowledge,** then pirates can never be entirely sure of how other pirates will behave, and can cover all their bases only by voting for their preferred outcomes. In that case the main conclusion is surely right and the alternative solution can be discarded.

So why not avoid all the muss by simply stating the problem a little more realistically in the first place? One answer is that it's quite standard in lower-level economics courses always to assume that everyone knows everyone else's strategies for certain. (This assumption gets dropped soon enough in higher-level

---

* This is the same sort of common knowledge we discussed in chapter 10, and it matters here just as it mattered there. In fact, the Ferocious Pirates problem, like the Obedient Prisoners problem of chapter 10, is a great illustration of the importance of distinguishing between *shared* knowledge (where all pirates know that all pirates are rational) and *common* knowledge (where all pirates know that all pirates know that all pirates know . . . that all pirates are rational).

courses.) Sometimes our students learn to think of that assumption as a harmless simplification. Occasionally even a professor falls into that trap. This problem, and others like it, is a good reminder that this particular simplification can be far from harmless.

A historical note: I assigned this problem to classes for years, expecting (and usually getting) the 96-0-1-0-1-0-1-0-1-0 answer. One day in class, while I was reviewing that "correct" answer, my student Matt Wampler-Doty raised his hand to point out the plethora of alternative solutions and the unjustified assumption in the "official" analysis. I was sure he was wrong and made some inane attempt to dismiss him, but to his credit, he persisted until I got the point. He made my day.

CHAPTER 12

How to Make Decisions

*L*ife is full of difficult choices. Should I go to the pizza parlor, or should I go to the gym? Should I go to college, or should I get a job? Should I be a welder, or should I be a philosopher? Should I seek serenity, or should I seek revenge? Should I hold out for Mr. Right, or settle for Mr. Right Here Right Now?

What's a good guideline for making choices? The obvious candidate is

> Aim to make yourself happy.

But decision theorists — yes, there is a subject called *decision theory;* it's taught in both economics and philosophy departments, and you're about to get a taste of it — generally find that a little too vague to be a useful guideline. (We'll soon see why.)

So those decision theorists have toyed with some less vague variations on the same theme. Like this one:

The Best Friend Rule: Make the choice that your (real or imaginary) best friend will be glad to hear about.

That's not a bad rule. I know quite a few people who, if they had followed this rule, would not have married the wrong person. But it's still imperfect. The Best Friend Rule (like, perhaps, best friends themselves) sometimes gives advice you'd be better off without. Try it on this problem:

1

The Persimmon Problem

Doctors have recently discovered that a single gene—they call it the P-gene—causes both cravings for persimmons and early-onset Alzheimer's. Persimmons themselves, though, are a very healthy food. You've just developed a craving for persimmons. Should you eat one?

Just about everybody agrees that the answer to this problem is yes. You've either got the P-gene or you don't, and nothing can change that. The persimmon is delicious, it's good for you, and it satisfies your craving. Have one. Have another.

But your best friend, on hearing that you chose to eat the persimmon, is likely to say, "Oh no! You ate a persimmon! Does that mean you had a craving? How are you set for long-term-care insurance?"

Your best friend, in other words, would be far happier to hear that you *didn't* eat the persimmon—so according to the Best

Friend Rule, you shouldn't eat it. In short, the Best Friend Rule gets this one wrong.*

Okay, so that rule was imperfect. Here's another try:

The Cause and Effect Rule: Make choices that you (or your best friend) believe will cause you (at least on average) to be happy.

The Cause and Effect Rule at least gets the Persimmon Problem right. Nobody believes that persimmons *cause* Alzheimer's, so as long as you stay focused on the *causes* of happiness (or unhappiness), there's no reason to avoid them.

Unfortunately, the same rule seems to get other things wrong. Try this one:

2

The Hiker's Problem

Scientists have discovered a gene that makes people both more eager and less able to jump over gorges. They call it the G-gene.

So there are two kinds of people: those who have the G-gene and often jump over gorges but unfortunately rarely make it, and those without the gene, who almost never jump but who, when they do, usually succeed.

As a result, almost all gorge jumps are fatal.

You're out hiking and you've just come to a gorge. On the

---

* Or maybe not. A best friend who already knows about your craving will be glad you ate the persimmon. A best friend who sees you eat the persimmon and therefore, for the first time, infers that you probably had a craving, will feel quite dismayed. I am envisioning the second type of best friend. I believe a nontrivial amount of confusion in the philosophy literature arises from a failure to specify exactly how much background information your best friend is assumed to have.

other side of the gorge is a lovely meadow you'd like to explore. You're pretty sure you don't have the G-gene, so you're pretty sure you can make it over. Should you jump?

Most people say, "For God's sake, don't jump. Don't you realize that almost all gorge jumps are fatal?"

Or to put this another way: "If you jump, you're likely to have the G-gene, and if you have the G-gene, you're likely to fall in."

But if you've bought into the Cause and Effect Rule, that argument cuts no ice. After all, jumping the gorge can't *cause* you to have the G-gene, any more than eating a persimmon can cause you to have the P-gene.

The fact of the matter is, you believe you don't have the G-gene. You therefore believe you can probably jump the gorge. There's a very lovely meadow on the other side. Why not take the leap?

The answer, presumably, is that the moment you decide to take the leap, you'll stop believing that you don't have the G-gene. And then you're off on a merry circle. "Wait a minute! I just decided to jump a gorge! I bet I have that gene after all! I'd better not jump. Aha! I just decided not to jump! I guess I probably don't have that gene after all. Which means I should jump. But wait a minute . . ." Foreseeing all this, and preferring not to spend an infinite amount of time deliberating back and forth, you'd best just enjoy the view from this side of the gorge.

But the Cause and Effect Rule isn't interested in your infinite chain of reasoning. Right now, you believe you don't have the G-gene. Jumping can't change that. So the Cause and Effect Rule says, "Jump already!"

And again, the problem is that most people think that's the wrong answer. So maybe the Cause and Effect Rule isn't quite right either.

Here's what *does* get the Hiker's Problem right: our old standby, the Best Friend Rule. Your best friend knows that almost all attempted gorge jumps fail, and therefore does not want to hear that you've attempted one. Therefore, according to the Best Friend Rule, you shouldn't jump. Period, end of story.

So here's where we stand: The Best Friend Rule (at least according to most people) gets the Persimmon Problem wrong and the Hiker's Problem right. The Cause and Effect Rule gets the Persimmon Problem right and the Hiker's Problem wrong. Decision theorists would like to find a rule that gets *everything* right. That's turned out to be more difficult than you might expect.

The ultimate testing ground for any rule is *Newcomb's Problem,* devised around the year 1960 by the physicist William Newcomb, popularized among academics in 1969 by the philosopher Robert Nozick, and then popularized to a wider audience by Martin Gardner in a 1974 *Scientific American* column. It has vexed philosophers, economists, game theorists, decision theorists, mathematicians, and computer scientists ever since.

3

Newcomb's Problem

Zorxon, a hyper-intelligent being from a nearby planet, has been studying life on earth for a while and considers himself an expert on human psychology — so much so that he's been boasting to all his hyper-intelligent friends that he can pretty much predict anything a human will do in pretty much any situation. They've challenged him to a bet.

The terms of the bet are these: Zorxon (who needs no sleep) will spend ten years meeting with earthlings, one-on-one, for five minutes at a time. This will allow him to meet about a million earthlings. He will present each one with a decision problem and predict each one's choice. He bets he can get all of them right.

Each earthling is presented with two boxes, one labeled M (for "mystery") and one labeled T (for "thousand"). The M box is sometimes empty. Other times it contains $1 million. The T box is guaranteed to contain $1,000.

Maybe $1 million in here
Maybe nothing

$1,000 in here

You can have M
or you can have both

When it's your turn to be the human subject, you have a choice: go home with just the M box, or go home with *both*.

If Zorxon expects you will take just the M box, he indicates his prediction by putting $1 million in the M box. If he expects you to take both, he indicates his prediction by putting nothing in the M box. You, of course, have to choose without knowing which he's done.

But you do know this: So far, Zorxon has met with 900,000 earthlings, and in every case his prediction has been correct — those who go home with just the M box invariably find that it contains $1 million. Those who go home with both boxes invariably find that they've got $1,000 and an empty box.

Now it's your turn. Which do you choose — one box or two?

Robert Nozick once observed that almost everyone thinks the answer is obvious. But the odd thing is that people often disagree violently about *which* answer is obvious. Is it obvious that you should take just the M box, or that you should take both?

Your friends, no doubt, will be rooting for you to take just the M box (and will immediately start planning one hell of a party if you do). After all, they have ample evidence that people who take just the M box (let's call them one-boxers) always end up a lot happier than two-boxers. So if you buy into the Best Friend Rule, the solution is clear: take just the M box.

But the Cause and Effect Rule disagrees. Your choice to take a single box cannot *cause* Zorxon to put $1 million into that box, because he makes his decision *before* you make yours. He's already decided. There's already $1 million in that box, or there isn't. Your decision can't change that. So take the M box, and while you're at it, you might as well take the T box also.

According to this reasoning, it's certainly true that you'd prefer to be the type of person who one-boxes. Zorxon, with his extraordinary insight, would surely perceive your one-boxing nature and make you rich. But sadly, you can't change the type of person you are (or, more precisely, you cannot now change the type of person you were back when Zorxon was making his prediction), so that shouldn't affect your decision. According to the Cause and Effect Rule, the only things that matter are things you can influence — and the only thing you can influence is whether you take the extra thousand or not. So (if you buy into the Cause and Effect Rule), take both boxes.

The Cause and Effect Rule, then, embodies the wisdom of the famous Serenity Prayer by the theologian Reinhold Niebuhr: "God grant me the serenity to accept the things I cannot change, the courage to change the things I can, and the wisdom always to know the difference."

You can't change your psychological makeup, and therefore can't change what Zorxon has put in the box. Maybe you should find the serenity to accept that and focus on the one thing you *can* change, namely, "Do I or do I not take the free thousand dollars? Well, of course I do."

The Best Friend Rule, though, disagrees. It tells you to one-box. But a souped-up version of the Best Friend Rule is on board with two-boxing. Remember the original Best Friend Rule:

The Best Friend Rule: Make the choice that your best friend will be happy to hear about.

Here's the souped-up version:

The Psychic Best Friend Rule: Make the choice that your best friend would be happy to hear about *if your best friend knew all the relevant facts.*

In this case, imagine that, unlike you, your psychic best friend knows *what's in the boxes* (either because she's psychic or because she was spying when Zorxon made his choice).

Then either your psychic best friend knows that the M box is empty, in which case she is surely rooting for you to take both boxes, or your psychic best friend knows that the M box contains $1 million, in which case . . . she is *still* rooting for you to take both boxes. Since your psychic best friend has all the relevant information and you don't, surely you should take her advice.

And even if you don't actually *have* a psychic best friend, *you still know for sure what that psychic best friend would want you to do,* which seems like reason enough to do it.*

That appears to be something like an airtight reason to take both boxes. Unfortunately, everyone who buys into that airtight reason goes home disappointed. So maybe it's not so airtight after all.

In the end, most one-boxers defend their choice with arguments that come down to some version of the original Best Friend

---

* The Psychic Best Friend Rule isn't always so useful. In the hiking problem, it says to imagine a psychic best friend who knows your genetic makeup, and to jump or not according to what that friend wants you to do. Unfortunately, there's no way to know what that psychic best friend wants you to do unless you know your genetic makeup, in which case you don't need the psychic best friend. What's unique about Newcomb's Problem is that we can be sure of what the psychic best friend would urge *without having to know what's in the boxes.*

Rule. If you meet a one-boxer, your first question should be, "Why are you using a rule that can't even get the Persimmon Problem right?"

But on the other hand, most two-boxers defend their choice with arguments that come down to some version of the Cause and Effect Rule. If you meet a two-boxer, you might want to ask, "Why are you using a rule that can't even get the Hiking Problem right?"

Two-boxers tend to argue (based on the Cause and Effect Rule, or the Psychic Best Friend Rule, or something like them) that two-boxing is the only rational choice. One-boxers tend to respond that two-boxing can't possibly be rational, because it's only the one-boxers who get rich.

To this, a two-boxer might respond with the tale of Zorxon's twin brother, Alknor, who comes to earth and gives a million dollars to every earthling who believes that two plus two equals five. Alknor makes irrational people rich and leaves rational people poor. Why, then, should we be surprised that Zorxon can do the same thing?

To this, one-boxers might reply that they'd rather be rich than rational.

Newcomb's Problem has puzzled philosophers and economists for well over half a century, and there's been a lot written about it, not all of which is worth repeating. But for what they're worth, here are a few more thoughts:

First: If we take the Zorxon story seriously, we've got to buy into the idea that human behavior is almost perfectly predictable. If that's so, then your choice, one way or the other, is already inevitable (or nearly so) and there's no point in agonizing over it. (Of course, that's likely to be useless advice, because your agonizing is probably just as inevitable as anything else you do.)

Second: Zorxon's perfect track record seems almost literally incredible. Maybe it should be treated as such. If you showed me a creature who had accurately predicted 900,000 out of 900,000 human decisions, I'd have to seriously entertain the possibility that I was hallucinating. How should that affect my decision? I'll leave you to ponder that.

Third: We've told a story in which you meet Zorxon once and only once. If instead this little game were repeated, say, once a year, you'd be well advised to try to *turn yourself into* the sort of person who one-boxes. I'm not sure exactly how you'd accomplish that, but it would sure be worth thinking about.

And finally: The computer scientist Scott Aaronson has pointed out that if Zorxon can confidently predict your choice, then he must know absolutely everything about you — because anything about you might affect your choice. You might, after all, take both boxes because the T on the second box reminds you of the monogrammed T on your grandmother's bathrobe. That means Zorxon must know about your memories of your grandmother's bathrobe.

But if Zorxon knows everything about you, he must, one way or another, be running the equivalent of a perfect simulation of you — a computer program that embodies all of your memories, all of your inclinations, all of your emotions, and all of your thoughts and perceptions — a computer program, in other words, that *thinks it is you.*

Which means that there's a good chance you *are* that computer program. If so, you've got an opportunity to remake yourself in a way that affects Zorxon's choice. You should strive to be the kind of person who one-boxes.

In the usual interpretation of Newcomb's Problem, any such commitment comes too late — Zorxon has already made his decision. But if you are the simulation that Zorxon consults, then remaking yourself can change his decision. So remake yourself into a one-boxer, collect the million, and invite me to the party.

For those who have gotten this far and still don't know what to think, I recently invented a decision-theory problem that I believe is both very easy and useful for clearing the air.

4

The Amnesia Problem

You have amnesia and cannot remember whether you once stashed a million dollars in your attic. You're on your way up to look around. But you're well acquainted with the vast psychological literature showing that amnesiacs who have stashed a million dollars in their attics virtually always burn a thousand-dollar bill before they go upstairs to search—and those who have *not* stashed a million virtually *never* burn the thousand.

Because of that odd psychological phenomenon, all and only those amnesiacs who have burned thousand-dollar bills have, upon going up to have a look, found a million dollars in their attics.

Should you burn a thousand-dollar bill before you go upstairs to search?

Unrealistic? Sure. But if we're demanding realism, we don't have to worry about Zorxon in the first place.

I contend that this problem is very easy. There either is or is not a million dollars in your attic, and either way, burning a thousand-dollar bill won't change that. So of course you should not burn the thousand-dollar bill.

It's true that the Best Friend Rule advises otherwise: your best friend wants to hear that you've burned the bill and are therefore likely a millionaire. But that doesn't impress me, because the

Best Friend Rule is already known to be fallible. (Remember how poorly it does with the Persimmon Problem.)

On the other hand, the Psychic Best Friend Rule is certainly on board with *not* burning the bill. Your psychic best friend already knows what's in your attic. Whatever's there, you can't change it by throwing away a thousand dollars.

My guess — although I have not tested this — is that almost everyone will choose "not burn" in this scenario. If I'm right, then the Amnesia Problem is easy. But I contend that it is, in all important respects, identical to Newcomb's Problem. If so, then Newcomb's Problem is easy too.

Here are the parallels:

- In Newcomb's Problem you are either a one-boxer (the sort of person who takes just one box) or a two-boxer (the sort of person who takes two boxes). In the Amnesia Problem you are either a burner or a non-burner.
- In Newcomb's Problem, if you're a one-boxer, there's just about sure to be a million dollars in the Mystery Box. In the Amnesia Problem, if you're a burner, there's just about sure to be a million in the attic.
- In Newcomb's Problem, one-boxing means throwing away the thousand dollars in the other box. In the Amnesia Problem, burning the bill means throwing away a thousand dollars.

The two problems, then, run perfectly parallel. If the Amnesia Problem is an easy call for non-burning, then Newcomb's Problem is an easy call for two-boxing.

The fundamental argument here is no different from the standard pro-two-boxing arguments we've already encountered, and in that sense the Amnesia Problem adds nothing to the discussion. But it seems to me — though perhaps you'll disagree — that when we replace the irrelevant science-fiction scenario with an equally irrelevant psychiatric scenario, the one-boxing (or pro-burning) argument suddenly seems far less plausible, while the two-boxing (or anti-burning) argument suddenly seems far more compelling. So much so, in fact, that it's hard to see why anyone ever considered this a problem in the first place.

But the problem keeps resurrecting itself in other guises:

5

The Riddle of the Ages

Why do people vote in US presidential elections?

The answer surely cannot be that they care about the outcome, because nobody's vote ever changes the outcome, and the probability that it ever will is small enough to be treated as zero. For your vote to change the outcome, the margin of victory would have to be exactly one vote. The 2000 US presidential election came down to five hundred thirty-seven votes in the state of Florida. Five hundred thirty-seven is a far cry from one.

So both economists (who want to find the rationality underlying as much human behavior as possible) and political scientists (who want to understand elections) worry a lot about this question. One popular theory is that people reason something like this:

It's true that my one vote can't change the outcome. But I've noticed that in years when I vote, many others who think like me tend to vote too. And I've noticed that in years when I don't vote, those people tend not to vote. I want those people to vote, and that's why I'm voting.

This, of course, is magical thinking insofar as your own vote can't *cause* other members of your demographic group to vote.

But is there any difference between people who think this way and the one-boxers in Newcomb's Problem who tell themselves (falsely) that taking just one box can *cause* that box to contain a million dollars, or the burners in the Amnesia Problem who tell themselves (falsely) that burning a thousand-dollar bill can *cause* there to be a million dollars in the attic?

There seems to be a general consensus that the "people like me" reasoning is faulty (though it might still explain why people vote, given that people are not always perfect logicians). Yet there is no general consensus against Newcomb one-boxing. I wonder what difference people see.

If I myself should ever be called as a subject in Zorxon's grand experiment, I cannot say for sure what I would do — but I know what I *hope* I'd do. I hope I'd take *zero* boxes.

That's because I like to think I'm the sort of person who can walk by an open cash register without helping myself to its contents.

Where, after all, does Zorxon get all this money? Given the quantity he's distributed, it's just about *got* to be counterfeit. And counterfeiting is the moral equivalent of emptying other people's cash registers. It debases the value of real money and therefore effectively steals from the people who own that money. That, after all, is why counterfeiting is against the law.

I'd feel a lot better about Newcomb's Problem if we could replace the million dollars with a million dollars' worth of crude oil or chocolate bars, all of which Zorxon creates at his own expense (or perhaps, if his technology is advanced enough to be indistinguishable from magic, at zero expense) back on his home planet. Those I could take without qualms.

You might be tempted to think that creating oil by magic is much like running counterfeit money off a printing press. Just as the counterfeit money debases the value of real money, so the magic oil debases the value of the "real" oil that people have worked so hard to extract from the ground.

But here's the difference: when Zorxon uses magic to create a gallon of oil, the price of oil goes down. That's bad for everyone who owns oil, but it's also good for everyone who's looking to *buy* oil. The good and the bad wash out. If I accept this gallon, I've done no *net* harm to the rest of the world.* Another way to say this is that Zorxon has created something of real value and made the world a richer place. I'm happy to be the recipient of those new riches.

By contrast, when Zorxon uses magic to create a dollar, the value of existing dollars goes down. That's bad for everyone who owns dollars, and there's no offsetting good.† If I accept this dollar, I'm effectively stealing it. Another way to say this is that Zorxon has created nothing of real value. (Unlike oil, a dollar bill cannot run my car.) Therefore whatever I gain must come at someone else's expense. I'd like to believe I'm the kind of person who would turn that down.

Having gotten that little digression out of my system, let me return briefly to decision theory. Here's one more decision rule to consider:

The No Sure Regrets Rule: Don't make choices that you're sure you'll regret.

We've encountered this rule (though not by name) elsewhere

---

* In the same way, every time I buy a carrot, I drive up the price of carrots, which hurts everyone else who's buying them. But I don't feel bad about that because I've helped the sellers just as much as I've hurt the buyers.

† A more complete accounting: People who owe money are winners (because they get to pay their debts in debased dollars); the people to whom they owe that money are losers, and that washes out. People who *own* money are losers, and for that loss, there is no offsetting gain.

in this book; it was, for example, the key to solving problem 7 (Art at Auction, Take Two) in chapter 5.

The No Sure Regrets Rule sounds hard to argue with (though it can be oddly difficult to implement when you're confronted with a bowl of M&M's), but it's subtler than it appears.

Every day I decide whether to spend a couple of seconds putting on my seat belt. That's a small cost, but it's a cost. If I make it to work without an accident, those couple of seconds have been wasted. I regret that.

Occasionally, though, I have an accident, and the seat belt saves my life. On those days you might expect me to say something like "Thank God I wore my seat belt." Nope. What I'll actually say is "If only I hadn't spent two seconds fastening my seat belt, I'd have arrived on the scene two seconds earlier, before the other driver swerved into my lane. Now my car is totaled, and all because I put on my seat belt. Man, do I ever regret that choice!"

Of course in the real world not all accidents can be prevented by getting a two-second head start. But if we're going to entertain a hypothetical near-omniscient extraterrestrial named Zorxon, we ought to be willing to entertain a hypothetical world where all accidents really do depend on the split-second timing of your arrival.

In that world, it seems like wearing my seat belt always guarantees regret. Either I don't have an accident and I regret the time I wasted, or I do have an accident and I regret that putting on the seat belt caused me to be in the wrong place at the wrong time.

So according to the No Sure Regrets Rule, it looks like I should never wear my seat belt, right? But that's likely to be the wrong answer, because people who wear their seat belts tend to live and people who don't wear their seat belts tend to die in car crashes.

In other words (unless I tricked you), the No Sure Regrets Rule gets this one wrong.

6

No Regrets

So does this mean that we should abandon the No Sure Regrets Rule?

SOLUTION: Nah. I *did* trick you. I left something out. Namely, it *is* true that I always regret wearing my seat belt on days when I have an accident. And it's also true that I regret wearing my seat belt on most days when I *don't* have an accident. But occasionally, there's going to be a day when the two seconds I spend fastening my seat belt will cause me to arrive at the accident site two seconds *after* the other driver swerves into my lane. On those days I'm very glad I took the time to put on my seat belt. So regret is not a certainty, and the No Sure Regrets Rule does not apply in the first place.

The real problem with the No Sure Regrets Rule is that most of the time there *is* no option that guarantees no regrets. Should I go to the party or stay home and work? If I go to the party and have a bad time, I'll regret my choice. If I stay home and accidentally erase my hard drive, I'll regret *that* choice. Which choice is better? The No Sure Regrets Rule is silent. But on those rare occasions when it speaks up, the No Sure Regrets Rule is worth listening to. You'll never regret it.

CHAPTER 13

Matters of Life and Death

S top me if you've heard this one. Five people are tied to a trolley track, with a trolley bearing down on them. You and a very fat man are standing on an overpass above the track. His body, but not yours, is massive enough to stop the train and save five lives. Should you throw him to his death?

There's a good chance you *have* heard that one, because it's been circulating for more than fifty years among professors of philosophy and has more recently started popping up in popular culture. But this is no mere academic exercise or Internet meme. The answer matters. It matters because policymakers (and the economists who advise them) confront problems like this every day. Should we save lives by spending more on fire protection, or save different lives by spending the same funds on highway guardrails? Should we save lives by banning carcinogenic insecticides, or save different lives by encouraging the use of those same insecticides so that fresh fruit (and its nutritional benefits) will be more plentiful?

Not only do we weigh lives against lives; we also weigh lives against pretty much everything else. Every year, about fifteen Americans are fatally poisoned by household batteries — but batteries remain readily available. Apparently we've collectively decided that we'd rather power our flashlights than save those lives.

Here's why we're okay with that: Fifteen deaths a year translates into about a .000005 percent annual chance of death for the average American. The average American, if you asked, would probably say something like *"That's a chance I'm willing to take* for the convenience of using batteries."

That seems to me (and to most economists) like a pretty good guideline in these matters: what matters is not the total number of deaths but whether people are comfortable with the individual risks they're facing. In other words, when we're making policy — for example, when we're deciding whether batteries should be legal — it's generally best (in the words of more than one hit song) to give the people what they want. (Of course this works only when it's clear what the people want. More on that later.)

Here's a test case that I wrote about in my book *The Big Questions*:

1

The Headache Problem

A billion people are experiencing fairly minor headaches, which will continue for another hour unless an innocent person is killed, in which case the headaches will cease immediately. Is it okay to kill that innocent person?

SOLUTION:

- First, virtually nobody will pay a dollar to avoid a one-in-a-billion chance of death. (We know this, for example, from studies of willingness to pay for auto-safety devices.)
- Second, most people — at least in the developed world, where I will assume all of this is taking place — would happily pay a dollar to cure a headache. (I don't actually know this, but given what I've seen in other people's medicine cabinets, it seems probable.)
- Taken together, this tells me that most people think a headache is worse than a one-in-a-billion chance of death. So if I can replace *your* headache with a one-in-a-billion chance of *your* death, I've done you a favor. And I can do you this favor by killing a headache sufferer chosen at random. It's good to do people favors, so of course I should do this.

If you're an economist (either by profession or by instinct), you're likely to be comfortable with that analysis. If you're a philosopher, you might not be. A number of philosophers have weighed in on the Headache Problem, and all seem to agree that the solution, even if correct, is at least counterintuitive. If you agree with them, keep in mind that people *have* died to cure your headaches. Like batteries, household painkillers are responsible for several accidental deaths every year. We could save those lives by getting all the painkillers off the shelves — but apparently we'd rather relieve headaches. Pretty much everybody is on board with that, and I've never heard anyone but a philosopher declare that there's something counterintuitive about wanting to keep aspirin legal.

Economists care about problems like this for two reasons. First, we care about getting the right answer. Second, we care about predicting the behavior of policymakers, who might care less about getting the right answer and more about advancing their careers. Here's a puzzle that combines both issues:

2

Rescue Operations

Ten people, all strangers to you and to one another, are trapped under rubble. You can mount a rescue operation that is guaranteed to save exactly five of them, or a different operation that has a 60 percent chance of saving all ten (and a 40 percent chance of failing completely). You have only enough resources to mount one of these operations or the other.

a) If you care only about what's best for the victims, which operation should you choose?
b) If you care also about your own reputation, which operation should you choose?

SOLUTION:

(a) If you were buried under that rubble, which would you prefer: a 50 percent chance of being rescued or a 60 percent chance? Clearly the latter. So if your goal is to give people what they want, this one's a no-brainer. Go with the second operation.

Were you tempted to prefer the first operation because it's a "sure thing"? Might it be better to be sure of saving five than to risk not saving anyone? The problem with that reasoning is that the first operation is *not* a sure thing in any relevant sense. To *any given victim,* the first operation provides a 50 percent chance of rescue, and 50 percent is no sure thing. As long as you care only about the victims, the only choice is 50 percent versus 60 percent—and 60 percent is definitely better.

(b) On the other hand, if you're worried not just about the victims but about how much praise *you're* in for, then you might want to go with the operation that's guaranteed to have you posing for pictures with five grateful survivors.

The policymaker who opts for the "sure thing" (the sure thing, that is, for the policymaker, though not for any of the victims) is following along a trail I blazed at the age of eight, when I realized it was a good idea to give my mother candy for her birthday — especially candy that I liked and she didn't. After I'd done this a couple of years in a row, my father caught on and started giving her cigars. Many years later, Homer Simpson joined the bandwagon when he gave his wife Marge a bowling ball engraved with the name Homer. None of us were giving the people what they want. All of us were falling prey to a natural temptation, which good policymakers must learn to resist.

Now let's move on to something a little harder. "Give the people what they want" is all well and good when all the relevant people want pretty much the same thing — as, for example, when they are all miners hoping to be rescued. But you can't always count on that. When different people face different risks, those people are likely to have different policy preferences. If you spend a lot of time on mountain roads, you'll want more guardrails. If your house is made of straw, you'll want more fire protection. If you like a drink after work, you'll want alcohol to be freely available. If you're a teetotaler with six kids who like to play in the street, you might want to give prohibition another try.

So if I ask "the people" what they want, all I'm likely to get is a lot of self-interested special pleading. The person I really want to ask is a person who *has* no special interests. The closest I can probably come to that person is an amnesiac — someone who can't remember his own driving habits, or where he lives, or what he drinks, or how many children he has, or indeed whether *his* and *he* are the right pronouns here. Economists have elevated that observation to a general principle:

The Amnesia Principle: to figure out whether a risk is acceptable, ask (or at least pretend to ask) an amnesiac.

In short: *give the amnesiacs what they want.*

(Actually, economists more often say: "Ask a not-yet-born soul, completely ignorant of the circumstances it's about to be born into." It comes down to pretty much the same thing, but I find amnesiacs a little easier to imagine.)

In the Trolley Problem, for example, we can't just "give the people what they want" because five people want you to push the fat man, while the fat man himself emphatically wants you not to. But the Amnesia Principle comes to the rescue and tells me to give him a shove. After all, if he and the five other victims have all managed to forget who's who, then each is thinking, "There's a five-sixths chance I'm tied to the tracks and a one-sixth chance I'm the fat man. Given that, I'd prefer you to save the people on the tracks, please."

Note the careful wording. I said that based on the Amnesia Principle, I *should* push the fat man. I did not say that I *would* push the fat man, and indeed I don't know whether I would or not, any more than I know whether I'd run into a burning building to save a child. Sometimes fear or squeamishness trumps our better instincts.

Surveys show that most people, when asked, say that they would *not* push the fat man. But if you change the problem slightly and ask, "Would you push a button that diverts the train to another track where it will run over one person instead of five?" most people say they *would* divert the train. Philosophers have devoted a lot of ink and pixels to the question of why our moral instincts are so different in the two cases. I suspect they're asking the wrong question. There's no evidence here of a conflict in moral instincts. My own moral instinct, for example, is exactly the same in both cases: you should sacrifice the one to save the five. But I am sure I would push the button and not at all sure I would push the fat man. I simply don't trust myself always to do the right thing.

So if I were taking this survey, I would answer very much as the majority does — I would not (or might not) push the fat man, but I would definitely divert the train. But if the survey is reworded to ask, *"Should* you push the fat man?" and *"Should* you divert the train?" I answer yes to both, leaving the philosophers with no apparent ambiguity to write about. A very cynical economist might suspect, then, that the wording of the actual surveys is carefully chosen to keep philosophers employed.

Now we have two principles for policymakers. First, give the people what they want, at least when all the people can agree on what that is. Second, when they *can't* all agree, at least give the amnesia victims what they want.

Taken together, these principles provide a framework for policy analysis. It's not the only possible framework, but most economists seem to think it's at least a pretty good starting point. It's the framework I'll be using for the rest of this chapter. Of course, if you don't like this framework, you might not agree with all my problem solutions. But I hope the logic of those solutions will at least give you something worth pondering.

3

Medical Research

An international philanthropy has hired you to allocate funds for medical research. You can afford to fund exactly one of two projects:

- The Kildare Study is seeking a cure for cancer. You estimate that it has a 1 percent chance of success. Worldwide, cancer kills about 10 million people a year.

- The Casey Study is seeking a cure for ALS (also known as Lou Gehrig's disease). You estimate that it has a 25 percent chance of success. Worldwide, ALS kills about 200,000 people a year.

a) If you care solely about the disease victims, which study should you fund?

b) If you care also about being hailed as a hero, which study should you fund?

SOLUTION:

(a) You can't just "give the victims what they want" because different victims want different things. Cancer victims want you to fund the Kildare Study, and ALS victims want you to fund the Casey Study.

Here's where the Amnesia Principle comes in. Imagine a victim—let's call her Betty—who has managed to forget which disease she's suffering from. Then the Kildare Study is twice as likely as the Casey Study to save Betty's life.* She wants you to fund the Kildare Study. That's what you should fund.

(b) If you fund the Kildare Study, there's a 99 percent chance it will fail, and you will be blamed (or at least not applauded). If you fund the Casey Study, there's a 25 percent chance of banner headlines touting a major breakthrough for which you were responsible. You might, then, be tempted to make the wrong choice—just like your cousin, who is in the business of rescuing people from rubble.

---

* There are 10.2 million disease victims altogether. Of these, 10 million are cancer victims, so Betty figures she's got cancer with probability 10 million/10.2 million or about 98 percent. The probability that the Kildare Study will save her life is the probability that she has cancer times the probability that the study succeeds, which comes to 98% × 1%, which is pretty close to 1%. The probability that the Casey Study will save her life is 2% × 25%, which is just half of 1%.

(I kept this example simple by assuming that Betty cares only about her survival probability. If she cares also about the alleviation of symptoms, and thinks that one disease has more unpleasant symptoms than the other, then the math gets a little more complicated.)

Most people are not in the business of mounting rescue operations, or allocating research funds, or choosing between guardrails and fire protection. But most of us still make decisions that are governed by similar logic. For example, we give to charity.

4

Charitable Giving

The Starving Children Fund is a well-established charity that reliably feeds one child with each $100 it collects. The Feeding Fund claims to be twice as efficient, and able to feed *two* children with each $100 it collects. I figure there's a 60 percent chance they're telling the truth and a 40 percent chance they're planning to abscond with everything they collect. I would like to make a $100 contribution to help starving children. Where should I send my check?

SOLUTION: Ask a starving child. Call him Billy. If there are, say, ten starving children altogether,* then my contribution to the Starving Children Fund gives Billy a 10 percent chance to get fed. By contrast, my contribution to the Feeding Fund gives

---

* The assumption that there are ten of them out there is purely for illustration. If you replace ten with a hundred or a thousand or a million, it won't change the outcome of the calculation.

Billy a 12 percent chance to get fed.* It's a safe bet that a starving child prefers a 12 percent chance of eating to a 10 percent
chance. I should give to the Feeding Fund.

Notice the conclusion: *I* should give to the Feeding Fund. I don't
know what *you* should do. That's because the problem specifies
only that *I* believe there's a 60 percent chance that the Feeding
Fund is legit. If you believe it's more like 20 percent or 30 percent,
you'll want to redo the calculations, and might end up making a
different choice.†

In other words, perfectly reasonable people can make different choices. This is all the more true when you're choosing between, say, the Starving Children Fund and the Fund to Cure Malaria. In principle, the Amnesia Principle stands ready to guide
you. Where would you want that money to go if you'd forgotten
whether you're a starving child or a potential malaria victim? In
practice, who knows? There are so many uncertainties, so many
unknown probabilities, and so many competing priorities, that
it's easy for people of goodwill to disagree about which cause is
worthiest. Some of us feed the children, others fight malaria, and
we can all be thankful for one another's generosity.

It's much harder, though, to imagine that people of goodwill
can disagree with *themselves* about which cause is worthiest. If
I've decided to give $100 to the Starving Children Fund, it's be-
cause, based on the information I've got, and after accounting
for all of my uncertainties, I believe the Starving Children Fund
is worthier than the Feeding Fund or the Fund to Cure Malaria.

---

* Twelve percent is the product of 60 percent (the probability the organization is
legit) times 20 percent (the probability that Billy will be one of the two out of ten
who gets fed).

† If you've read chapter 10, you might ask why either of us should trust our own
opinions more than we trust one another's. In the interest of staying focused on
the key points here, I'm sweeping that issue under the rug.

If I then decide to give another $100, I still want to give it to the charity I believe is worthiest — and unless something relevant has changed, that will be the Starving Children Fund again.

But oddly enough, there are people who write checks to three different charities all on the same day — as if they'd decided at 10:00 that the Starving Children Fund is the worthiest, then at 10:01 that actually the Feeding Fund is worthier, and then at 10:02 that actually the Fund to Cure Malaria is worthiest of all — but then didn't take the trouble to tear up the first two checks.*

The likeliest explanation seems to be that these people are motivated by something other than purely charitable impulses. Maybe they find it more gratifying to get three thank-you notes instead of one.†

If people give to charity for reasons that are not entirely charitable, I'm still all for it — just as I'm glad that there are people in the business of rescuing people from rubble, even if their motives are impure and their choices are imperfect. *Most* of what we do is not entirely charitable, and almost everyone seems to be fine with that. But I think it's a good idea, every now and then, to stop and think about what you're doing and whether there's a way to do it better.

---

* It's (just barely) possible that these people happen to have judged all three charities to be exactly equally worthy, but even then, there's no particular reason to donate to all three of them. If you write one check for $300 instead of three for $100 each, you can save the cost of two stamps and contribute a little more.

† For a much longer catalog of possible explanations, see chapter 12 of my book *More Sex Is Safer Sex*.

CHAPTER 14

The Coin Flipper's Dilemma

*B*ob has challenged Alice to a game of Deep Pockets. When they meet tomorrow, they'll empty their pockets, and whoever has the most cash takes everything on the table. But Alice, having read and digested the solution to problem 4 in chapter 5, knows how boring that game would be. Rational players never carry any money.

So Bob suggests a twist: instead of *choosing* how much cash to carry, they'll each commit to the same random procedure. Tonight before he goes to bed, Bob will flip a coin repeatedly until it comes up heads. If he gets heads on the first flip, he'll carry $1 in his pocket tomorrow. If he gets heads on the second flip, he'll carry $4. If he gets heads on the third flip, he'll carry $16, and so on, multiplying his pocket cash by 4 for each additional flip. Alice, if she accepts the challenge, must do the same.

1

The Coin Flipper's Dilemma

Should Alice play this game?

Obviously, the answer is that she should play if (and only if) she wants to. This game is a risky prospect, and only Alice can know how she feels about that risk.

So let's start by assuming we know a little more about Alice, namely, that she wants to play if (and only if) the odds are in her favor. Then we can replace our question with this one:

2

The Coin Flipper's Odds

In this game, do the odds favor Alice?

That's the sort of question economists are usually good at answering. But in this case I do not believe that economics, or game theory, or decision theory, or any other formal discipline can help very much.

Oh, game theory will try to make you *think* it has something to say here. In fact, game theory offers an apparently irrefutable argument against playing. The problem is that it also offers an apparently irrefutable argument *for* playing. The next several problems will illustrate those arguments. You should approach them all on the assumption that Alice has agreed to play Bob's game.

3

If Alice Needs One Try

Suppose Alice flips heads on her first try, so she's required to carry $1. Are the odds in her favor?

SOLUTION: Well, she can't possibly win, because Bob always brings at least a dollar.

In fact, there's a 50 percent chance that Bob also flips heads on his first try and brings $1, in which case they tie and no money changes hands.

There's also a 50 percent chance Bob does not flip heads on his first try, in which case he brings more than $1, and Alice loses her dollar.

In expectation,* then, she loses 50 cents. This means the odds are against her.

4

If Alice Needs Two Tries

Suppose Alice flips heads on her second try, so she's required to carry $4. Are the odds in her favor?

SOLUTION: There's a 50 percent chance that Bob flips heads on his first try and brings $1, in which case Alice wins his dollar.

---

* Remember that "in expectation" means "on average, if we were to repeat this experiment a great number of times." To say that Alice comes out ahead in expectation is the same thing as saying the odds are in her favor.

There's a 25 percent chance that Bob flips tails, then heads, and brings $4, in which case they tie.

The remaining 25 percent of the time, Bob brings more than $4 and Alice loses her $4.

In expectation, then, she loses 50 cents. This means the odds are against her.

5

If Alice Needs More Tries

Suppose Alice flips heads on her third try, so she's required to carry $16. Are the odds in her favor?

What if she flips heads on her fourth try, or her fifth or her sixth?

SOLUTION: Regardless of whether she flips heads on her third, fourth, fifth, or ninety-seventh try, Alice always loses 50 cents in expectation. (You can check this with exactly the sort of calculation we did in the preceding two problems.) The odds are always against her.

Alice's friend Carol, who studies economics, has chimed in on the question of whether Alice should play this game:

> Alice, this game is totally stacked against you!
>
> If you flip heads on the first try, your expected loss is fifty cents. If you flip heads on the *second* try, your expected loss is fifty cents. Likewise, if you flip heads on the third or the fourth or the ninety-seventh try.
>
> So *no matter how your coins turn up,* after you flip them,

you're going to say "Rats! I wish I'd never agreed to play this game!"

How can it possibly make sense to play if you know in advance that you're sure to regret it?* Just say no.

This makes so much sense that Alice is almost convinced. But here's what bothers her: Surely Bob's economist friends are making exactly the same argument for why *he* shouldn't play. And if the game is bad for Bob, it must be good for Alice.

Check it out.

6

If Bob Needs One Try

Suppose Bob flips heads on his first try, so he's required to carry $1. Do the odds favor Alice?

SOLUTION: Alice can't possibly lose; she can only tie or win Bob's dollar.

There's a 50 percent chance that Alice also flips heads on her first try and brings $1, in which case they tie and no money changes hands.

There's a 50 percent chance that Alice does not flip heads on her first try, in which case she brings more than a dollar and Alice wins Bob's dollar.

In expectation, then, she gains 50 cents. The odds are in her favor.

---

* Carol might want to call Alice's attention to the No Sure Regrets Rule that we met in chapter 12.

7

If Bob Needs Two Tries

Suppose Bob flips heads on his second try, so he's required to carry $4. Do the odds favor Alice?

SOLUTION: There's a 50 percent chance Alice flips heads on her first try and brings $1, in which case she loses her dollar.

There's a 25 percent chance that Alice flips tails, then heads, and brings $4, in which case they tie.

The remaining 25 percent of the time, Alice brings more than $4 and wins Bob's $4.

In expectation, then, she wins 50 cents. The odds are in her favor.

8

If Bob Needs More Tries

Suppose Bob flips heads on his third try, so he's required to carry $16. Are the odds in Alice's favor?

What if he flips heads on his fourth try, or his fifth or his sixth?

SOLUTION: Regardless of whether Bob flips heads on his third, fourth, fifth, or ninety-seventh try, Alice always gains 50 cents in expectation. The odds are always in her favor.

This prompts Alice's friend Doreen, who also studies economics, to make this argument:

Alice, of course you should play! The odds are totally with you!

Imagine spying on Bob while he flips his coins.*

If you see him flip heads on the first try, you will, in expectation, gain fifty cents. The odds will be with you and you'll be high-fiving yourself for agreeing to play. If he flips heads on the second try, it's the same story. And likewise if he flips heads on the third or the fourth or the ninety-seventh try.

Once you see Bob flip his coins, you're sure to be glad you agreed to play. How can you turn down an opportunity that's sure to make you glad?

Go for it!

Doreen's argument seems airtight. But so does Carol's. To break the tie, Alice goes to her one remaining economist friend, Eddie. Eddie has yet another take on the situation:

Alice, this game is perfectly symmetric. If it's good for you, it's got to be good for Bob, and if it's bad for you, it's got to be bad for Bob.

But obviously it can't be good for both of you or bad for both of you, because whatever one wins, the other loses. So it must be neither bad nor good for either of you.

The only possible conclusion is that it doesn't make a bit of difference whether you play or not. Pardon the expression, but you might as well flip a coin.

Like Carol and Doreen, Eddie appears to be making perfect sense. Unfortunately, while they've all done excellent jobs of explaining why their own arguments are right, none of them has even attempted to explain why the others' arguments are wrong.

To keep track of the arguments, here's a chart showing (along the side) the various amounts Alice might carry and (along the top) the various amounts Bob might carry. The sizes of the boxes

---

* Doreen is imagining that Bob flips his coins before Alice does — but that's a harmless assumption, because it clearly doesn't matter who flips first.

are proportional to their probabilities, and the entries in the boxes show Alice's payoffs.

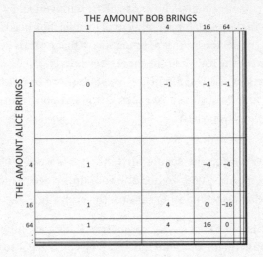

THE AMOUNT BOB BRINGS

THE AMOUNT ALICE BRINGS	1	4	16	64 ...
1	0	−1	−1	−1
4	1	0	−4	−4
16	1	4	0	−16
64	1	4	16	0

The gist of problems 3, 4, and 5 is that if you average the cells in any given row, weighting them by their sizes, you always get −.50.

The gist of problems 6, 7, and 8 is that if you average the cells in any given column, weighting them by their sizes, you always get +.50.

Carol's argument is that every day you're going to be in *some* row, every row is bad, and therefore every day is bad, so you should avoid this game. Doreen's argument is that every day you're going to be in some column, every column is good, and therefore every day is good, so you should embrace this game.

After musing on this chart, Alice asks a question:

Can somebody please just tell me, if I were to play this game repeatedly, how much I should expect to win or lose on the average day?

Carol has already told us that each row in the chart averages out to −.50. Doreen has told us that each column averages out to

+.50. But Alice is asking, What is the average of all the boxes *in the entire chart?*

It's a great question. Unfortunately, it has no answer. There are infinitely many boxes in this chart. Not every infinite collection of numbers has a meaningful "average." This is one that doesn't.

As we've seen, each row and each column has an average. But if the whole chart had an average, it would have to coincide with the average of the row averages, which is −.50, and it would also have to coincide with the average of the column averages, which is +.50. Obviously, that's impossible, so the full-chart average can't exist.

In other words, Alice's perfectly reasonable question — "How much can I expect to win or lose on the average day?" — has no answer. You might find that disturbing, but that's how life is sometimes.

But...

But surely *something* must happen if Alice agrees to play the game repeatedly. What could that something be?

Eddie, one of Alice's economist friends, was on to something when he pointed out that the game is symmetric. The probability that Alice will win, say, $64 on a given day is equal to the probability that she'll lose $64. You might be tempted to conclude, then, that if she plays enough times, her gains and losses will largely cancel out, so that on average she'll neither win nor lose very much.

In other contexts, you might be entirely right. Here's what happens when two evenly matched baseball teams wager $100 per game:

- If they play 1 game, one team or the other is sure to lose $100.
- If they play a sequence of 10 games, it's over 95 percent certain that neither team will lose (on average) more than $60 per game.
- If they play a sequence of 100 games, it's roughly 95 percent certain that neither team will lose more than $20 per game.

(It's also 99 percent certain that neither team will lose more than $26 per game, and 99.9999 percent certain that neither team will lose more than $46 per game.)

That's all due to the *law of large numbers,* which says that if you repeat a fair game enough times, you're almost sure to come extremely close to breaking even on average.

For that matter, if you keep repeating a game that's stacked in your favor, you're almost sure to come out ahead, and if you keep repeating a game that's stacked against you, you're almost sure to come out behind. That's why casinos make money and almost nobody gets rich playing slot machines.

The law of large numbers applies to every kind of casino game or sports wager, and for that matter almost any situation that is ever likely to cross the desk of an economist. But the law admits one loophole: it does not apply in situations where averages can't be computed. So it doesn't apply to Alice and Bob.

This brings us back to Alice's question: If she and Bob play a great many times, what *does* happen on average? The answer is that *no matter how long they play,* there's no reason to think they'll ever come close to breaking even.

Here's what happens:

- If Alice and Bob play 50 games, there's about a 50 percent chance that one or the other will lose more than 55 cents per game — which comes to $27.50 altogether.
- If Alice and Bob play 500 games, there's *still* about a 50 percent chance that one or the other will lose more than 55 cents per game — which comes to $275 altogether.
- If Alice and Bob play 5 million games, there's *still* a 50 percent chance that one or the other will lose more than 55 cents per game — which comes to $2,750,000 altogether.

That answers the immediate question, but let's not lose sight of the even bigger question — the one we started with. Alice wants to know whether she should play this game. What useful advice can she get from an economist?

I promise to come back to that question, but first let's warm up with some easier questions.

9

The Insane Bookmaker

Suppose you've found a clinically insane bookie who will allow you to bet $100,000 on a fair coin flip at two-to-one odds. Should you take that bet?

SOLUTION: I dunno. It depends on your attitude toward risk. *Having the odds in your favor is not the same thing as eliminating risk.* In this case, if you flip that coin, the odds are in your favor, but you're facing a world of risk.

10

The More Accommodating Bookmaker

Suppose that same bookie will allow you to bet $1 each on 100,000 flips of that same fair coin at those same favorable odds. Should you take that bet?

SOLUTION: Absolutely! With that many flips, the law of large numbers says it's almost certain you'll come extremely close to doubling your money. It would be crazy to turn that opportunity down.

In other words: the law of large numbers has all but eliminated your risk, so feel free to focus entirely on those enticing odds.

Economists can give a lot of good advice along those lines. If you think the roulette wheel is tilted in your favor, you still might not want to bet $1,000 on a single spin — but you shouldn't hesitate to bet $1 each on a thousand spins. If you think the stock market is headed generally upward, you still might not want to invest your entire nest egg in a single company — but you shouldn't hesitate to divide your nest egg out over a great many companies. (Probably the best way to do this is by buying shares in a mutual fund that holds a diversified stock portfolio.) As long as you spread out your bets, you can rely on the law of large numbers to protect you. Risk is not an issue.

And ordinarily, if a game is completely fair, and you have the same sort of opportunity to diversify — for example, if Bob is willing to play a hundred times for pennies instead of playing once for dollars — you can count on the law of large numbers to insure that you'll come extremely close to breaking even on your average play. Because Eddie has convinced Alice that her tournament against Bob is fair, Alice takes some comfort in this. I suspect that that's why she said upfront (on the first page of this chapter) that all she cares about is the odds.

But her comfort is illusory. In fact, she finds herself in one of those rare situations where the law of large numbers is simply not true, and the economists' usual advice does not apply. She can spread her play out over a thousand days or a million or a billion, without eliminating any risk. Economics and game theory are just not designed to dispense advice in that kind of situation.

Which means that Alice, unlike almost everyone else, should probably — just this once — stop listening to economists and follow her heart, wherever it leads her.

CHAPTER 15

Albert and the Dinosaurs

*E*very day Albert leaves his office (at the bottom of the map below), gets on the main highway, and attempts to drive home to his house on Second Street. If he turns too soon (onto First Street), or if he overshoots (going all the way to the north end of the main highway), he is mauled by dinosaurs.

Obviously, Albert's best strategy is to go straight at the first intersection and turn right at the second. Unfortunately, the intersections look identical. Doubly unfortunately, Albert is extremely absent-minded and can never remember whether he's already passed the first intersection.

That makes Albert very interesting to economists. After all, absent-mindedness is part of the human condition, so if you want to understand how real-world humans make choices, Albert, though fictional, is one good place to start.

Because Albert can't tell the intersections apart, he needs a single strategy for both of them. One option is "always turn right" — but that delivers him directly to the First Street dinosaur mob. Another is "always go straight" — but that puts him on a direct route to the North Side crew. Neither of these strategies has any chance of getting him home.

It turns out that his best hope is to flip a fair coin at each intersection, with the faces labeled "straight" and "right" instead of "heads" and "tails." This gives him a $1/2$ chance of going straight at First Street and a $1/2$ chance of going right at Second, so his chance of getting home is $1/2 \times 1/2 = 1/4$. With this strategy, in other words, he makes it home safely one day out of four.*

So that's what he does.

In fact, he's on his way home right now and is just pulling up to an intersection. Of course, he has no idea which intersection it is. Can you help him?

---

* There are other options, but they all turn out to be worse than the fair coin. For example, Albert could flip a *weighted* coin that leads him to go straight $1/4$ of the time and turn right $3/4$ of the time. But this gives him a $1/4$ chance of going straight at First Street and a $3/4$ chance of turning right at Second, giving him only a $1/4 \times 3/4 = 3/16$ chance of getting home. That's worse than the $1/4$ chance he gets from the fair coin.

1

The Upcoming Intersection

What's the probability that Albert is approaching First Street?

SOLUTION: Albert gets to First Street every day. He gets to Second Street only (on average) every other day—the days when his first coin flip tells him to go straight. So out of every three times he approaches an intersection, there are two approaches to First Street and one to Second Street. So the probability that the current intersection is First Street is ⅔.

2

Albert's Survival Probability

Albert is still approaching that intersection. What's the probability that he'll make it home?

I'll give you the solution. Better yet, I'll give you *two* solutions. Unfortunately, they contradict each other.

SOLUTION 1: We've already solved this problem. When Albert left the office, his survival probability was ¼. Nothing has changed since then, so it's still ¼.

Or to be more precise: the only so-called news is that Albert is now approaching an intersection. But *we knew all along* that Albert would eventually approach at least one intersection, so this can't count as news. Therefore there's no reason to recalculate. The probability remains ¼.

SOLUTION 2: Albert is approaching either First Street or Second Street.

If it's First Street, he needs two lucky coin flips to get home (one to send him straight and one to send him right). The probability of two lucky coin flips is ¼.

If it's Second Street, he needs only one lucky coin flip (to send him right). The probability of one lucky coin flip is ½.

We know from problem 1 that Albert is at First Street with probability ⅔ and at Second with probability ⅓. Putting all this together, we get this survival probability:

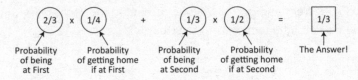

So which is it? Is Albert's survival probability ¼, or is it ⅓? The answer appears to depend on which of two perfectly reasonable calculations we choose to go with, which means it depends on exactly how we interpret the word *probability*.

This brings us to a more fundamental question: Who cares? Albert either makes it home or doesn't. What does it matter how he chooses to calculate his survival probability along the way?

Actually, it matters a lot, and here's why: Albert is currently rethinking his strategy, and as we'll soon see, his decision depends on getting this stuff right.

Remember that Albert's strategy is to flip a fair coin at each intersection. But he also happens to have a *weighted* coin in his glove box — a coin that sends him straight with probability ¼ and right with probability ¾.

Here are his coins:

COIN F:
THE FAIR COIN

STRAIGHT with
PROBABILITY 1/2

RIGHT with
PROBABILITY 1/2

COIN W:
THE WEIGHTED
COIN

STRAIGHT with
PROBABILITY 1/4

RIGHT with
PROBABILITY 3/4

3

Switching Coins

As Albert approaches the unknown intersection, he contemplates discarding his fair coin (coin F) and flipping the weighted (coin W) instead.

a) If Albert switches coins, what is the probability that he'll make it home?

b) Should he switch coins?

SOLUTION:

a) Albert might (or might not, as we'll see soon enough!) reason like this:

Step 1: Either I'm at First Street or I'm at Second, with probabilities ⅔ and ⅓.

Step 2: If this is First Street, I make it home by going straight and then right. With coin W, the probability of that is ¼ × ¾ = ³⁄₁₆.

Step 3: If this is Second Street, I make it home by going right. With coin W, the probability of that is ¾.

Conclusion: So with coin W, I have an overall survival probability of

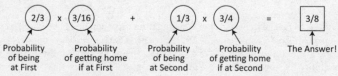

| 2/3 | x | 3/16 | + | 1/3 | x | 3/4 | = | 3/8 |

Probability of being at First · Probability of getting home if at First · Probability of being at Second · Probability of getting home if at Second · The Answer!

b) If Albert reasons as in (a), he figures that coin W gives him a
⅜ chance to make it home. According to the calculations in
problem 2, coin F gives him a survival probability of either
¼ (which is more than ⅜) or ⅓ (which is less than ⅜). So he
should either stick with coin F or switch to coin W, depending
on which calculation you buy into.

Well, that's pretty ambiguous. But even before you get to that ambiguity, there's something very odd about the calculation in part
(a). Step 1 assumes that the current intersection is First Street
with probability ⅔. Albert got that from the solution to problem
1, which assumed that in the past Albert has always flipped coin F.

But why would Albert believe that? Remember that every intersection Albert approaches looks the same to him — and at *this*
intersection, he's thinking about switching to coin W. If he's willing to switch now, he was probably willing to switch at the *last* intersection. Which means that maybe he *did* switch at the last intersection! If so, his calculation goes wrong right at the first step.*

And that's not the only thing that's a little odd here! Step 2 of
Albert's calculation assumes that if he switches to coin W, he'll
be flipping it both now and at any future intersection (so that the
probability of turning right at the next intersection is ¾). But if
he's willing to switch to W now, maybe he'll be willing to switch
some third coin X in the future — giving a different probability
for a right turn. That's another reason his calculation might (or
might not) be incorrect.

Is Albert sophisticated enough to think of all that? And if so,
how does he factor it all in? How *should* he factor it all in? *Can*

* If Albert in fact switched to coin W a long time ago, then he's been going straight
with probability ¼, which means he reaches First Street four days out of four and
Second Street only one day out of four, which means he's now at First Street with
probability ⅘, not ⅔.

Pepper ...
And Salt

THE WALL STREET JOURNAL

*"The key to making the right decision
is knowing which coin to flip."*

he trust his memory of what coins he's flipped in the past (even if
he can't trust his memory of which intersection he's reached)? I
have no idea. *Can* he commit himself now to flipping a particular
coin at the *next* intersection? I have no idea. There's a lot about
Albert's mind that we haven't specified.

What additional assumptions should we make? If our only goal
is to construct a brain teaser, we can assume anything we want.
But if we want Albert's behavior to shed some light on the work-
ings of real (and occasionally absent-minded) people navigating
their way through a real (and occasionally confusing) world, then
some assumptions are better than others.

There is a substantial literature on this question, and on the
more general questions of how rational but absent-minded ac-
tors both do and should make decisions. Recently, an entire issue
of the prestigious journal *Games and Economic Behavior* was devoted to the problem of poor Albert, who, if he's read that issue, is
surely now more confused than ever.

Here are a few possible visions of Albert:

Albert Mark Zero is totally inflexible. Once he makes a plan, he sticks to it. This Albert, of course, chooses the fair coin F and never even contemplates a change of plans.

Albert Mark One is capable of changing plans once but believes (either correctly or incorrectly) that he can't change plans twice. This is the Albert who buys into solution 2 in problem 2. He contemplates switching from the fair coin F to strategy W, then computes his survival probabilities *on the twin assumptions that he always employed strategy F in the past and that if he switches, he'll stick with strategy W in the future.* But if he believes he can switch from F to W at this intersection, why doesn't he believe he might switch from W to one of the differently weighted coins X, Y, or Z at the next one? This Albert is a bit of an odd duck.

Albert Mark Two is capable of changing plans for the *current intersection* but believes (either correctly or incorrectly) that when he gets to the *next* intersection, he'll revert to the old plan. He arrives at an intersection planning to flip coin F and asks himself whether he should switch to W for *this intersection only,* fully confident that he'll revert to strategy F at the next intersection (if any). He computes his survival probabilities accordingly and gets yet a third solution to problem 2. If you work that solution out, you'll discover that this Albert has nothing to gain from switching. So he *contemplates* a switch but ends up sticking with the original fair coin F.

Or more precisely, he sticks with strategy F *if* he starts with that strategy in the first place. But he can do much better if he's prescient enough to pick a different starting strategy. Specifically, he can start off with the strategy "always turn right." Given that, and given what we've assumed about his cognitive abilities, he updates his strategy to "always go straight" when he reaches the first intersection and then updates again to "always turn right" at the second. This gets him home with certainty.

Moreover, this alternative requires no more skill on Albert's part than the fair-coin solution — either way he's remembering the same amount of information and performing the same calculations — so this is what I'd expect him to do.*

In any event, none of these visions of Albert rings true to me. Here's my own preferred vision:

Albert Mark Three is capable of remembering the coin he previously chose. He also remembers one *rule* for updating to a new strategy each time he reaches an intersection. For example:

Rule A: Always square the probability you started with, so if you started with coin W ($1/4$ probability of going straight), switch to coin X ($1/16$ probability of going straight).

Another example of a rule would be:

Rule B: Always add 1 to the probability you started with and divide by 2, so if you started with coin W, you'll switch to coin Y (with $5/8$ probability of going straight).

He's even allowed to build some randomness into his rule, so this one is also valid:

Rule C: Always flip a fair coin. If it comes up heads, use rule A. If it comes up tails, use rule B. Albert applies his rule, flips an appropriately chosen new coin, either goes straight or turns, and carries the memory of the coin he flipped to the next intersection.

Now Albert's problem is recast. It's not "What does Albert do right now?" but "What rule does Albert live by?"

---

* A widely cited paper by the economists R. Aumann, S. Hart, and M. Perry defends both "Mark Two" as the proper vision of Albert and the fair coin as his starting strategy. From this, they derive correctly that he'll always stick with the fair coin. They explicitly entertain the alternative possibility that he'll start with the "always go right" strategy and get home with certainty but then reject this possibility as contrary to the spirit of the problem. But it seems to me that Albert is unlikely to care about the spirit of the problem. If you've designed him so that he's capable of doing something, you ought not arbitrarily prohibit him from doing it.

It's natural to suppose that the rule must be one from which Albert will never want to deviate in the present, given that he expects to follow it in the future.

It's not obvious that there are any rules that satisfy this criterion, but it turns out that in fact there is exactly one. Moreover, no matter how you change the environment (say by replacing one set of dinosaurs with a band of Chihuahuas who are exactly $1/10$ as annoying as the dinosaurs), there is always exactly one rule that satisfies these conditions (though for different environments, the rule is different). A full description of those rules — together with a proof that there's always exactly one of them — is more technical than most readers of this book will want to see, but the appendix contains a reference to a paper with all the details.

It might strike you that Albert Mark Three can remember an awful lot for a guy who's supposed to be absent-minded. But I claim that the same is true of Alberts Mark Zero, One, and Two, all of whom remember what coins they've flipped in the past, and all of whom can remember enough about themselves to predict what coins they'll flip in the future.*

I prefer Albert Mark Three because his behavior is entirely consistent. Unlike Albert Mark One, who believes both that he can and that he can't change his strategy, or Albert Mark Two, who believes (sometimes incorrectly) that he'll always revert to his past strategy in the future, Albert Mark Three always assumes — correctly! — that he'll use the same updating rule in the future that he does in the present and the past. Absent-minded though he may be, Albert Mark Three is a rational man.

---

* It's also important to distinguish between what Albert can remember and what sort of rules he can follow — if you think of Albert as a computer, this is analogous to the difference between how much disk space he's got and how sophisticated a program he's running. On the memory front, all of our Alberts are capable of remembering exactly the same thing, namely, "Which coin have I been planning to flip?" They differ only in the "programs" they are running to convert that single input into a single output, namely, "Which coin will I actually flip?"

CHAPTER 16

Money, Trade, and Finance

*B*ecause you've just bought a book with the word *economist* on the cover, you're likely to be interested in such traditional topics as financial markets, monetary matters, and international trade. We've touched on all those subjects, but in this final chapter I'll use our puzzling skills to focus directly on them, and reveal more about how economists think.

I once had dinner with Fischer Black, a legend in the field of finance for his pioneering work in the design and pricing of financial derivatives. Black had recently left academia and gone to work on Wall Street, earning what his former colleagues considered to be Very Big Bucks. One thing I asked him was "When you go into that fancy office, what exactly do you do all day?"

His answer: "I design complicated financial instruments to sell to people who would be better off with nothing but Chase CDs and Vanguard mutual funds." (I'm pretty sure that the only reason he mentioned Chase instead of, say, Wells Fargo or Bank of America, is that our third dinner companion was a Chase vice president.)

Having said this, Black turned his gaze downward, thought for a moment, and then half muttered: "People like me should be taxed out of existence."

I wish in retrospect that I'd pursued this with him a little further than I did. In fact, my only follow-up question was "Why don't your clients realize this?" His answer was that the clients mostly don't manage their own affairs; instead they hire financial managers who are easily bribed with a lot of fancy dinners. I didn't ask why honest managers (with, presumably, better track records for their clients) don't drive dishonest managers out of business, or why you can't bribe the financial manager just as well *without* bothering to cook up an inferior product. Nor did I challenge him with a list of plausible scenarios in which novel financial products can fill real and obvious needs. The conversation had moved on.*

Whether Fischer Black was fully, partly, or not at all justified in his grim assessment is a subject for a very different book. But other questions about derivatives — what they are, how they work, and how they're priced — will fit right in here. If you work through the next few problems, you'll have mastered the main idea that made Fischer Black legendary among economists and netted him a high-paying job on Wall Street.

The simplest example of a financial derivative is a *call option* — a piece of paper (or its electronic equivalent) that says something like this:

---

* The conversation had in fact moved on to the topic of Black's recently completed book manuscript, where he'd found a novel solution to a problem that plagues many authors. Having written several dozen short chapters, he gave them all appropriate titles and then ordered them alphabetically by title. No more agonizing about what goes where!

> Issued on: (today's date here)
>
> The holder of this piece of paper
> is entitled to purchase
>
> 10 shares of stock
> in Generic Conglomerate Corporation (GCC)
>
> at a price of $12 per share
> exactly one year from the issue date shown above

If you are the owner of this call option, and if a year from today GCC stock is selling for $15 a share, you'll be able to make a quick $30 profit by buying ten shares at $12 each and immediately selling them at the market price of $15 each. So this call option has a chance of being valuable next year — and that makes it valuable today. That is, people are willing to pay something for it today. But how *much* should we expect them to pay? The next series of questions will show you how economists answer that question.

1

Foreseeing the Future

a) Suppose that one year from today GCC's stock sells for $15 a share. How much will the call option pictured above be worth on that day?
b) Suppose instead that one year from today GCC's stock sells for $10 a share. How much will this call option be worth on that day?

SOLUTION:

a) The call option will allow you to buy ten shares, worth a total of $150, for a total of $120. If you want, you can turn around and sell those shares for $150 cash. The call option, in other words, is effectively a machine for turning $120 into $150. A machine like that is worth $30.

b) If you want to buy GCC stock, you can buy it in the marketplace for $10 a share. It would be crazy to buy it for $12 a share just because you're holding a call option. In other words, you might as well throw your call option away. It has the same value as any other piece of trash, namely, $0.

To summarize:

- One year from today, if the stock is worth $15, the call option will be worth $30.
- One year from today, if the stock is worth $10, the call option will be worth $0.

This still doesn't tell us what we want to know: What is the value of the call option *today?*

To answer that, I need two more bits of information and one imaginary cousin. The two bits of information are the current price of the stock and the going interest rate. I'll make these assumptions:

- The current price of GCC stock is $12 a share.
- The going interest rate is 50 percent per year (not terribly realistic, I know, but I'm trying to make the arithmetic easy).

As for the imaginary cousin, his name is Jeter and he has absolutely no interest in call options. His wheeling and dealing takes a different form.

2

Jeter's Game

This morning Jeter borrowed $40, withdrew $32 from his bank account, and used the total of $72 to buy six shares of GCC stock at $12 per share.

a) One year from today, if GCC's stock is selling at $15 a share, how much will Jeter pocket from his investment scheme on that day?
b) One year from today, if GCC's stock is selling at $10 a share, how much will Jeter pocket from his investment scheme on that day?

SOLUTION:

a) Jeter's six shares will be worth $90, out of which he needs $60 to repay his loan at the going 50 percent interest rate. He pockets $30.
b) Jeter's six shares will be worth $60, out of which he needs $60 to repay his loan. He pockets $0.

To summarize:

- One year from today, if the stock is worth $15, Jeter pockets $30.
- One year from today, if the stock is worth $10, Jeter pockets $0.

3

Comparison

You've just bought the call option from problem 1. Jeter has just borrowed $40, withdrawn $32 from his savings, and bought six shares of stock at the current price of $12 per share.

Suppose (admittedly unrealistically) that next year's stock price must be either $15 or $10 and cannot be anything else.

Who pockets more money next year — you or Jeter?

SOLUTION: If next year's stock price is $15, we know from problem 1 that you pocket $30 and from problem 2 that Jeter pockets $30.

If next year's stock price is $10, we know from problem 1 that you pocket $0 and from problem 2 that Jeter pockets $0.

Either way, you're sure to both pocket the same amounts.

That's a very strong conclusion. It doesn't just say that you and Jeter will do equally well on average. It says that you are *guaranteed* to do equally well, no matter what the future brings.

4

Option Pricing

Given the results of the previous few problems, what is that call option worth today?

SOLUTION: When two things are guaranteed to be equally desirable, and both are traded in the marketplace, they had better sell for exactly the same price; otherwise nobody would ever buy the more expensive one.

It costs Jeter $32 out of pocket to implement his strategy. The call option is guaranteed to be exactly as desirable as Jeter's plan, so it had better cost $32 out of pocket to buy the call option. The option sells today for $32.

It's quite stunning that we can solve this problem with so little information. We did make some assumptions about the stock price and the interest rate, but we made absolutely no assumptions about how *likely* the stock price is to go up or down; all we assumed was that both things were possible. We also made absolutely no assumptions about how much risk investors are willing to tolerate. Your first guess should have been that without such information, it's impossible to know what the option is worth. But that first guess would be wrong.

Now, suppose you want to figure out the fair price of some real-world call option, say, an option to buy a hundred shares of Coca-Cola ten years from today at a price of $50 a share. How do you do it? It was the solution to this problem that made academic superstars out of Fischer Black and his coauthor Myron Scholes. (Scholes won a Nobel Prize for this work; Black would surely have won also had he not made the mistake of dying too soon.)

The first thing you need is an imaginary cousin Jeter, who follows some imaginary investment strategy that involves borrowing, buying shares of stock, and selling shares of stock. You rig all the imaginary numbers — the amount Jeter borrows, the number of shares he buys and sells, and the adjustments he makes every day — so that *no matter what happens to the stock price,* Jeter's portfolio is certain to be exactly equal in value to the option you want to price. Then you calculate the cost of Jeter's strategy, and that must be the price of the option.

For example, to price the option pictured on page 261, I rigged all the numbers in problems 2 and 3 so that Jeter's strategy would always have exactly the same value as the call option. This rigging process was pretty easy because I was prepared to make the thoroughly unrealistic assumption that there are only two possible future prices for the stock ($15 and $10). To solve a real-world problem, you must allow for a great many more possible future prices, which makes it a whole lot harder to rig the numbers. Black and Scholes got rich and famous by figuring out better ways to do exactly that.

As financial assets go, call options are somewhat exotic. Now let's go to the other end of the spectrum and talk about the least exotic of all financial assets, namely, money.

5

Vaults Full of Cash

Scrooge McDuck is a fabulously wealthy eccentric who keeps a vault full of cash so he can bathe in it. *True or False:* McDuck's propensity to hoard cash benefits nobody but himself. The rest of us would be better off if he spent some of that money.

SOLUTION: False. When McDuck buys, say, a turkey, there's one less turkey for the rest of us. Or, alternatively, when McDuck buys a turkey, he induces some farmer to produce one more turkey — using labor, food, and fuel that are then unavailable to produce, say, one more hop plant, in which case there's one less quart of beer for the rest of us.

So when McDuck spends his money, the rest of us get poorer, not richer.

Beer and turkeys are produced at substantial resource costs. Paper money is produced at almost no cost whatsoever. (It takes a million dollars' worth of resources to produce a million dollars' worth of turkeys, but it takes far, far less than a million dollars' worth of paper and ink to produce a million dollars' worth of cash.) There is no better neighbor than one who places almost no demands on the community's resources. There is no better neighbor, that is, than one who bathes in his cash instead of spending it.

If McDuck starts buying turkeys, cheese, or Hula-Hoops, there will soon be fewer turkeys, cheese, or Hula-Hoops, and the prices of those goods will rise. You and I will then be able to buy fewer of them, and eat less well (or hoop less well) than we do today.

You might object that if McDuck starts buying turkeys, the rest of us will have fewer turkeys, but we'll be compensated by having more money. Alas, when there are fewer turkeys, the price of turkeys gets bid up, which lowers the value of that money. In any event, the quality of our lives depends on how well we eat and how well we live, not the number of zeroes on our bank balances.

I should acknowledge one possible exception: in recessionary times, if markets are functioning badly (which means, for example, that prices are failing to adjust to changing market conditions), then it is possible (through complicated mechanisms I'm not describing here) for a McDuck spending spree — or even a government spending spree — to "jump-start" the economy. But this exception applies only under unusual circumstances, and even then is beneficial only in the short run. I am not aware of any thinking person, or any economist (thinking or not), who believes that McDuck can make us better off by spending his money in ordinary circumstances.

We can squeeze one more lesson out of our friend McDuck.

6

Taxing the Rich

Scrooge McDuck, you'll remember, keeps a vault full of cash so he can bathe in it. In fact, he almost never spends money, because he prefers to keep adding it to his vault. *True or False:* If McDuck's tax rate (and nobody else's) goes up, the government will be able to provide more services to the rest of us, all at McDuck's expense.

SOLUTION: Alas, nothing of the sort is true. In order to provide the rest of us with, say, more or better roads, the government needs asphalt, workers, and construction equipment—all of which must come from somewhere. They can't come from McDuck, because McDuck owns no asphalt or construction equipment, and he employs no workers. Instead, all of those resources will be diverted from other projects—so to get more roads, we must have fewer factories or parking lots or movie theaters. None of that comes from McDuck.

The way this plays out is that McDuck turns over some money to the government, the government pays for construction materials, the price of those materials is bid up, and therefore someone somewhere decides to build one less movie theater. The losers are the people who would have profited from that theater and the people who would have enjoyed watching movies there.*

---

* Or there could be a multistep process: the government takes resources from the theater project; the theater project goes ahead using resources that had been slated for a department store project; the department store project goes ahead with resources that had been slated for a restaurant project. But the chain has to end *somewhere*.

The (much) more general lesson is that the people who are *required by law* to pay taxes and the people who are *actually hurt by those taxes* are often not the same people. It's worth spelling out the underlying logic here:

If the government undertakes a new project, the resources have to come from somewhere.

If Scrooge McDuck does not reduce his resource consumption, then the resources don't come from McDuck.

Therefore, if the government funds a new project with a tax that doesn't affect McDuck's resource consumption, the cost of that tax must fall on somebody other than McDuck — even if it's McDuck who's required by law to pay the tax.

The same logic would apply even if McDuck didn't bathe in cash. It would apply, for example, to Warren Buffett, who is a very rich man with a very modest lifestyle. If you fund a new hospital by raising Warren Buffett's taxes, he is unlikely to reduce his resource consumption. Therefore someone other than Warren Buffett will bear the cost of the hospital. Probably the way this one plays out is that Buffett pays his taxes by withdrawing funds from a savings account, leading his bank to make fewer loans and leaving one less movie theater or restaurant able to get funding. But the (much) larger point is that it's got to play out *somehow*.

This does not, of course, mean that the government should never build a road or a hospital. It does mean that these projects have costs, that we should be aware of those costs, and that if you want to know who's really paying those costs, you've got to think beyond the obvious.

And now on to our final topic: trade, between individuals and between countries.

7

The Electrician and the Carpenter

Earl the electrician and Carla the carpenter live across the street from each other. They both want to rewire their houses and panel their dens.

Earl can rewire a house in 10 hours. Carla can also rewire a house, but because she's not a skilled electrician, it takes her 20 hours to do the same quality job.

Earl can panel a den in 15 hours. You might expect Carla, the professional carpenter, to do it faster. But Carla is in fact not a terribly good carpenter, and in order to do just as good a job as Earl, she needs 18 hours, including all the time she spends correcting mistakes.

Carla has suggested to Earl that they swap some labor — she'll work on his den if he'll rewire her house. Earl, who was never known for his tact, points out that he's not only a better electrician than Carla, he's also a better carpenter — and therefore has nothing to gain by trading.

Is he right?

SOLUTION: If Earl does all his own work, he spends 10 hours rewiring and 15 hours paneling, for a total of 25 hours. If Carla does all her own work, she spends 20 hours rewiring and 18 hours paneling, for a total of 38 hours.

If Earl does all the rewiring while Carla does all the paneling, Earl spends 20 hours on two rewiring jobs and Carla spends 36 hours on two paneling jobs. This saves Earl 8 hours and saves Carla 2 hours. Everybody wins.

An economist would say that Carla has a *comparative advantage* at paneling, even though she's a slower paneler than Earl. All that means is that if Carla does Earl's paneling for him, they can both be better off. The surprise is that you don't have to be good at anything to have a comparative advantage.

George and Mary run a business together. George types 40 words a minute; Mary types 120. Who has the comparative advantage at typing? Based on the information given, we cannot know. Now suppose I tell you that the business is an engineering firm, Mary's a first-class engineer, and George barely made it through high school algebra. Conclusion: George has the comparative advantage at typing. He and Mary can both come out ahead as long as he does all the typing and frees her up to work on other things where she can be more valuable.

Comparative advantage is one of the cornerstones of international trade theory. It means that if, for example, it takes more labor to produce a refrigerator in Mexico than in the United States, it can still make sense for Americans to buy their refrigerators from Mexico — thereby freeing up American effort and resources to produce, say, more airplanes or more semiconductors.

It means too that a small country with widespread starvation should not necessarily concentrate on producing more food. It might be better to concentrate on producing decorative jewelry, which can be traded for food.

It is a matter of mathematical fact that whenever two trading partners come together, each of them must have a comparative advantage at *something*. In other words, two people — or two countries — can *always* gain from trade.

Here's a quick bonus puzzle to check your understanding:

8

Midwesterners

Suppose an acre of land in Iowa can yield either 50 bushels of wheat or 100 bushels of corn, while an acre of land in Oklahoma can yield either 20 bushels of wheat or 30 bushels of corn.

Each state currently produces 200 bushels of wheat and 360 bushels of corn.

Can they gain from trade? And which state has the comparative advantage at growing wheat?

SOLUTION: Oklahoma has the comparative advantage in wheat (and Iowa does in corn). This is so despite an Oklahoma acre producing only 40 percent as much wheat as an Iowa acre.

Currently Iowa devotes 7.6 acres to farming (4 acres for wheat and 3.6 acres for corn), while Oklahoma devotes 22 acres (10 for wheat and 12 for corn).

If Iowa produces all 720 bushels of corn for both states while Oklahoma produces all 400 bushels of wheat, Iowa will need only 7.2 acres and Oklahoma will need only 20. The extra land is available to produce even more food, or to build public parks. Both states gain from trade.*

If your job title is "economist," you will sooner or later be accosted at a party by someone who has figured out how to solve all

---

* The quick way to discover that Oklahoma has the comparative advantage in wheat is to notice that a bushel of wheat grown in Oklahoma requires $\frac{1}{20}$ of an acre, which could otherwise be used to grow 1.5 bushels of corn, while a bushel of wheat grown in Iowa requires $\frac{1}{50}$ of an acre, which could otherwise be used to grow 2 bushels of corn. That the opportunity cost of wheat is lower in Oklahoma tells us that Oklahoma has the comparative advantage in growing wheat, and that there is a mutually beneficial trade in which Iowa gets at least some of its wheat from Oklahoma.

the world's financial problems by eliminating taxes, or outlawing banks, or canceling all debts every fifty years, or using cows for money.

You will also be accosted, perhaps at the same party, by someone who has figured out that the real solution to all of our problems lies in restrictive trade agreements. That person will offer many arguments, all of which were thoroughly debunked two centuries ago.* Sometimes that person will be aware that these arguments fly in the face of something called the theory of comparative advantage, and will try to inoculate him- or herself against that objection by saying, "I fully understand the theory of comparative advantage, but . . ."

I always stop them right there and ask this: "Earl can rewire a house in ten hours or panel a den in fifteen hours. Carla can rewire a house in twenty hours or panel a den in eighteen hours. Who has the comparative advantage at paneling?" If they can't answer this (and they rarely can), they most definitely do not understand the theory of comparative advantage.

That's not a moral failing. Nobody understands everything. It's also not a moral failing to believe you understand something when you actually don't. Claiming to understand something when you *know* you don't is a little dicier.

When those partygoers can't answer my question about Earl and Carla, some are grateful to have been brought up short, and resolve either to go do a little reading or to stop being quite so sure of themselves. Others try to bluster through. This book is dedicated to everyone in the first group, and everyone else who would rather be right than win an argument.

---

* There are also some arguments in favor of restrictive trade agreements that have *not* been thoroughly debunked (though these arguments tend to apply only in very special circumstances). These are not the arguments one hears from strangers at parties.

Appendix

1. Warm-Ups

State Boundaries was suggested by my old friend Steve Maguire, who teaches statistics at the College of DuPage.

Get Off the Earth: I remember seeing a version of this in a puzzle book from my childhood; I believe it was old even then. The title is a shout-out to an unrelated but classic puzzle designed by the legendary puzzle maker Sam Loyd.

Doctors and Lawyers is a disguised version of a neat trick that first appeared in what might be the shortest math paper ever published — a three-line article[1] where the Israeli mathematician Dov Jarden solved this math problem:

Rationality Test

Let's use the word *offspring* for the result of raising one number to the power of another. For example, the offspring of 2 and 3 is 2^3, or 8. *True or False:* The offspring of two irrational numbers is always irrational.

SOLUTION: False, though this solution won't tell you exactly why. Consider the following "family tree" of numerical offspring:

$$\sqrt{2} \;\rule{1cm}{0.4pt}\; \sqrt{2}$$
$$\mid$$
$$X \;\rule{1cm}{0.4pt}\; \sqrt{2}$$
$$\mid$$
$$2$$

Here I've used X as an abbreviation for $\sqrt{2}^{\sqrt{2}}$, and I've used the laws of exponents to calculate that the offspring of X with $\sqrt{2}$ is

$$X^{\sqrt{2}} = (\sqrt{2}^{\sqrt{2}})^{\sqrt{2}} = \sqrt{2}^{(\sqrt{2}\times\sqrt{2})} = \sqrt{2}^2 = 2$$

Now X either is or is not irrational. So:

If X is rational, then X is the rational offspring of two irrational parents (namely $\sqrt{2}$ and $\sqrt{2}$).

If X is irrational, then 2 is the rational offspring of two irrational parents (namely X and $\sqrt{2}$).

Even if we don't know which bullet point applies, we certainly know that *one* of them applies, and either way the statement is false.

The Hungry Bookworm: V. I. Arnold's book *Problems for Children from 5 to 15* was first published in Russian in 2004. An English version appears on the web at https://imaginary.org/sites/default/files/taskbook_arnold_en_0.pdf.

More Boys was invented by puzzle maker Gary Foshee, who caused a sensation when he presented it to the puzzle aficionados who met for the 2009 Gathering 4 Gardner Biennial Conference, devoted to the playful exchange of ideas and critical thinking in recreational math, magic, science, literature, and puzzles to honor the memory of the great writer and polymath Martin Gardner. You can get information about upcoming Gathering 4 Gardner conferences at www.gathering4gardner.org.

The Tortoise and the Hare was invented by Professor Stan Wagon of Macalester College and appears in the quite wonderful book of (mostly mathematical) puzzles *Which Way Did the Bicycle Go?* by Joseph Konhauser, Dan Velleman, and Stan Wagon.

The discussion following **Fuel Efficiency, Take Three** references work by economists estimating the number of additional infant lives that would be lost in car accidents if parents were required to buy extra seats for their infants on airlines. If you want to see what those calculations look like, you can visit the web page for MIT's open courses on economics at https://ocw.mit.edu/courses/economics/, click through to course number 14.03 (Microeconomic Theory and Public Policy, fall 2016, taught by David Autor), and then click through to the notes for lecture 18.

2. Inferences

The gender-discrimination case at Berkeley (which illustrates that aggregate statistics can tell a misleading story) and the comparison between Babe Ruth's and Lou Gehrig's batting averages (which illustrates that broken-down statistics can tell an equally misleading story) are both such perfect examples that they've become standard fare in college statistics courses. The Berkeley case came to the widespread attention of college professors through an article in the journal *Science*.[2]

I think it would probably be impossible to determine who first noticed the Gehrig/Ruth example.

Jury Selection is inspired by real-world statistics first observed by the New Zealand statistician Ian Westbrooke.[3]

Income Trends: The numbers are lifted from the book *Unintended Consequences: Why Everything You've Been Told About the Economy Is Wrong* by the businessman, author, and scholar Edward Conard.

The numbers on student math scores at the bottom of page 24 come from the National Center for Education Statistics, a branch of the US Department of Education, Trends in Academic Progress, 2012.

Alex Tabarrok and Jonathan Klick's study on the effectiveness of policing appeared in *The Journal of Law and Economics*.[4]

The University of Nevada researchers who seem to have missed the point of **Good-Looking Teachers** reported their findings in *The Journal of General Psychology*.[5]

Checking Cards is based on the work of psychologist Peter Cathcart Wason, who reported[6] that only about 10 percent of his subjects got it right.

Barefoot Cheaters and **Which Is Harder?** are based on the work of psychologists Leda Cosmides and John Tooby, which has inspired a great deal of study in evolutionary psychology.[7]

3. Predictions

The Wonderful Future Invention Checklist appears on page 73 of Tom Weller's *Science Made Stupid* (Houghton Mifflin, 1985).

Pigs in a Box is based on experiments reported by the biologist John Maynard Smith in his book *Evolution and the Theory of Games* (Cambridge University Press, 1982).

Boys or Girls? references my two *Slate* columns on whether parents prefer boys. The first is "Oh, No! It's a Girl!," published October 2, 2003, and the second is "Maybe Parents Don't Like Boys Better," published October 16, 2003.

My blog commenter Mark Westling pointed me to Amazon's baby-sex predictor and suggests the following business model: Offer baby-sex prediction over the web, charge $75 (so consumers know it's good), and offer a full refund if you're wrong (upon review of relevant documents).

Kids at School: Much of what's known about the effects of family size, demographics, and birth order can be found in the work of Sandra Black, Paul Devereux, and Kjell Salvanes.[8]

In **Cutting Hairs** the Baumol effect takes its name from the economist William Baumol, who explored it along with coauthor William Bowen.[9]

The discussion following **The Organ Eater** refers to evidence that in certain parts of contemporary Asia, increases in the price of some grains can lead to increases in their consumption. That evidence can be found in a paper by Robert Jensen and Nolan Miller.[10]

4. Explanations

Why Don't Jews Farm? is based on the thoughtful and carefully researched book *The Chosen Few* by Maristella Botticini and Zvi Eckstein (Princeton University Press, 2012).

What Do Police Officers Want? is based on a passage from my book *More Sex Is Safer Sex: The Unconventional Wisdom of Economics* (Simon & Schuster, 2007), which in turn is based on research by economists John Knowles, Nicola Persico, and Petra Todd.[11]

For the sake of brevity, the discussion in the text ignores some subtleties. For example, it ignores the possibility that, say, white men in Volkswagens (or blacks or whites with some other identifiable characteristic) are especially likely to carry drugs. If so, then police who are out to maximize arrests will concentrate on white men in Volkswagens, so that on average whites will be stopped more frequently than blacks, even though the police bear them no racial animus. The counterargument is that if white men in Volkswagens were stopped more frequently than white men in general, then white male drug carriers would stop driving Volkswagens, so that this effect cannot persist.

5. Strategy

The Prisoner's Dilemma is probably the most frequently invoked metaphor in all of social science. It was developed by a group of researchers led by Merril Flood and Melvin Dresher at the RAND Corporation around 1950.

The Two-Sided Card Game is adapted from an odd and lovely little book called *A Mathematician's Miscellany,* published in 1953 by the great British mathematician J. E. Littlewood.[12] In Littlewood's version the winner's prize is equal to the loser's penalty. I've doubled the winner's prize (a prize that is never collected) to illustrate the moral that mutual rationality can be a curse.

Art at Auction, Take Two is standard classroom fare, first analyzed in print by William Vickrey.[13] Vickrey later made history of a sort by dying just three days after winning the Nobel Prize in Economics (and before collecting it).

The Hundred-Dollar Auction was introduced by the economist Martin Shubik.[14]

6. How Irrational Are You?

Economists, by nature and by training, are always looking for loopholes, and my friend Romans Pancs has pointed out the loophole in my story about Sidney Morgenbesser, who chooses apple pie until he learns the restaurant is out of blueberry, whereupon Morgenbesser switches to cherry. The challenge is to explain how Morgenbesser can have these preferences but (contrary to my claim in the text) still be rational. Here is Romans's effort:

> Suppose that only the best of chefs can prepare a good blueberry pie or a good cherry pie. An apple pie is easy; every grandmother can do it. So, upon learning that the restaurant ran out of blueberry pies, Morgenbesser reasoned: "That the restaurant has run out of blueberry pies means that they are very popular at this restaurant, which, in turn, means that the chef is very good. Because the chef is very good, I need no longer go for the safe option of the apple pie. I can order cherry." This argument is thanks to [the Nobel Prize–winning economist] Amartya Sen.

I agree that this chain of reasoning would absolve Morgenbesser of the charge of irrationality. I believe Romans would agree that this is not the chain of reasoning that Morgenbesser had in mind.

Problems 1 and 2 are collectively known to economists as the *Allais paradox* — in honor of the Nobel laureate Maurice Allais, who first thought of using such questions to test for conformity to the rationality axioms, and "paradox" because a great many people fail that test.[15] (Allais's Nobel Prize was awarded for work quite unrelated to this paradox.)

For readers who are uncomfortable with the discussion of problems 1 and 2 on pages 126-131, here's a slightly different version of the same argument.

As in the chapter, we start here: It's okay to prefer dogs to cats, and it's okay to prefer cats to dogs. But *if* you prefer dogs to cats, you'd better prefer, say, an 11 percent chance of winning a dog to an 11 percent chance of winning a cat.

Suppose, for example, that I offer you the chance to draw a pet from either of two urns (after thoroughly mixing their contents). One contains 11 cats and 89 mystery pets; the other contains 11 dogs and the same 89 mystery pets:

 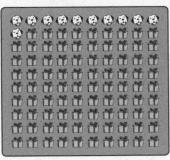

A rational person is one who can make this choice without having to ask what's in the mystery boxes. Rational cat lovers choose the first; rational dog lovers choose the second. The only thing that's *ir*rational is to say, "I can't decide without knowing what's in those mystery boxes."

Likewise, if you're rational, you won't need to know what's in the mystery boxes to choose between *these* urns, where the first contains 11 one-million-dollar prizes (shaded gray), while the second contains 10 five-million-dollar prizes (shaded black) plus one white box with an X that's worth nothing. Both urns contain the same 89 mystery prizes:

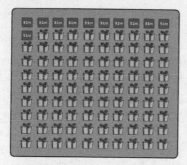 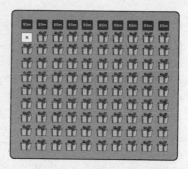

After all, 89 percent of the time you'll get a mystery box and your choice won't matter anyway. The other 11 percent of the time you'll either get a million dollars for sure or a 10/11 chance at $5 million. Some people prefer the million; others prefer the 10/11 chance at $5 million. All of them can be rational — as long as their choice of urns doesn't depend on what's in the mystery boxes.

So go ahead. Make your choice. Do you prefer urn A or urn B?

Now that you've decided, I can reveal that all the mystery boxes in both urns contain $1 million. So if you picked urn A, you're guaranteed $1 million. If you picked urn B, you'll be choosing from an 89 percent chance to win $1 million, a 10 percent chance to win $5 million, and a 1 percent chance to draw the X box and win nothing at all. That's *exactly the same* choice you were called on to make in quiz question 1. If you preferred urn A *before* I told you what was in the mystery boxes, you should still prefer it after — and you should have answered A to question 1. If you preferred urn B, you should have answered B.

Oh — wait — I made a mistake. Did I say the mystery boxes all contain $1 million? I meant to say that they're all empty. So if you picked urn A, you have an 11 percent chance at $1 million, and if you picked urn B, you have a 10 percent chance at $5 million. This is *exactly the same* as the choice you were called upon to make when you answered quiz question 2. Once again, if you preferred urn A, you should have answered A when you took the quiz; if you preferred urn B, you should have answered B.

So the only difference between questions 1 and 2 is what's in the mystery boxes. And we've already agreed that rational people choose their urns without regard to what's in those mystery boxes! In other words, some rational people answer A to both questions, and other rational people answer B to both questions, but no rational person can answer A to one question and B to the other. If you did that, you earned an irrationality point.

Problems 3 and 4 are also the inventions of Maurice Allais.

Problems 5 and 6 are collectively known to economists as the *Zeckhauser paradox.* It was widely and informally circulated by Professor Richard Zeckhauser of Harvard, though I'm not sure he ever published anything about it.

Problems 8 and 9 are collectively known to economists as the *Ellsberg paradox,* named for the decision theorist Daniel Ellsberg.[16] Readers of a certain age might recognize Ellsberg's name; he played a key and very public role in the downfall of former US president Richard Nixon.

7. Law School Admissions Test

Reasonable Doubt is, as noted in the text, inspired by the decision theorist Howard Raiffa, and more specifically from the anecdote on pages 20–21 of Raiffa's exceptionally readable text *Decision Analysis: Introductory Lectures on Choices Under Uncertainty* (Addison-Wesley, 1968).

William Blackstone's "Ten Guilty Men" formulation is from his *Commentaries on the Laws of England* (Clarendon Press, 1765). Alexander Volokh's survey of variations on the Blackstone theme appeared in the *University of Pennsylvania Law Review.*[17]

Medieval Justice is, as noted in the text, lifted from the economist Peter Leeson, and more specifically from Leeson's provocative book *WTF?! An Economic Tour of the Weird* (Stanford University Press, 2017), where readers can find (among many other economic oddities!) a substantially more detailed defense of Leeson's thesis about the effectiveness of trial by ordeal.

Settling Lawsuits is from J. E. Littlewood's *Mathematician's Miscellany.*

8. Are You Smarter Than Google?

Are You Smarter Than Google? first came to my attention via a post on the research-level math site MathOverflow.[18] Much of the discussion there, especially the response from Douglas Zare, is exceptionally illuminating if you're into math. Zare is a mathematician and a figure of some note in the worlds of competitive backgammon and poker.

Here's how to calculate the expected fraction of girls in a country with two families. Here are some possible configurations with their associated probabilities:

PROBABILITY	FIRST FAMILY	SECOND FAMILY	FRACTION FEMALE
¼	B	B	0
⅛	B	GB	⅓
⅛	GB	B	⅓
1⁄16	GB	GB	½
1⁄16	GGB	B	½

That gives me a ¼ chance of 0 girls, a ⅛ chance of ⅓ girls, a ⅛ chance of ⅓ girls, a 1⁄16 chance of ½ girls, a 1⁄16 chance of ½ girls, et cetera. I can add all this up, beginning like this:

$(1/4) \times 0 + (1/8) \times (1/3) + (1/8) \times (1/3) + (1/16) \times (1/2) + (1/16) \times (1/2) + \ldots$ and get an answer that is not ½.

(In fact the sum is $\log(4) - 1$, which is less than .4. I don't claim this is obvious, but I do claim it's true.)

For a country with three, four, five, a thousand, or a million families, a similar calculation will always give a number that is less than ½.

For the **Wanna Play?** problem, my frequent blog commenter Bennett Haselton suggests a nice intuitive way to explain the result: "The sequences that have more Hs in them will tend to have more HX strings in them. But, the sequences that have more Hs in them will likewise tend to have more HH strings in them. So, HH strings contribute less on average to the percentages, because they tend to appear in sequences with more HX strings in them, diluting their contribution."

The researchers called GVT in the text are Thomas Gilovich, Robert Vallone, and Amos Tversky.[19] The researchers who uncovered the error in GVT's analysis are Joshua Miller and Adam Sanjurjo.[20]

9. Backward Reasoning

The Hungry Lions and **Selling Snake Oil** are variations on standard classroom examples whose origins would be hard to trace.

The Surprise Quiz (sometimes recast as an Unexpected Hanging) was first proposed by the philosopher D. J. O'Connor.[21] It was widely popularized by Martin Gardner in a 1968 *Scientific American* column[22] and has received far more attention from philosophers than it can possibly deserve.

10. Knowledge

The long passage by Joel David Hamkins is from a post at the website MathOverflow.[23]

The Obedient Prisoners: The earliest source I know for this problem is once again J. E. Littlewood's *Mathematician's Miscellany*. Here is Little-wood's version of the problem, together with his commentary:

> Three ladies, *A, B, C,* in a railway carriage all have dirty faces and are all laughing. It suddenly dawns on *A:* Why doesn't *B* realize *C* is laugh-ing at her? — Heavens! *I* must be laughable. (Formally: if I, *A,* am not laughable, *B* will be arguing: If I, *B* am not laughable, *C* has nothing to laugh at. Since *B* does not so argue, I, *A,* must be laughable.)
>
> This is genuine mathematical reasoning, and surely with mini-mum material. But further, what has not got into the books so far as I know, there is an extension, in principle, to *n* ladies, all dirty and all laughing. There is an induction: in the *(n+1)*-situation A argues: If I am not laughable, *B, C,* . . . constitute an *n*-situation and *B* would stop laughing, but does not.

In **The Obedient Prisoners** I've replaced the ladies with prisoners, the dirty faces with red dots, the laughing with leaving the prison (which, unlike the laughing, can happen only once a day), and the arbitrary num-ber *n* with 40. Various other versions of this problem have circulated on the web, sometimes under the title The Blue-Eyed Islanders.

Elk or Moose?: This problem is a shout-out to the extensive literature on "agreeing to disagree," much of which asserts that it is quite impossible as long as everyone is honest and everyone's honesty is common knowledge.

This literature begins with the Nobel laureate Robert Aumann's paper "Agreeing to Disagree" (*Annals of Statistics* 4 [1976]: 1236–39). He gave a rigorous proof that Ed and Marsha, if they are honest truth seekers, cannot simply agree to disagree. This leaves two possibilities: either they come to an agreement, or they continue yelling "Elk!," "Moose!," "Elk!," "Moose!" forever. The economists John Geanakoplos and Heraklis Polemarchakis analyzed the problem further and ruled out the latter possibility.[24]

This still leaves the possibility that Ed and Marsha will go back and forth for an extremely long time before agreeing. That loophole was pretty much ruled out by the computer scientist Scott Aaronson.[25]

Another potential loophole is that not all of our beliefs stem from logic and evidence. George Mason University economist Robin Hanson closed this loophole by showing that *even so,* we cannot honestly agree to disagree.[26]

Economists Paul Milgrom and Nancy Stokey have explored the implications of all this for financial markets.[27]

If this topic fascinates you (as it fascinates me), you can read more about it in chapter 9 of my book *The Big Questions*.

The Sudoku Dilemma is solved (and solved again, in multiple ways) in a paper by the computer scientists R. Gradwohl et al.[28]

12. How to Make Decisions

The **Best Friend Rule** and the **Cause and Effect Rule** are meant to capture the essence (but perhaps not every nuance) of what philosophers call "evidentiary decision theory" and "causal decision theory." Some of the issues raised by **The Persimmon Problem** and **The Hiker's Problem** are well illuminated in a paper titled "Some Counterexamples to Causal Decision Theory" by the philosopher Andy Egan (*Philosophical Review* 116 [2007]: 93–114).

Newcomb's Problem: The argument that Zorxon must be, in essence, running a simulation of you, and that in this case you are likely to *be* that simulation, and hence able to influence Zorxon's choice, was advanced by the computer scientist Scott Aaronson in a blog post (https://www.scottaaronson.com/blog/?p=30). Essentially the same idea emerges from the "timeless decision theory" proposed in a long and thoughtful essay by the computer scientist Eliezer Yudkowsky.[29]

The Amnesia Problem appears for the first time in this book, though I'd be unsurprised to learn that someone else had long ago proposed something very similar. I dare to hope that it will put Newcomb's Problem permanently to bed, but given the history of the problem, there are limits to my optimism.

13. Matters of Life and Death

The Headache Problem was raised by the philosopher Alistair Norcross.[30] He got what seems to me to be the self-evidently correct answer but (bizarrely in my opinion) labeled it "counterintuitive." Other philosophers, even more bizarrely, have labeled Norcross's conclusion not just counterintuitive but wrong.[31]

Rescue Operations: Although I've argued that the right policy is the risky one that might save all and might fail completely, my contrarian friend Romans Pancs observes that if we suspect the policymaker of both laziness and dishonesty, we might not want to allow him this option. That's because he might announce that he's chosen the risky operation, then make no actual effort to carry it out, and then declare that sadly, the operation has failed.

14. The Coin Flipper's Dilemma

Game theory beings with the monumental work of John von Neumann and Oskar Morgenstern.[32] They proved (among a great many other things) that under quite general conditions, all rational agents must be "expected utility maximizers," from which we can infer a great deal about how they choose among risky options. This non-obvious truth is so widely applicable that it pervades almost all of economics. But Bob's coin-flipping game presents one of the rare situations in which the "quite general conditions" of the von Neumann–Morgenstern theorem does not apply, which leaves economists with remarkably little left to say.

15. Albert and the Dinosaurs

The problem of the absent-minded driver was first raised by the game theorists Michele Piccione and Ariel Rubinstein in the journal *Games and Economic Behavior.*[33]

Albert Mark Two is the version of Albert proposed by Robert Aumann, Sergiu Hart, and Motty Perry.[34]

Albert Mark Three makes his debut in my paper "Albert and the Dinosaurs."[35]

16. Money, Trade, and Finance

The idea of pricing financial instruments by comparing them to portfolios guaranteed to produce the same results (as in **Jeter's Game** and **Comparison**) originated with the economist Stephen Ross.[36]

In **Option Pricing,** the Black-Scholes model of option pricing[37] makes good use of Stephen Ross's insight.

The Electrician and the Carpenter: The principle of comparative advantage was introduced by David Ricardo in his book *On the Principles of Political Economy and Taxation,* published in 1817. It has dominated the theory of international trade ever since.

Notes

1. D. Jarden, "Curiosa," *Scripta Mathematica* 19 (1953): 229.
2. P. J. Hickel, E. A. Hammond, and J. W. O'Connell, "Sex Bias in Graduate Admissions: Data from Berkeley," *Science* 187 (1975): 398–404.
3. I. Westbrooke, "Simpson's Paradox: An Example in a New Zealand Survey of Jury Composition," *Chance* 2 (1998): 40–42.
4. A. Tabarrok and J. Klick, "Using Terror Alert Levels to Estimate the Effect of Police on Crime," *Journal of Law and Economics* 48 (April 2005): 267–79.
5. R. Westfall, M. Millar, and M. Walsh, "Effects of Instructor Attractiveness on Learning," *Journal of General Psychology* 143 (2016): 161–71.
6. P. C. Wason, "Reasoning About a Rule," *Quarterly Journal of Experimental Psychology* 20 (1968): 273–81.
7. This work appears in *The Adapted Mind: Evolutionary Psychology and the Generation of Culture,* edited by L. Cosmides, J. Tooby, and J. Barkow (Oxford University Press, 1992).
8. S. Black, P. Devereux, and K. Salvanes, "The More the Merrier," *Quarterly Journal of Economics* (May 2005): 669–700.
9. W. Baumol and W. Bowen, "On the Performing Arts: The Anatomy of Their Economic Problems," *American Economic Review* 55 (1965): 495–502.
10. R. Jensen and N. Miller, "Giffen Behavior and Subsistence Consumption," *American Economic Review* 98 (2008): 1553–77.
11. J. Knowles, N. Persico, and P. Todd, "Racial Bias in Motor Vehicle Searches: Theory and Evidence," *Journal of Political Economy* 109 (Feb. 2001): 203–29.
12. See also the book *Littlewood's Miscellany* (Cambridge University Press, 1986), a collection of Littlewood's essays that overlaps substantially with the 1953 book.
13. W. Vickrey, "Counterspeculation, Auctions and Competitive Sealed Tenders," *Journal of Finance* 16 (1961): 8–37.
14. M. Shubik, "The Dollar Auction Game: A Paradox in Noncooperative Behavior and Escalation," *Journal of Conflict Resolution* 15 (1971): 109–11.
15. M. Allais, "Le comportement de l'homme rationnel devant le risque: Critique des postulats et axiomes de l'ecole Americaine," Rational man's behavior in the presence of risk: Critique of the postulates and axioms of the American school, *Econometrica* 21 (1953): 503–46.
16. D. Ellsberg, "Risk, Ambiguity, and the Savage Axioms," *Quarterly Journal of Economics* 75 (1961): 643–69.
17. A. Volokh, "*n* Guilty Men," *University of Pennsylvania Law Review* 146 (1997): 173–216.

18. "Google question: In a country in which people only want boys," question on Math Overflow, www.mathoverflow.net/questions/17960.

19. T. Gilovich, R. Vallone, and A. Tversky, "The Hot Hand in Basketball: On the Misperception of Random Sequences," *Cognitive Psychology* 17 (1985): 295–314.

20. J. Miller and A. Sanjurjo, "Surprised by the Gambler's and Hot Hand Fallacies? A Truth in the Law of Small Numbers," IGIER Working Paper no. 552, Nov. 15, 2016, available at SSRN: https://ssrn.com/abstract=2627354 or http://dx.doi.org/10.2139/ssrn.2627354 .

21. D. J. O'Connor, "Pragmatic Paradoxes," *Mind* 227 (1948): 358–59.

22. This column is reproduced in Gardner's book *The Unexpected Hanging and Other Mathematical Diversions* (University of Chicago Press, 1991).

23. https//www.mathoverflow.net/questions/114245/i-know-that-you-know.

24. J. Geanakoplos and H. Polemarchakis, "We Can't Disagree Forever," *Journal of Economic Theory* 28 (1982): 192–200.

25. S. Aaronson, "The Complexity of Agreement," in *Symposium on the Theory of Computing* (Association for Computing Machinery, 2005): 634–43.

26. R. Hanson, "Uncommon Priors Require Origin Disputes," *Theory and Decision* 61 (2006): 318–28.

27. P. Milgrom and N. Stokey, "Information, Trade and Common Knowledge," *Journal of Economic Theory* 26 (1982): 17–27.

28. R. Gradwohl et al., "Cryptographic and Physical Zero-Knowledge Proof Systems for Solutions of Sudoku Puzzles," in the book *Fun with Algorithms : 7th International Conference, FUN 2014,* eds. A. Ferro, F. Luccio, and P. Widmayer (Springer-Verlag, 2014).

29. E. Yudkowsky, "Timeless Decision Theory" (Machine Intelligence Research Institute, 2010).

30. A. Norcross, "Comparing Harms: Headaches and Human Lives," *Philosophy and Public Affairs* 26 (1997): 135–67.

31. One example: D. Dorsey, "Headaches, Lives and Value," *Utilitas* 21 (2009): 36–58.

32. J. von Neumann and O. Morgenstern, *Theory of Games and Economic Behavior* (Princeton University Press, 1953).

33. M. Piccione and A. Rubinstein, "On the Interpretation of Decision Problems with Imperfect Recall," *Games and Economic Behavior* 20 (1997): 3–24.

34. R. Aumann, S. Hart, and M. Perry, "The Absent-Minded Driver," *Games and Economic Behavior* 20 (1997): 102–16.

35. S. Landsburg, "Albert and the Dinosaurs," preliminary version at www.landsburg.com/amd.pdf.

36. S. Ross, "The Arbitrage Theory of Capital Asset Pricing," *Journal of Economic Theory* 13 (1976): 341–60.

37. F. Black and M. Scholes, "The Pricing of Corporate Liabilities," *Journal of Political Economy* 81 (1973): 637–54.